Psychosocial Pathology and Social Work Practice

Psychosocial Pathology and Social Work Practice

Shawn Lawrence, Reshawna Chapple, and Linda Manning
University of Central Florida

cognella®
SAN DIEGO

Bassim Hamadeh, CEO and Publisher
Amy Smith, Senior Project Editor
Alia Bales, Production Editor
Jess Estrella, Senior Graphic Designer
Alexa Lucido, Licensing Manager
Stephanie Adams, Senior Marketing Program Manager
Natalie Piccotti, Director of Marketing
Kassie Graves, Senior Vice President, Editorial
Jamie Giganti, Director of Academic Publishing

Cover image copyright © 2021 iStockphoto LP/draganab.

Printed in the United States of America.

cognella® | ACADEMIC PUBLISHING
3970 Sorrento Valley Blvd., Ste. 500, San Diego, CA 92121

This book was written during the course of the COVID-19 pandemic and is dedicated to all of those who were lost to the pandemic and their families.

BRIEF CONTENTS

DETAILED CONTENTS

CHAPTER 4   **Bipolar and Related Disorders**   **65**

with Celine Rodriguez

PREFACE

The desired outcome of social work pedagogy is to enable future practitioners to perform like social workers through the development of the professional self. One significant challenge in the field of social work is the misconception held by other medical and mental health professionals (and the general public) that social work practitioners are concerned only with social justice and that social workers are paraprofessionals. In fact, social work is a licensed mental health profession that comes with a large number of professional responsibilities.

Social work students often struggle with diagnosing because of the subjectivity of diagnosing and overlap among similar diagnoses. The purpose of writing this text is for it to serve as an adjunctive source to the DSM-5 (APA, 2013), providing not only an overview of the disorders and their criteria but a guide through the assessment and differential diagnosing process. This text is intended to provide master level social work students (and those in other mental health professions) with the skills necessary to make an informed diagnosis to assist with treatment modalities. What makes this text different from other psychosocial pathology texts is that each chapter provides racial and ethnic cultural and gendered considerations of each diagnosis, a complex multidimensional case study, a full diagnosis, a detailed explanation of how the diagnoses were reached, and a decision tree for each diagnosis. Instructors can use this text to prepare their students to develop practical skills in applying the DSM-5 diagnostic criteria to actual cases. Finally, this text can be used by practitioners as a reference tool for assessing and treatment planning.

ACKNOWLEDGMENTS

Shawn

I want to start by thanking two of my friends and former colleagues, Drs. Eileen Abel and Mary Ann Burg. Your unwavering support and laughter throughout the writing of this text and throughout my academic career has provided me the foundation and motivation to keep striving to achieve and reach beyond my goals. Thank you to my family, the Lawrences' and the Hayes', for your love, support, and endless understanding. Thank you to Dr. Teresa Chmelir and Abi Bell for your unconditional friendship, keeping me healthy both emotionally and physically, and reminding me that yes, I can "do all the things" and to Steve Adrian for being my voice of reason. Katherine Van Patten, you have been my inspiration even long after you were gone. Finally, thank you J.K. for being "my person."

Reshawna

Acknowledgments are difficult because we are nothing without our tribe. That said, I would like to thank my amazing husband, Jay. You are my rock, my sun, my moon, my stars, and my consistent cheerleader. I love you more than you will ever know. I would like to thank my kids Kiara and Jailen. You two have taught me so much about unconditional love and acceptance. I am so honored to be your mom. I would like to thank my mom and grandmother for believing in me so much that I am still harvesting your positive energy long after you both have passed on. I would also like to thank my brother James for being unapologetically honest and real with me about everything. Lastly, I would like to thank my chosen family. You know who you are.

Linda

My gratitude goes to Dr. Shawn Lawrence for inviting me into this project and for being kind, patient, and a great friend. I would like to thank my dear friends for their unwavering support. Thank you, Dr. Eileen Abel, Jane Pawlowski, and Heidi Peckham, for your wise counsel wrapped in laughter.

CHAPTER 1

Introduction to Psychopathology and Social Work Practice

LEARNING OBJECTIVES

1. Gain a basic understanding of the history of mental illness.

2. Explain the basic theories surrounding the etiology of mental illness.

3. Become familiar with the *Diagnostic and Statistical Manual of Mental Disorders*, including the pros and cons of its use.

4. Understand the ethics of diagnosing mental illness from a strengths and multicultural perspective.

History of Mental Illness

To begin, it is important to understand the history of mental illness. For much of history, people believed that mental illness was caused by demon possession, witchcraft, or an angry god or gods. Treatments for mental illness included exorcism, prayer, medicinal drinks, and even drilling holes in a person's skull. By the 1700s, people who were considered "odd" were placed in asylums specifically created for people with mental health disorders to keep them away from the rest of society. By the end of the 1700s, Phillipe Pinel, the founder of psychiatry in France, called for more humane treatment of people with mental health disorders. He stated that, to diagnose mental illness, the physician must observe and listen to a patient, as well as take an accurate history (Weiner, 1992). In the United States in the 19th century, Dorothea Dix led reforms for mental healthcare. Despite her efforts and the efforts of others, patients were subjected to freezing baths, electroshock therapy, and inhumane living conditions. This remained commonplace well into the 20th century.

A shift in how U.S. society viewed mental illness occurred in 1963 when President John F. Kennedy signed the Mental Retardation Facilities and Community Mental Health Centers Construction Act (now referred to the Community Mental Health Act). This act shifted the paradigm of how community mental health centers operated and how mental health services were delivered in the United States. Until this momentous act, care and housing standards for mental health facilities differed from state to state, without federal oversight. The premise for the act was for each state to develop mental health facilities to fit the needs of its population. President Kennedy also called for an increase in research and training surrounding mental illness (Prioleau, 2016), another area that had been neglected for decades. In 2008, Senator Edward Kennedy and Representative Patrick Kennedy updated the Community Mental Health Act of 1963 with the Mental Health Parity and Addiction Equity Act (MHPAEA), which requires that health insurers cover mental health and/or substance abuse disorders the same way they cover other illnesses (Prioleau, 2016).

Today, most psychiatric hospitals run by state or local healthcare organizations are focused on short-term care, and the vast majority of people who are experiencing mental health issues are not hospitalized but receive treatment on an outpatient basis. This is where social workers and other mental health professionals play a significant role in assessment, diagnosis, and treatment. A psychopathology, or diagnosing, class will help you develop the skills needed to diagnose major psychiatric disorders. The intent of this text is not to provide an overview all psychiatric disorders, but rather to focus on those you are most likely to encounter as a new practitioner. However, before assessment, diagnosis, and treatment, it is important to have a basic understanding of the etiology (cause) of mental illnesses.

Theories of Etiology

Psychosocial Theories

A number of psychosocial theories have been developed to explain mental illness. Two of these theories are Piaget's stages of development and Bowlby's attachment theory.

COGNITIVE DEVELOPMENT

Jean Piaget identified four major stages that lead to adult thought: sensorimotor, preoperational thought, concrete operations, and formal operations. Each stage leads to the next, but the pace at which individuals move through the various stages is based on their biological makeup and environment (Sadock et al., 2015). Children who do not transition successfully to the next stage of development may develop psychological issues. For example, in the sensorimotor stage, infants learn through observation and gain control over their motor functions through activities and manipulation of their environment. The critical point in this period is the development of object permanence. This relates to the child's ability to understand that objects exist even when the child is not involved with them. Children who do not develop object permanence because of a lack of stimulation (such as a hospitalization) may develop separation anxiety, because they need their caregivers to be present to be sure they still exist.

ATTACHMENT THEORY

Attachment theory originated from the work of John Bowlby. Bowlby posited that the attachment between a mother and child was an essential part of human interaction and had significant consequences for later development and functioning (Sadock et al., 2015). A child relies on caregivers to provide comfort in stressful situations. When the caregiver is unavailable to the infant physically and/or psychologically, the child will develop anxiety. Once in adulthood, the individual may have relationship issues, such as having an *anxious ambivalent* attachment style, which can manifest in jealousy and an obsessive nature with romantic partners. An individual with an *avoidant attachment* style can appear uninvested, despite feeling lonely. They may present with fears of intimacy and become withdrawn. An individual with a *secure* attachment style can present with high investment in the relationship with very little jealousy or fear of rejection.

Neurobiology

Social work practice continues to be profoundly influenced by advances in neuroscience. New imaging techniques, gene sequencing technology, and discoveries on a molecular level are making it imperative for clinical social workers to understand the neurobiological contribution to several mental health disorders. Evidence-based research leads us to consider some of these as brain disorders rather than mental illness, which will better encompass environmental influences, genetics, and neurobiological differences. This overview covers four areas:

- Basics of brain structure

- Neurotransmission, neuroplasticity, and neurotransmitters

- Influences of genetics and the environment on the brain

- Microbiomes and the gut–brain axis

A review of recent neurobiology research will be included in each chapter, specific to a major diagnoses.

Basics of Brain Structure

The nervous system is composed of the brain and spinal cord, which together are referred to as the central nervous system (CNS), and the cranial, peripheral, and spinal nerves, which are referred to as the peripheral nervous system (PNS). The brain and spinal cord are encased in the bony structures of the skull and spinal column. The PNS is outside the skull and spine, making it sensitive to environmental influences. The brainstem is an extension of the spinal cord and is the oldest structure of the brain in evolutionary terms. The brainstem regulates respiration, heart rate, temperature, and sleep (Applegate & Shapiro, 2005).

The cerebral cortex is the part of the brain that functions to make human beings unique. Located on the outside layer of the brain, the cerebral cortex is the center of thought, reason, and imagination (Figure 1.1). The cerebral cortex is divided into two hemispheres, or halves, connected by white matter called the corpus callosum. The right hemisphere primarily processes emotions, gestures, and other nonverbal

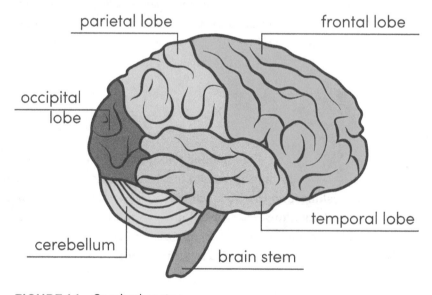

FIGURE 1.1   Cerebral cortex

communication, whereas language and fine motor development are the province of the left hemisphere.

The cerebral cortex is further divided into four sections, or lobes. The frontal lobe, parietal lobe, occipital lobe, and temporal lobe have been associated with distinct functions ranging from reasoning to auditory perception:

- *Frontal lobe*: Located at the front of the brain, the frontal lobe is known as the brain's executive center (Cozolino, 2002). Damage to the frontal lobe can lead to changes in movement, language, and attention, as well as increased risk-taking.

- *Parietal lobe:* The parietal lobe is located in the middle of the brain, and it processes information such as pressure, touch, and pain. The somatosensory cortex is located in this lobe and connects sensory and motor functions, including proprioception, or orientation, of the body in its space. Damage to this lobe can lead to difficulty reading, recognizing people or objects, and perceiving one's own body and/or limbs.

- *Temporal lobe*: Located at the lower front of the brain, the temporal lobe contains the primary auditory cortex, which aids in interpreting sounds and language. It is also the location of the hippocampus, which is associated with the formation of memories. Damage to the temporal lobe can lead to problems with memory, speech, and language.

- *Occipital lobe:* The occipital lobe is located near the back of the brain and processes visual stimuli. Damage to this lobe can cause problems such as an inability to identify colors and difficulty with word recognition.

Sometimes referred to as the "little brain," the cerebellum lies behind the brainstem. It receives information from the balance system of the inner ear, sensory nerves, and the auditory and visual systems. The cerebellum also assists in the coordination of movements, as well as motor learning. It helps with posture, balance, and the coordination of voluntary movements.

Located above the brainstem, the thalamus takes in sensory information and relays it to the cerebral cortex. The hypothalamus controls huger, thirst, emotions, and body temperature. The hypothalamus influences the pituitary gland to secrete hormones, giving the hypothalamus considerable control over many body functions.

The four main regions of the limbic system include the amygdala, the hippocampus, the anterior cingulate, and the orbitofrontal cortex. Essential connections exist between the limbic system and the hypothalamus, thalamus, and cerebral cortex. The hippocampus, as noted above, is important in memory and learning (Siegel, 1999), while the entire limbic system controls emotional responses.

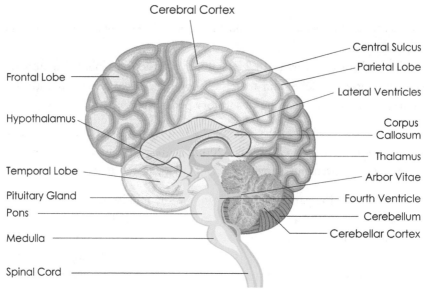

FIGURE 1.2   Anatomy of the human brain

Neurotransmission and the Concept of Neuroplasticity

Neurons are cells in the brain and nervous system that send information to other neurons throughout the body through a process called neurotransmission. A neuron is composed of a cell body, sending points called axons, and receiving points called dendrites. Chemical and electrical signals transmit messages from one neuron to another. The transfer of information happens in the space between the neurons called the synaptic cleft or synapse. The axons carry a message in electrical form to the synapse, where it is converted into a chemical message by neurotransmitters (discussed below). The message is received by the dendrites of the other cell. The human brain has approximately 100 billion neurons and as many as 1,000 trillion synapses.

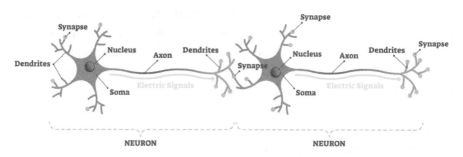

FIGURE 1.3   Neuron

Neuroplasticity is defined as the brain's ability to form new neural and synaptic connections over a lifetime in response to experiences, including injuries to the brain, learning, and external stimulation. After a traumatic brain injury (TBI), stroke, or even surgical removal of an entire brain hemisphere, an impressive amount of neurological recovery often occurs. Neurological recovery has been seen with TBIs resulting from motor vehicle accidents; assaults; sports-related injuries, such as concussions; falls; and combat. In 2017, Galetto and Sacco conducted a meta-analysis of research published between 1985 and 2016 and found that cognitive rehabilitation following TBI resulted in some neuroplastic recovery regardless of the severity of the injury.

Strokes occur due to blockage of blood vessels in the brain or bleeding in the brain (i.e., cerebral hemorrhage). If a stroke occurs in the left hemisphere of the brain, language may be negatively affected. Neuroimaging provides evidence that the right hemisphere can take over language tasks in some adults unless and until the left-brain language function improves (Blasi et al., 2002).

Children with drug-resistant epilepsy are sometimes treated by a hemispherectomy, the surgical removal of part or all of one brain hemisphere. Studies using a neuroimaging technology called functional magnetic resonance imaging (fMRI) have shown that many children who have a left hemispherectomy are able to develop language skills due to changes in the intact right hemisphere (Holloway et al., 2000; Ivanova et al., 2017).

Note that the mechanisms of neuroplasticity vary significantly among individuals. These variations include gender, age, physical and mental health, and many other factors. One such mechanism is axonal sprouting, in which undamaged axons sprout new nerve endings to reconnect damaged neurons or to connect with other undamaged cells. In some instances, dendrites thicken, allowing for increased reception of information (Galetto & Sacco, 2017). Neurogenesis is the production of entire new nerve cells. This process occurs in adults when neural stem cells differentiate and become new neurons. It was formerly thought that neurogenesis only happened in infants and very young children up to 2 to 3 years of age. We now know that it also occurs, through different mechanisms, in adults (Galetto & Sacco, 2017).

In normal human development, neurogenesis and synaptogenesis begin in the prenatal period. By 5 months' gestation, most neural networks are established, though they continue to grow through the gestation period. After birth, these processes continue rapidly until a child is about 2 years old, at which point a pruning process begins. This pruning process operates on the principle of "use it or lose it"—if the neurons and synapses are not engaged, brain cells are lost, and development may be affected. The pruning continues through approximately age 16, after which neuronal and synaptic density remain stable throughout adulthood. Researchers have reported that synaptic density abnormalities in some individuals with intellectual impairment, schizophrenia, and autism may indicate that synaptic pruning is essential for normal brain development (Murray et al., 2017; Packer, 2016).

Neurotransmitters

Neurotransmitters are the chemical messengers found in the synapses between neurons. The three main types of neurotransmitters can be classified based on their function: excitatory, inhibitory, or modulatory. Neuromodulators work on a large scale, are slower than other neurotransmitters, and affect several neurons at one time. They are found in the synapses, so they can regulate populations of neurons over a slower time course than excitatory and inhibitory neurotransmitters. Excitatory neurotransmitters enhance the ability of an axon to send a message to the dendrite of another cell, whereas inhibitory neurotransmitters have the opposite effect, slowing the action potential of the message (Kolb &Whishaw, 2016). Whether a neurotransmitter is excitatory or inhibitory depends on the receptor it binds to (Purves et al., 2001). More than 100 neurotransmitters have been identified. In the recent past, it was thought that each had a single role to play in communication, but now we know that they interact in a variety of ways and demonstrate a sophisticated complexity (Schwartz, 2002). Several important neurotransmitters that are known to affect mental health are described briefly below.

Dopamine is sometimes referred to as the "pleasure chemical." Scientists originally discovered that dopamine, specifically the loss of the neurotransmitter, interfered with the ability of people with Parkinson's disease to use their executive function (e.g., to make decisions). Ghorayeb and colleagues (2017) note that dopamine has been linked to Parkinson's disease, schizophrenia, obsessive compulsive disorder (OCD), addictions, and Tourette syndrome. Dopamine, or a lack of it, also affects learning, motivation, attention, movement, and reward processing.

Acetylcholine (Ach) has the distinction of being the first neurotransmitter identified. It plays a role in attention and is also thought to influence neuroplasticity in the brain's cortex. New research has shown that the release of acetylcholine prompts the release of dopamine, influencing reward processing and learning (Surmeier & Graybiel, 2012). This is an example of neurotransmitters interacting with each other.

Serotonin is sometimes called the "calming chemical" and is best known for its mood-modulating effects. A lack of serotonin has been linked to depression and related neuropsychiatric disorders (Meyer, 2012). Serotonin has been found to affect appetite, sleep, memory, sex drive, and, most recently, decision-making behaviors (Sukel, 2012). Neurons that use serotonin are found in various parts of the nervous system. As a result, serotonin is involved in functions such as sleep, memory, appetite, mood, and others. It is also produced in the gastrointestinal tract in response to food.

Norepinephrine is both a hormone and a neurotransmitter. It has been linked to mood, arousal, vigilance, memory, and stress. Newer research has focused on its role in both posttraumatic stress disorder (PTSD) and Parkinson's disease (Vazey & Ashton-Jones, 2012).

Glutamate is the most abundant excitatory neurotransmitter, active in approximately 50% of synapses (Snyder & Ferris, 2000). Glutamate has been connected to learning and memory. It is distributed in the brain's cortex, subcortical structures, and other areas. An excess of glutamate can result in the death of neurons, such as in amyotrophic lateral sclerosis (ALS), often referred to as Lou Gehrig's disease; stroke; or traumatic brain injury (TBI) (Mukherjee & Manahan-Vaughn, 2002). Glutamate has also been implicated in several brain disorders such as bipolar disorder, schizophrenia, and major depressive disorder.

Gamma-aminobutyric acid, or GABA, is an inhibitory neurotransmitter and has the opposite effect of glutamate. GABA is thought to be involved in seizure activity, anxiety, and neurodegenerative diseases such as Alzheimer's.

Influences of Genetics and the Environment on Brain Disorders

Defining the boundaries between disorders and determining the sometimes fine line between normal and pathological behavior can be difficult. For example, consider autism spectrum disorder, mild (formerly referred to as Asperger's disorder). Some of the key characteristics of the disorder are limited social skills, deficits in communication, and difficulty with relationships. Although these are characteristics of a disorder, they may, in fact, just be part of the individual's personality. Where is the line drawn between "normal" and disordered behavior? Recent advances in research on the human genome have found many genetic variations that influence our understanding of the neurobiological basis for several mental health disorders. Similarly, research demonstrates a connection between environment and mental health. Some studies look specifically at the interplay of genetics and childhood environment and the effect on later behavior and vulnerability regarding mental health. Each chapter of this text will address recent research on both the genetic and the environmental basis, or contributory effect, on diagnoses such as schizophrenia, major depressive disorder, and substance use.

Microbiomes and the Gut–Brain Axis

Compelling evidence suggests that gut microbiota has a key role in bidirectional interactions between the gut and the nervous system. The gut interacts with the CNS by regulating brain chemistry and influencing neuroendocrine systems associated with the stress response, anxiety, and memory function. Some symptoms can look like mental health issues, but actually be more biologically rooted. The gut–brain axis (GBA) consists of two-way communication between the central and the enteric nervous system (part of the autonomic nervous system), connecting the emotional and cognitive centers of the brain with peripheral intestinal functions (Carabotti et al., 2016). Research has described the importance of gut microbiota in influencing these interactions. The intestinal or gut microbiome contains approximately 100 trillion bacteria with more than 1,000 distinct bacterial species (Qin et al., 2010).

At birth, babies are exposed to their mothers' microbiota, influencing the babies' microbial identity. This gut microbiota is essential for the development of the CNS and produces certain neurotransmitters (Mueller et al., 2015). The vagus nerve carries information back and forth between the gut and the brainstem, engaging the hypothalamus and limbic system (which regulates emotion). This suggests a relevant role of gut microbiota in the development of disorders such as anxiety and depression.

Diagnostic and Statistical Manual of Mental Disorders (DSM)

Something that always needs to be considered is that there really is no such thing as a textbook diagnosis (even though you are reading a textbook about diagnosing). It is important to remember that each person is unique, and that sometimes you will be convinced that an individual has a certain disorder, but they just do not meet the criteria, or they meet criteria for another diagnosis as well. As a clinician, it is your job to determine the thoughts and features (the clinical indicators) that fit with the diagnosis. Your job is not to label people; it is to determine the best course of action for a person who is suffering. To do this, it is crucial that you are self-aware, both in terms of nature and nurture. The lens by which you view the behaviors of others becomes the lens by which you diagnose behavior.

History of the DSM

The *Diagnostic and Statistical Manual of Mental Disorders*, or DSM, is an evolving tool for clinical diagnosis, research, and administrative tasks, such as third-party reimbursement. Classification of mental disorders has been the interest of healing practitioners around the globe for centuries. In the United States, the effort to classify mental disorders reflected a simple need to collect statistical information on the mental health of the populace. The 1840 U.S. Census attempted to record the frequency of "idiocy and insanity." Seven categories were used in the 1880 U.S. Census: dementia, dipsomania (an uncontrollable craving for alcohol), epilepsy, mania, melancholia, monomania (obsessive enthusiasm), and paresis (muscular weakness) (Kawa & Giordano, 2012). In the latter part of the 19th century and for almost half of the 20th, statistics on mental disorders were collected on people in public or private hospitals, or what were referred to as mental institutions. Diagnostic criteria were largely nonexistent, and the causes of the disorders were speculative and not based on empirical research.

The American Psychiatric Association (APA) was formed in 1921 and worked to develop a classification system for mental disorders with a focus on clinical use. In 1952, the first edition of the DSM (DSM-I) was published and accepted. This early version was approximately 130 pages. There was a distinction between "organic brain syndromes" and "functional disorders. The functional disorders included neurotic, psychotic, and character disorders. Interestingly, the DSM-I reflected the psychobiological view popular at that time that mental disorders were reactions to social, biological, and psychological factors. This early version, however, had little reliability and validity.

The second edition, DSM-II, was published in 1968 and had 193 diagnostic categories. It was an improvement over the DSM-1, in that it had a focus on clinical disorders that would likely present on an outpatient basis. This version had a stronger focus on anxiety-related and depressive, personality, and childhood disorders. However, much like the DSM-I, the DSM-II lacked validity and reliability. A study of clinicians indicated that the conceptualizations in the clinicians' minds of what the disorders should look like were very different than the actual patient symptoms (Blashfield et al., 2014). A project led by Overall and Woodward in 1975 (as cited in Blashfield et al., 2014) found that when eight videotapes of patients were shown to American and British psychiatrists, the diagnosis by most of the American psychiatrists was schizophrenia. However, the British diagnoses ranged from manic depression (now bipolar disorder) to schizophrenia and personality disorders. This indicated that there was a lack of reliability in the diagnostic criteria. Some have claimed that this was indicative of "sloppy" diagnosing on the part of Americans and their tendency to be overly dependent on the diagnosis of schizophrenia (Blashfield et al., 2014). A significant improvement of the DSM-II is that by its seventh printing homosexuality was removed and "sexual orientation disturbance" was added.

The publication of the DSM-III (1980) was led by Robert Spitzer. This version represented a shift away from psychoanalysis and one that was more consistent with the International Classification of Mental and Behavioral Disorders (ICD). The ICD is published by the World Health Organization (WHO) and provides a set of codes to report diagnosis and procedures. DSM-III diagnoses were subjected to field trials sponsored by the National Institute of Mental Health to improve reliability. Although it has been criticized by some for creating several new categories of mental health diagnosis that had no empirical support (Robbins, 2014), this version formalized many disorders, including posttraumatic stress disorder (PTSD), attention deficit hyperactivity disorder (ADHD), and a number of childhood disorders. The DSM-III attempted to have a strong biomedical model, but it was inconsistent in terms of diagnostic measures. The DSM-III did have more detailed descriptions of the disorders, differential diagnoses, and an explanation of the course and onset of the disorder if it was known (Blashfield et al., 2014). The DSM-III included the multiaxial system, which included the primary diagnoses, personality or developmental disorders, medical issues, psychosocial stressors, and an assessment of overall level of functioning. It also included flow charts and tables. In this version, homosexuality was now referred to as "ego-dystonic homosexuality." The DSM-III-R was released in 1987 and was intended to correct the diagnostic criteria. This edition also had higher interclinician reliability. "Ego-dystonic homosexuality" was removed from this version, as well.

The DSM-IV (1994) was published in 1994 and had 383 categories, 201 of which were diagnostic categories defined by criteria. This version had an appendix that addressed 17 possible diagnoses that needed further investigation. The DSM-IV-TR was published in 2000. The intention with the DSM-IV-TR was not to change criteria (though some were indeed changed) but to add supporting narrative. The updated version, however, did increase in length by 54 pages, and the cost increased by $26.

The APA released the DSM-5 in 2013. This is the edition currently used by mental health practitioners, and it follows ICD-10 coding. The DSM-5 had several changes from the DSM-IV-TR. One of the most notable changes was the removal of the multiaxial system. Another significant change was the replacement of the term *mental retardation* with *intellectual disability*. In addition, the category of intellectual disability was expanded to require a cognitive and functional assessment. Autism, Asperger's, and childhood disintegrative disorder have become one disorder under the umbrella of autism spectrum disorders. Although the criteria for ADHD remain the same, some changes have been made, including, but not limited to the use of examples, that the individual must be impaired in several settings, and that the symptoms must have been present before the age of 7 years. Most notable, however, is that ADHD has been moved into the chapter on neurodevelopmental disorders (Sadock et al., 2015). The DSM-5 eliminated the subtypes of schizophrenia and changed the criteria for schizoaffective disorder. The DSM-5 no longer includes mood disorders, but has two distinct categories of depressive disorders and bipolar disorders. In the same vein, the anxiety disorders chapter no longer includes trauma-related disorders or OCD; both have their own chapters. These and other changes will be discussed later in the text.

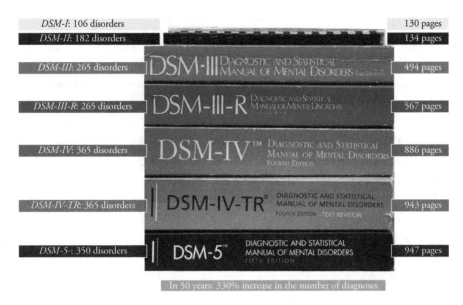

FIGURE 1.4   DSM history

Pros and Cons of the DSM

The DSM has become a fairly reliable describer of behaviors and symptoms that ultimately result in a diagnosis. The DSM has been translated into over 20 languages and is utilized by clinicians from many disciplines; researchers; policymakers; criminal courts; and, of course, third-party reimbursement providers (Kawa & Giordano, 2012). It allows practitioners from a variety of disciplines to communicate with common language about clients or patients. The DSM also provides practitioners a way to begin a comprehensive biopsychosocial assessment, set goals, and develop a suitable treatment plan.

The DSM is not without its flaws. Some disorders have an emphasis on the biological cause, such as ADHD. Although there is certainly a biological cause of ADHD, the behavioral contributions may be minimized. This, in turn, may lead to an increase in pharmacological treatment, as opposed to focusing on behavioral strategies (Krauss Whitbourne, 2013).

One of the biggest criticisms of the DSM by mental health clinicians is its strong focus on the medical model, because it is written by psychiatrists. Social workers have long advocated for the medical community to look at the entire client system. The DSM does not consider the person in the environment (PIE); in other words, the environment in which the client lives, the *reason* the person is behaving the way he/she/they are. Mental health practitioners often encounter situations in which the root cause of the problem of the presenting client does not lie within the client but rather in the environment.

Diagnosing a mental illness is based on a deficit model, labeling the individual's deficits or shortcomings, not what is functional. This flies in the face of social work, which is based on the strengths perspective. Some argue that the DSM pathologizes "normal" behaviors such as temper tantrums (disruptive mood dysregulation disorder) and PMS (premenstrual dysphoric disorder) (Krauss Whitbourne, 2013).

The ICD is the diagnostic classification system used in medical practices and by researchers. It is rarely used by the mental health community. The ICD defines diseases, disorders, injuries, and other health conditions, including mental health disorders. The first edition of the *International List of Causes of Death* was created in 1893, though some scholars trace the origins of the ICD back to 1763. In 1948, the WHO took over the classification system and added coding for causes of morbidity, in addition to mortality. The first five editions consisted of one volume. The ICD-6 contained two volumes and was the first to include a section on psychiatric disorders. The seventh and eighth revisions were published in 1957 and 1968, respectively. In 1977, the ICD-9 was moved out of the WHO and into the public domain. At this time, the United States created the ICD-9-Clinical Modification, which allowed for diagnostic coding at physicians' offices, in addition to inpatient and outpatient facilities. The ICD-10 was released in October of 2015. It allowed for better disease tracking than the previous volumes. However, the ICD is not without its challenges. With each new ICD release, healthcare systems must spend an enormous amount of money to update their billing systems. In addition, as with the DSM, individuals are labeled and put into categories, which may lead to the depersonalization of care (Hirsh et al., 2016). A version of the ICD-11 was released in June of 2018 to allow for preparation, translation, and implementation. Use of the ICD-11 will begin January 2022.

Cultural Considerations in Psychosocial Pathology

Black/African American, Latinx/Hispanic American, American Indian/Alaskan Native, Native Hawaiian/Pacific Islander, and Asian American communities; women; and lesbian, gay, bisexual, transgender, queer, intersex, and asexual (LGBTQIA) often suffer from poor mental health outcomes due to multiple factors, including a lack of access to high-quality mental health care services, the stigma surrounding mental health care, discrimination, and overall lack of awareness about mental health (APA, 2013). It is also important to consider issues of intersectionality, ,the interconnection of all aspects of a person's social and/or political identities. (APA, 2017; Crenshaw, 1991).

Considerations Related to Racial and Ethnic Culture

In general, racial and ethnic minoritized groups have rates of mental health disorders similar to those of White Americans but experience more adverse mental health outcomes (APA, 2017). According to the National Institute of Mental Health (NIMH), 20.4% of White adults are living with a mental health condition, compared to 15.2% of Hispanic Americans/Latinx, 14.5% of Asian Americans, 16.2% of Black/African Americans, and 19.4% of Native Americans/Alaskan Natives (NIMH, 2019). Although rates of mental illness are similar among cultures, individuals from some racial and ethnic cultural backgrounds are overdiagnosed but underserved in terms of treatment. For example, Black/African Americans are less likely to have private insurance, are more likely to be covered by Medicaid, and are twice as likely to be uninsured compared to Whites. Black/African Americans are more likely to have jobs in which healthcare benefits are not provided, are less likely to have a stable source of healthcare services (Smedley et al., 2003, as cited in Copeland, 2005), tend to have less access to treatment, are less likely to receive treatment, and receive a poorer level of care.

An observational study of elderly individuals enrolled in Medicare + Choice plans found that mental health care for the elderly is not optimal and that the quality of care was worse for non-White patients compared to White patients (Virnig et al., 2004). In addition, there were significant differences in follow-up care: 38% of White patients received 7-day follow-up care, compared 25% for Black/African American patients. The same trend was seen at 30-day follow-up, with 60% of White patients receiving care, compared to 42.4% of Black/African American patients (Virnig et al., 2004).

People who have mental illness are often criminalized and placed in jails or prisons. Black/African Americans with mental health conditions, particularly schizophrenia, bipolar disorders, and other psychoses, are more likely to be incarcerated than people of other racial or ethnic groups (APA, 2017). Mental health treatment in jails and prisons is subpar or nonexistent. This, combined with the disproportionate number of underrepresented multicultural groups in U.S. prisons, serves as an additional barrier to mental health services (Ward & Willis, 2010).

Considerations Related to Gender and Sexuality

Consideration of one's biological sex and individual self-representation is important when assessing and diagnosing women and individuals from the LGBTQIA community. The DSM-5 classifies differences between men and women in terms of variations that result from biological sex as well as an individual's self-representation, which includes the psychological, behavioral, and social consequences of one's perceived gender. (APA, 2013). LGBTQIA individuals are more than twice as likely as heterosexual, cisgender men and women to have a mental health disorder in their lifetime. LGBTQIA individuals are 2.5 times more likely to experience depression, anxiety, and substance use disorders compared with heterosexual individuals. Women who identify as lesbian/bisexual are more than twice as likely to engage in alcohol misuse. The rate of suicide attempts is four times greater for lesbian, gay, and bisexual youth and two times greater for questioning youth than that of heterosexual youth (APA, 2017).

Mental Health Stigma

In addition to receiving a lack of quality care, many ethnic groups hold stronger stigmatizing attitudes or stereotypes toward mental illness, making them less likely to seek treatment than Whites (Nadeem et al., 2007). Gary (2005) provides the example of the stereotype that Asian Americans are the "model minority" (p. 985). The societal construct is often that Asian Americans do not have substance abuse or socioeconomic issues. This stereotype can then, in turn, serve as a deterrent for someone who is Asian American to seek mental health treatment. Labels can also contribute to stigma and poor health outcomes. By simply assigning a diagnosis, particularly one such as schizophrenia, stigma is a possible outcome (Gary, 2005). People who have mental illnesses often experience a lowered self-esteem (Link et al., 1999). This lowered self-esteem, combined with the stigma of a diagnosis and the negative perception (public stigma) (Corrigan, 2004) that others may have of that individual, can lead to an internalization of the stigma, often resulting in the belief that they are less valuable than others in society (self-stigma) (Corrigan, 2004; Hudson, 2005). LGBTQIA older adults face a number of unique challenges, including issues of intersectionality pertaining to the combination of anti-LGBTQIA stigma and ageism. Approximately 31% of LGBTQIA older adults report depressive symptoms, with 39% reporting serious thoughts suicide. Many LGBTQIA individuals have reported experiencing stigma and discrimination when accessing health services, leading some individuals to delay necessary health care or forego it altogether. LGBTQIA individuals may have less social support than heterosexual individuals, particularly if they live in a region without a large LGBTQIA population or if they have experienced rejection by their family of origin. Bisexual people may feel particularly isolated, experiencing stigma both in society at-large and within the LGBTQIA community (APA, 2017).

Assessment and Diagnosis

Diagnosis is the process of identifying a problem and its underlying causes and for-mulating a solution. Diagnosing is guided by determining the identity of the disease or disorder supported by evidence, determining the cause, and formulating a diag-nostic impression based on examination. In the case of mental health diagnosing, the disorder is diagnosed using the DSM criteria (evidence) and determining the severity. The examination in this case is a detailed psychosocial history of the client. This will assist in helping to determine the potential causes of the disorder.

Assessment involves "determining the nature, cause, progression, and prognosis of a problem and the personalities and situations involved" (Barker, 1995, p. 27). Biological, psychological, and social and environmental factors need to be considered when assessing a client. In terms of psychological factors, the client's mental function-ing needs to be considered. One must ask, how is the person functioning mentally? In this case, a mental status exam is often helpful. Cognitive functioning must also be considered. Is the client able to think and apply sound and responsible decision making? And, most important, an assessment of lethality must be conducted. Is the individual a harm to themselves or to others? In terms of social and environmental factors, it is important to determine if the individual is open to receiving assistance and whether they have social support from family, friends, and/or neighbors. Occupation and level of education need to be considered. Is the client's work environment sup-portive, or is it a source of stress? What is their level of cognitive functioning? Ethnic and religious affiliations should also be considered. Is the individual a member of a religious or ethnic organization, and if so, is it a source of support or is it a source of stress?

Although diagnosis and assessment are often used interchangeably, they are processed differently. A diagnosis focuses on symptoms and what is "wrong" with the individual, whereas assessment focuses on the person in the environment (PIE). Assessment is an ongoing process; it does not just happen once during the first ses-sion. Agencies often have their own guidelines or requirements; however, assessment should occur at least every 6 months. It is important to ask specific questions when reassessing a client:

1. *What is happening in your life right now?* All too often, mental health clinicians get hung up on the past. Yes, the past is important; it shapes who we are today. However, there is a reason the client is sitting in front of you right now.

2. *What does the client expect from treatment?* Does the client have realistic goals? Is their goal something you can help them with? This is a time to make sure that you and your client are on the same page.

3. *What is the client learning from treatment?* This is an important question to assess your effectiveness, as well. The client, of course, does the majority of the work (hopefully), but you provide the appropriate tools. If the client is not learning anything or has stopped learning, it is time not only to update the treatment plan, but also perhaps look at your own toolbox to determine if your approach needs to be changed or tweaked.

4. *How is the client applying what they have learned?* Your client may be coming to every session and learning what you have provided them, in terms of skills. However, it is important that they apply this information and can generalize it outside of their sessions. For example, if you are working with your client on communicating with his husband by role-playing, but the client never goes home and speaks to his husband, the sessions are not effective. In this case, it is very important not to judge the client or blame them for being "noncompliant"; there is quite likely a reason for the lack of follow-through.

Finally, it is important for mental health practitioners to learn and apply culturally responsive practices to assessment and diagnosis of clients from racial and ethnic minoritized groups (Ponterotto et al., 2010; Pope-Davis & Coleman, 1997). Lack of cultural understanding by healthcare providers may contribute to overdiagnosis, underdiagnosis, and misdiagnosis of mental illness in certain cultural groups. Overdiagnosing often occurs when clinicians mistakenly ascribe pathology or a mental health diagnosis to a culture-related phenomenon (Paniagua, 2014). Factors that can contribute to underdiognoses and misdiagnoses include language differences between patient and provider, stigma of mental illness among underrepresented groups, and cultural presentation of symptoms (APA, 2017).

Ethical Considerations

The National Association of Social Workers (NASW) Code of Ethics requires that social workers respect the dignity and worth of all people and allow clients the time, space, and support to have control over their lives (empowerment) (NASW, 2021). Social workers are to be nonjudgmental and focus on a strengths perspective. Some argue that because the DSM is based on a medical model, by diagnosing a client with a mental health disorder, the focus is on their negative traits and highlighting their perceived weaknesses, as opposed to their strengths. However, a diagnosis allows for the provision of services and reimbursement through insurance companies. In addition, the medical model may be beneficial in that the client is provided a medical label rather than a moral one, which would imply that the individual has a disease and is not personally responsible or has a moral weakness (Barksy, 2019). However, does a medical diagnosis mean that the individual has little control over the disorder? Does this reduce their empowerment? A study of social workers found that clinicians reported that there were, in fact, advantages to diagnosing, including a sense of control for the clinician and the client, a reduction of anxiety or blame, and opening a path to recovery (Probst, 2005). However, the respondents did report that diagnoses must be used with caution because of the haste with which they are typically made, due to agency and reimbursement requirements. According to Barsky (2019), a social worker can increase a client's level of empowerment by including them in the diagnostic process, educating the client about the suspected disorder, and coming to a mutual consensus about diagnosis. Although the client and the worker may not agree on the diagnosis, the diagnostic process provides an opportunity to explore the client's views on mental illness and the stigmas attached. Interestingly, social workers report that sharing a diagnosis with a client raised ethical concerns such as confidentiality, stigma, and making someone in the family the "sick one" or "identified" patient (Probst, 2005).

Mental health providers often struggle whether or not to diagnose a client. Other times, mental health providers assign a diagnosis without much thought. This is often because the agency in which the worker is employed requires a diagnosis for reimbursement purposes. As mentioned earlier, a diagnosis stays with the client as their label. A diagnosis can prevent someone from getting a new job, cause them to lose their current job, and lead to stigmatization by friends and family. It is important for mental health providers to consider all these factors when assigning a diagnosis. One of the most important things to remember is that a diagnosis is only warranted when the client is experiencing an impairment socially, occupationally, or educationally. If there is no impairment, a diagnosis is not warranted; however, this does not mean the client does not need treatment (which is a conundrum with today's reimbursement systems), but remember, a diagnosis will stay with the person. This is often an ethical dilemma for clinicians: the client clearly needs assistance, but oftentimes you (your agency) cannot provide services without a diagnosis. Social workers often struggle with the ethics of having to assign a more "serious diagnosis" in order to receive reimbursement (Probst, 2005, p. 188). Sometimes mental health professionals will choose a "mild" diagnosis such as (major depressive disorder, mild, or adjustment disorder) (Barsky, 2019). Choosing a mild diagnosis may solve the problem in terms of reimbursement; however, it is still a diagnosis. If the symptoms are indeed mild, why is it necessary to diagnose? The short answer has to do with the benefits outweighing the costs. Do the potential services outweigh the risks, or should the worker explore other alternatives? Are there other services available (in the agency or elsewhere) that do not require a DSM diagnosis? There is no easy answer. Striking a balance between upholding the NASW Code of Ethics and the policies of the agency is often difficult; however, in the end, the dignity and worth of the clients must be considered first and foremost.

SUMMARY

Social workers provide more mental health therapeutic services than any other profession (Kirk, 2005). Social workers and other mental health practitioners are tasked with balancing diagnosing using the DSM (as required by agencies and third-party insurers) and upholding the NASW Code of Ethics. To assess, diagnose, and treat clients, it is imperative that social workers do so in the context of the person in the environment (PIE). Throughout the course of this text, the authors will guide you through the diagnostic process from the social work perspective.

REFLECTION QUESTIONS

1. What are the pros and cons of using the DSM for diagnostic purposes?

2. What are the differences between the DSM and ICD?

3. What are the ethical implications of diagnosing clients who have mild symptoms?

CREDITS

CHAPTER 2

Neurodevelopmental Disorders

with Teresa Michaelson Chmelir

LEARNING OBJECTIVES

1. Gain a basic understanding of the causes, prevalence, and comorbidities of neurodevelopmental disorders.

2. Become familiar with the criteria for autism spectrum disorder.

3. Become familiar with the criteria for ADHD.

4. Be able to differentially diagnose neurodevelopmental disorders.

Characteristics of the Disorders

Neurodevelopmenal disorders are disorders that have an onset during the developmental period (APA, 2013). The disorders typically manifest in early development and typically begin before the child is school aged. The disorders are characterized by developmental impairments that impact social, occupational and academic functioning. The neurodevelopmental chapter is the DSM-5 is comprised of intellectual disabilities, communication disorders, autism spectrum disorder, attention-deficit-hyperactivity-disorder, specific learning disorder, and motor disorders (APA, 2013). For the purposes of this chapter we will focus on autism spectrum disorder and attention deficit hyperactivity disorder as these are the disorders that social works will more commonly diagnose. Intellectual disorders, tic disorders and motor disorders are typically diagnosed by medical professionals after all physiological causes have been ruled out. The communication disorders are typically diagnosed by those who specialize in communication disorders.

Autism Spectrum Disorder

The two primary characteristics of autism spectrum disorder (ASD) are deficits in social communication and interaction and restricted or repetitive behaviors (American Psychiatric Association [APA], 2013). Children with ASD often struggle with nonverbal communication, such as interpreting facial expressions/body language or maintaining eye contact. Younger children with ASD often have difficulty making friends and engaging in imaginative play and tend to play by themselves. Adolescents and adults with ASD have difficulties understanding and maintaining relationships and therefore tend to be isolated from their peers.

One of the hallmarks of early childhood is the desire for repetition (Richler et al., 2007)—asking the same question over and over or requesting the same story. Although these behaviors are common for most children between the ages of 2 and 5 years, repetitive behaviors or mannerisms are one of the primary behaviors of ASD in the DSM-5 (APA, 2013). Children with ASD often engage in repetitive movements, use of objects, or verbalizations. For example, a child may line up objects in a very specific way, engage in echolalia (repeating words), or spin the wheel of a toy truck for prolonged periods of time. Another characteristic of ASD is the need for sameness in routines and surroundings. A colleague once told me a story about a child he was working with who had ASD. The mother came to the session looking very stressed and visibly upset. She stated that she was on her way to take her son to school, using the same route they had used every day for the past 2 years. There was a detour, and she was forced to take a different road. Her son, who was 8 years old at the time, noticed the change in routine and began getting very upset. He started screaming and crying, pulling at his hair, and scratching at his face. The mother was so afraid that he would seriously harm himself that she drove through the construction zone. Although this is an extreme example of the need for sameness, it illustrates that, in many cases, routine is especially important for children with ASD, and any changes need to be carefully considered in advance.

Attention-Deficit Hyperactivity Disorder

Attention deficit hyperactivity disorder (ADHD; often referred to by the general public as ADD) is a neurodevelopmental disorder and one of the most common mental health disorders to affect children. Historically, it was thought that ADHD was a childhood disorder; however, it is now known that ADHD can persist into adulthood.

ADHD is characterized by chronic inattention, chronic hyperactivity, or both. It is important to note that "ADD" is not a disorder, it is a term used by the general population but it is not an acutal diagnosis. An individual with chronic inattention who meets the DSM-5 criteria is diagnosed with ADHD, predominately inattentive presentation (which lay people refer to as "ADD"). Individuals with this presentation tend to make careless mistakes and fail to attend to details. Individuals with ADHD, predominately hyperactive presentation, tend to exhibit restlessness and impulsivity. ADHD has been linked to significant impairment in cognitive, academic, familial, and social functioning (Farone et al., 2001). Children with ADHD often struggle with the attention and social cues that are necessary for positive social interaction. These children are often seen as awkward or nervous. Children who are struggling with impulsivity are often seen as intrusive and overbearing by their peers. These behaviors often lead to rejection. In fact, it is estimated that over half of children with ADHD are rejected by their peers, compared to 10% to 15% of children without a diagnosis of ADHD (Hoza et al., 2005).

History

Autism Spectrum Disorder

The term *autism* is derived from the Greek word *autos* meaning "self." The first use of the term was by Eugen Bleuler, a Swiss psychiatrist, referring to a group of symptoms related to schizophrenia. In 1943, Leo Kanner wrote about 11 children who exhibited symptoms of a yet-to-be recognized disorder. He noted symptoms such as an inability to develop relationships with others, aloofness, and a delay in speech and communication. The 11 children presented differently in terms of symptoms; however, he believed that two general symptoms were of diagnostic importance: "autistic aloneness" and an "obsessive insistence on sameness" (Tsai & Ghaziuddin, 2014, p. 322). He labeled the condition "infantile autism" because the symptoms were present beginning in infancy. In 1944, Hans Asperger, an Austrian pediatrician, reported on four boys who exhibited symptoms of "autistic psychopathy in childhood" (Tsai & Ghaziuddin, 2014, p. 322). Not knowing that a Russian neuroscientist had reported on six children with symptoms similar to those described by Asperger, his paper was published. According to Asperger, children with "autistic psychopathy" begin speaking at the same time as children without the disorder; however, the content of their speech was different. The children often focused on long explanations of a favorite subject or engaged in echolalia. Other observed traits included verbal abuse and aggression toward others. Initially, Asperger noted that the children with "autistic psychopathy" exhibited high levels of abstract thinking and creativity; he later indicated that children with the disorder exhibited all levels of intelligence, including developmental delay (Tsai & Ghazuiddin, 2014).

Infantile autism was introduced into the DSM-III (APA, 1980) and ICD-9-CM (U.S. Department of Health and Human Services, 1980) with similar criteria but different conceptualizations of the disorder. In the DSM-III, infantile autism was classified under the broader category of pervasive developmental disorders (PDD), but the ICD-9-CM classified it as a subtype of childhood psychosis. At the time of the printing of the DSM-III, Asperger's disorder was unknown in the English literature, and therefore not a subtype of the PDD. The DSM-III-R (APA, 1987), however, did include autistic disorder as an Axis II disorder.

After a series of clinical studies, Asperger's disorder was added to the DSM-IV. The DSM-IV (APA, 1994) and the ICD-10 (World Health Organization [WHO], 1992) now included five categories of PDD: autistic disorder, Asperger's disorder (seen as a milder form of autistic disorder), Rett syndrome, child disintegrative disorder, and pervasive developmental disorder not otherwise specified (NOS). Numerous authors, however, claimed that Asperger's disorder was actually indistinguishable from what is termed a high-functioning autism. It was argued that original cases described by Asperger would actually meet the criteria and ultimately, by today's criteria, be diagnosed with ASD. A study conducted with 26 children who had been diagnosed with Asperger's disorder revealed that 20 of them met full criteria for autism and that none truly independently met the criteria for Asperger's disorder (Tryon et al., 2006). This may be, in part, due to the fact that some children were given a diagnosis of Asperger's disorder largely based on their obsessive and sometimes unusual interests. Some authors have argued that this is actually pathologizing children who are seen as "different" (Allred, 2009) and that these strong interests may be useful as the child becomes an adult, raising the question of whether these children are actually impaired or simply do not conform to the social norms.

The APA eliminated the category of pervasive developmental disorders from the DSM-5 (APA, 2013) and replaced it with ASD, a multilevel classification system based on level of severity. Level 1 indicates that the individual "requires support," level 2 indicates the individual "requires substantial support," and level 3 indicates that the individual "requires very substantial support" (APA, 2013, p. 52). Asperger's disorder was eliminated as a diagnosis from the DSM-5 and is now encompassed in level 1. The elimination of Asperger's disorder from the DSM was not without controversy; several studies have revealed that the number of people diagnosed with what was formerly called PDD in the DSM-IV-TR will no longer meet the criteria for ASD in the DSM-5 (de Giambattista et al., 2019). These studies indicate that only 50% to 75% of people with a DSM-IV-TR diagnosis will maintain their diagnosis in the DSM-5. This is particularly true for those individuals considered to be high functioning or who were diagnosed with Asperger's disorder (Smith et al., 2015; Young & Rodi, 2014). Other studies, however, estimate that approximately 92% to 97% of those diagnosed with Asperger's disorder will maintain their diagnosis (de Giambattista et al., 2019; Kim et al., 2015). Regardless, despite the elimination of Asperger's disorder, researchers continue to debate Asperger's disorder's conceptualization under the umbrella of ASD (de Giambattista et al., 2019).

Some individuals have come to find personal meaning from the label of Asperger's disorder, with some referring to themselves as "Aspies" and referring to people without Asperger's disorder as "neurotypical." Lorna Wing, who is often credited for the term *Asperger's syndrome*, after describing 34 case studies of children who matched the symptoms outline by Hans Asperger, stated that there is an ethical question surrounding changing an individual's diagnosis from Asperger's disorder to ASD. These individuals will be forced to reconfigure their long-established identities based on their diagnosis (Wing et al., 2011).

Attention Deficit Hyperactivity Disorder

ADHD-type symptoms were first described by Alexander Crichton in 1798. Crichton described a condition in which the individual experienced external senses or thoughts that occupied the mind, rendering the individual incapable of attending to the thought. His definition of the symptoms was very similar to the criteria used today to diagnose ADHD (Lange et al., 2010).

In the 1960s, hyperactivity was recognized as a behavioral syndrome that had either an organic or an environmental cause. In 1968, a definition of hyperactivity was added to the DSM-II (APA, 1968). The diagnosis was labeled as hyperkinetic reaction of childhood and was characterized by overactivity, distractibility, short attention span, and restlessness. It was stated that the disorder would typically diminish by adolescence. In 1980, the APA renamed the disorder as attention deficit disorder, with or without hyperactivity. It was now indicated that hyperactivity was no longer required for a diagnosis; however, reduced impulse control was considered a significant symptom of the disorder. The DSM-III-R (APA, 1987) removed the subtypes of with or without hyperactivity and renamed the disorder attention deficit hyperactivity disorder. The symptoms of hyperactivity, inattention, and impulsivity were combined into a single list of symptoms. The DSM-IV (APA, 1994) classified ADHD into three subtypes: predominately inattentive type, predominantly hyperactivity type, and combined type. The DSM-IV also recognized that ADHD is not exclusively a childhood disorder that recedes before adulthood. The DSM-IV-TR (APA, 2000) kept the criteria from the DSM-IV. As noted in Chapter 1, the DSM-5 (APA, 2013) had significant revisions. Most notable was the elimination of the chapter on disorders usually first diagnosed in infancy, childhood, or adolescence. The disorders in this chapter were included in the new chapter on neurodevelopmental disorders or added to existing chapters of the DSM. The criteria for ADHD remained the same in the DSM-5, with examples added. The requirement of impairment in two settings was strengthened to say several symptoms in each setting. The previous requirement that symptoms must be present before the age of 7 years was changed to several symptoms were present prior to the age of 12 years. Further changes included a cut off of five symptoms (rather than six) for adults.

Etiology

Autism Spectrum Disorder

There has been much debate about the cause of autism, particularly in relation to the measles, mumps, and rubella (MMR) vaccine. In 1998, Dr. Andrew Wakefield and his colleagues published an article in *Lancet* stating that the MMR vaccine may predispose children to "behavioral regression" and pervasive developmental disorder in children (Wakefield et al., 1998). The study consisted of a sample of only 12 participants, included a largely speculative conclusion, and relied on a nonexperimental design. Despite the issues with the reliability and validity of the study, the paper received much publicity, and MMR vaccinations began to drop because parents were worried about the risk of vaccinating their children (Sathyanarayana et al., 2011). Within a year of the Wakefield publication, epidemiological studies were conducted refuting the link between MMR vaccines and autism. In 2004, a retraction of the original paper was published by 10 of the original 12 authors, stating that there was insufficient data and that no causal link was found between the MMR and vaccines (Murch et al., 2004). In addition, *Lancet* acknowledged that Wakefield and his colleagues failed to disclose financial conflicts of interests such as funding sources (the lawyers of the parents suing the drug companies that created the vaccines). Interestingly, it was not until 2010 that *Lancet* retracted the original paper. Wakefield and two of his colleagues had their medical licenses revoked after being found guilty of ethical violations (not obtaining proper approvals for invasive procedures on children), not having ethical approval for the research, and data misrepresentations. There has been no reputable evidence to link autism to MMR. Seventeen major trials have looked at Wakefield's findings and found no relationship.

The cause of autism still remains unknown. However, there are a number of theories as to some possible causes of autism, including pre- and perinatal factors, neurobiological or genetic factors, or a combination of all three.

PRE- AND PERINATAL FACTORS

Increased parental age has been indicated as being a risk factor for increased risk for ASD. Research has indicated that children born to older mothers (older than 40 years) are 51% more likely of having ASD compared to children born to younger mothers (25 to 29 years) (Shelton, 2010). A study conducted with an Israeli birth cohort in 2006 revealed a sixfold increase for ASD among fathers older than 40 years as compared with fathers 30 years and younger (Reichenberg et al., 2006). This is consistent with a more recent meta-analysis conducted in 2017 that found that higher maternal age was associated with a 41% increased risk of ASD, and higher paternal age was associated with a 55% increased risk of ASD. The authors found that for every 10-year increase in maternal and paternal age, there was an 18% and 21% higher risk, respectively (Wu et al., 2017). The mechanism for the increased risk from parental age is not well understood. The increased paternal risk may be due to biological mechanisms or genetic mutations. The increased maternal risk may be associated with nutritional deficiencies, medications, pollution, a higher rate of obstetric complications, or increased opportunity to be exposed to more toxins.

Numerous studies have indicated an increased risk of ASD with a short interpregnancy interval (fewer than 12 months between pregnancies) (Cheslack-Postova et al., 2011; Coo et al., 2015; Dodds et al., 2011; Gunnes et al., 2013), whereas other studies have indicated an increased risk with long interpregnancy intervals (more than 60 to 84 months) (Cheslack-Postova, 2014; Zerbo et al., 2015). The reason for this increased risk in unknown, but it is thought to be related to nutritional intake, stress, or issues surrounding fertility.

Recent studies have indicated an association between the prenatal use of certain psychotropic medications (antidepressants and antiepileptics) and increased risk of ASD. Serotonin reuptake inhibitors (SSRIs) used to treat depression and anxiety disorders have been the most studied of the antidepressants. Of 11 studies investigating the association between SSRIs and ASD, 6 reported an increased risk, whereas 5 found no relationship (Lyall et al., 2017). Antiepileptics are often used as mood stabilizers for bipolar disorders, and studies have consistently indicated an increase of ASD and exposure to antiepileptics during pregnancy (Lyall et al., 2017).

GENETIC FACTORS

The heritability of ASD is strongly supported by twin and family studies, with estimates ranging from 50% to 90% (Colvert et al., 2015). Estimates of recurrent risk among siblings (the chances of subsequent siblings having the disorder) range from 3% to 18% (Gronberg et al., 2013). Research has also indicated a rare genetic variation related to autism and autistic features (Bourgeron, 2015).

NEUROBIOLOGICAL FACTORS

The neurobiological mechanisms and impairments in ASD remain largely unknown. However, studies consistently indicate early brain overgrowth in patients with ASD (Sacco et al., 2015). Further evidence suggest difference in brain substructures, specifically the cerebral cortex and the cerebeullum, though the magnitude of the differences differ among studies (Chen et al., 2015; Lefebvre, et al., 2015).

Functional studies implicate glucose and blood flow differences in individuals with ASD, as well as compromised white matter connectivity, although findings are highly variable across studies. Differences across functional imaging studies may reflect the heterogeneity of ASD and/or methodological and procedural differences between studies (Lyall, et al., 2017).

Attention Deficit Hyperactivity Disorder

The cause of ADHD is thought to be a combination of many factors, including biological (genetics and brain abnormalities) and environmental (neglect, exposure to lead, and maternal stress).

BIOLOGICAL FACTORS

It has been found that ADHD is highly genetic. Research has indicated that a child has a greater than 50% chance of having ADHD if one parent has been diagnosed with the disorder (Tandon & Pergjika, 2017). First-degree relatives (mother, father, brother, sister) of those with ADHD are two to eight times more likely to have a diagnosis than relatives of those without ADHD; twin studies have indicated a heritability rate of 71% to 90% for the combined and inattentive presentations (Tandon & Pergjika, 2017). Although ADHD is considered to be one of the most inherited disorders, no single genetic factor appears to be associated with the disorder; rather, ADHD is likely caused by an interplay of genetics, other biological factors, and/or environmental causes.

Researchers can use neuroimaging techniques to explore the relationship between functional and structural anatomy and behavior and mental health disorders. Functional neuroimaging indirectly measures brain function. Structural neuro-imaging is used to show the contrast between tissues, including white matter, grey matter, and cerebrospinal fluid, for example. Numerous neuroimaging techniques are available. One technique is magnetic resonance imaging (MRI), which can be used to examine brain structure; another is functional MRI, or fMRI, which can be used to look at brain function. Other neuroimaging techniques include computed tomography (CT), positron emission tomography (PET), and single photon emission computed tomography (SPECT).

Both functional and structural abnormalities have been identified in the brains of people diagnosed with ADHD. Functional and structural neuroimaging studies indicate that the frontal-stria regions of the brain are involved in ADHD. In terms of functional findings, research by Andersen and Teicher (2000) reported increased blood flow in the striatum of boys who were diagnosed with ADHD. At the same time, Lorberboym et al. (2004) found reduced blood flow in the frontal lobes and basal ganglia in children with ADHD.

Research on possible structural anomalies in the brain contributing to ADHD have produced varied and sometimes contradictory results. Studies, including those by Marcos-Vidal et al. (2018) and Ouhaz et al. (2018), have reported reduced grey matter, cortical thinning, and white matter connectivity in children with ADHD. Other studies (e.g., Friedman & Rapoport, 2015) have not found these same reductions in children with or without ADHD.

The source of the structural differences associated with ADHD is not always found to be directly related to the disorder. The best conclusion from these studies is that there are no changes in any investigated brain structure that is certain to be diagnostic of ADHD.

Some studies of the density of dopamine transporters have found decreased transporter density in the striatum of people with ADHD compared to healthy controls, whereas other studies have found increased density or no difference (Cheon et al., 2003; Chu et al., 2017). Vles et al. (2003) found that a 3-month course of the drug methylphenidate (Ritalin) in male children with ADHD reduced dopamine receptors by 20% and reduced dopamine transporter density in the striatal system by 74%. These reductions were associated with improved cognitive functioning and ADHD symptoms.

ENVIRONMENTAL FACTORS

Many environmental factors have been associated with ADHD, including diet, family stress, exposure to toxins, and maternal exposure to substances. Exposure to toxins such as PCBs (chemicals widely used in coolants, electrical equipment, and other manufacturing) and lead have been linked to increases in ADHD. Human and animal studies have indicated that exposure causes impairments in memory, impulsivity, and cognitive flexibility, which are comparable to symptoms of ADHD (Eugbig et al., 2010). The same study found similar results with regard to lead exposure, with cognitive flexibility, vigilance, and alertness being impacted.

Maternal smoking is one of the most cited prenatal risks associated with an increase of ADHD diagnoses. As is seen with toxins, there seems to be a dose-response relationship with smoking, meaning that the more the mother smokes, the higher the risk of ADHD. Exposure to alcohol has also been associated with an increased risk of ADHD.

The role of diet in the prevention of ADHD has been a topic of research since the 1980s. Results of two recent meta-analyses (Nigg et al., 2012; Pelsser et al., 2017) have indicated that an elimination diet can be effective in reducing ADHD symptoms. This diet involves a total change of food intake, where the child is only permitted to eat a limited number of nonallergenic foods, such as chicken, lettuce, and pears. After the symptoms diminish, other foods are slowly introduced, to determine if any trigger symptoms. Bosch et al. (2020) are currently conducting a randomized controlled trial to compare a 5-week and 1-year elimination diet and a healthy diet, as compared with a typical diet, in children with ADHD.

Prevalence and Comorbidities

Autism Spectrum Disorder

Identifying the actual prevalence of ASD is difficult due to several factors, including differing symptoms from child to child, lack of genetic markers, and changing of diagnostic criteria. The autism and developmental disabilities monitoring network (ADDM) is a surveillance system that provides estimates on the prevalence of ASD among children 8 years of age in 11 states (see Baio et al., 2018). The ADDM has reported that, in 2014, the overall prevalence was estimated at 16.8 children per 1,000 (1 in 29) (Centers for Disease Control and Prevention [CDC], 2018). A large telephone survey collecting parents' reports of ASD diagnoses in their children showed rates at approximately 2.2% for children 3 to 17 years of age from 2011 to 2014 (Zablotsky et al., 2015). Prevalence rates in the United States indicate that being non-White, Hispanic, and/or low socioeconomic status have been associated with lower rates and delayed diagnosing (Christensen et al., 2016). Interestingly, in Scandinavian countries, lower socioeconomic status is associated with higher rates of ASD (Lyall et al., 2017).

Globally, the WHO estimates that, in 2010, .76% of the world's children had ASD (Baxter et al., 2015); however, this estimate was based on only 16% of the global children's population (Lyall et al., 2017). China reported having lower estimates of ASD. The highest prevalence estimate for ASD diagnoses was in South Korea for the years 2005–2009, with a rate of 2.64% for children ages 7 to 12 years (Lyall et al., 2017).

People diagnosed with ASD often meet criteria for a least one other mental health disorder. In fact, according to a recent study by Mosner et al. (2019), 91% of children diagnosed with ASD had one or more comorbid disorders. This is consistent with previous research (see Gjevik et al., 2011; Joshi et al., 2010). Additional research has indicated that 41% to 60% of children with ASD have two comorbid disorders, and up to 24% of children have three or more comorbid disorders (Di Martino et al.,

2017, as cited in Mosner et al., 2019). The most common comorbid disorder is intellectual disorder, impacting 30% to 80% of children and adolescents with ASD (Baio, 2018). Children with a dual diagnosis of ASD and intellectual disability often have behavioral problems at rates higher than children without the diagnoses. These problems include aggression, self-injury, pica (the ingestion of nonnutritive items), and elopement (leaving supervised areas without permission) (Newcomb & Hagopian, 2018). These behaviors put the child at risk for self-harm, harm to others, and/or a decrease in quality of life. Other common comorbid disorders include ADHD (37% to 85%) (Stevens et al., 2016), OCD, depression, and oppositional defiant disorder (ODD). A comorbidity of ADHD with ASD is typically associated with more severe ASD symptoms and higher levels of impairment (Zachor & Ben-Itzchak, 2019). Some studies on the impact of anxiety on ASD have found that anxiety has a negative impact on adaptive functioning (Hallett et al., 2013).

Attention Deficit Hyperactivity Disorder

According to data presented by the Centers for Disease Control and Prevention (CDC, 2019), the estimated child prevalence rate of ADHD in the United States in 2016 was 6.4%, or 6.1 million. The CDC indicated that, of this 6.1 million, 388,000 were aged 2 to 5 years, 4 million were aged 6 to 11 years, and 3 million were aged 12 to 17 years.

As many as 60% of children with ADHD have a comorbid disorder. The most common comorbid disorders (50%) include ODD and conduct disorder. Preschoolers with a diagnosis of ADHD are eight times more likely to have comorbid ODD, 26 times more likely to have a diagnosis of conduct disorder, and nine times more likely to have depressive symptoms. School-aged children may display more physical or aggressive behaviors. This is often a manifestation of frustration at their inability to focus or complete tasks. The behavioral issues associated with these disorders puts the child at risk for poorer long-term outcomes, due to the increased risk of social and family strife and substance abuse (CDC, 2019).

Course and Prognosis

Autism Spectrum Disorder

ASD is typically considered to be a lifelong condition. The long-term outcomes for individuals with an ASD diagnosis depend on the level of impairment. These outcomes range from having minor difficulties and nearly typical function in adulthood to severe social and functional impairment. Although there have been reports of individuals "outgrowing" their ASD diagnosis, this is most likely due to the lack of use of standardized diagnostic measures (Zachor & Ben-Itzchak, 2020). A few studies have indicated that some children who met the diagnostic criteria in childhood no longer met the criteria in adulthood but still had communication and language difficulties, occasional repetitive movements, and attention issues, but the severity did not rise to the level of diagnosis (Fein et al., 2005; Orinstein et al., 2015). An 11-year follow-up study found that those adolescents who had the best outcomes (average IQ and no longer met criteria) had less severe symptoms in toddlerhood and had fewer attention and anxiety symptoms than those in the lower-functioning group.

Attention Deficit Hyperactivity Disorder

The symptoms of ADHD typically manifest in toddlerhood; however, the symptoms can sometimes be difficult to distinguish from normal developmental behaviors. Preschoolers are more likely to show hyperactive symptoms, while in the elementary school years inattentiveness tends to be more prominent. The symptoms of ADHD tend to persist into adulthood. A study conducted by Uchida et al. (2018) found that 77% of children with an ADHD diagnosis continued to display full or partial symptomatology into adulthood. Individuals with comorbid disorders such as depression or anxiety, a familial history of ADHD, and/or psychosocial stressors were more likely to have symptoms into adulthood.

Cultural and Gender-Related Considerations

Autism Spectrum Disorder

Cultural differences often exist in social interactions and cues, nonverbal communication and formulation of personal and professional relationships. Individuals with neurodevelopmental disorders have significant impairments identifying social cues and adhering to social norms within their cultural context. These cultual factors can contribute to late or underdiagnosis in Black/African American, Latinx/Hispanic American, and Asian American children (APA, 2013). Black/African American, Latinx/Hispanic and Asian children are less likely than White children to be diagnosed with ASD (Ennis-Cole et al., 2013).

The prevalence rate of ASD is four times higher in boys than in girls, at 26.6 and 6.6 per 1,000, respectively (Fombonne, 2003). The difference in rates between the sexes has remained consistent over time; however, some studies have identified moderating factors. One such factor is parental age. What is interesting, however, is that, as paternal age increases, the male-to-female ratio decreases (Anello et al., 2009); that is, the gap in rates of males and females diagnosed with ASD becomes smaller. This was not found to be true of maternal age. Another possible explanation may lie within diagnostic practices: females are often being underdiagnosed, due to current diagnostic practices. Females tend to be diagnosed with ASD at later ages (adolescence and adulthood) and tend to have greater delays between initial evaluation or intake and actual diagnosis (Begeer et al., 2013). Females who are diagnosed later in life often receive incorrect diagnoses prior to their diagnosis of ASD. Males are more likely to present with restricted/repetitive behaviors (Mandy et al., 2012). Females with ASD tend to be more advanced with vocabulary and core language skills than males. Because language delays are typically what are reported first by parents, this may play a role in diagnostics. Interestingly, research has indicated that females are more likely to camouflage their communicative impairments to fit in with their peers. A qualitative study indicated greater discrepancies between clinician-rated and self-rated autistic traits and core cognitive abilities, with the clinician reporting less impairment than the client (Lai, 2015).

Attention Deficit Hypeactivity Disorder

Studies have indicated that there are sex differences in ADHD presentation. Some studies indicate that boys present with more severe symptomatology, both in inattentive and hyperactive presentations (Arnett et al., 2015), whereas others found that boys tend to be more impulsive than girls (Gaub & Carlson, 1997). Boys are more likely to be diagnosed with ADHD, with a male/female ratio of 3 to 10:1 (Biederman, 2005). It has been long debated as to whether boys are being overdiagnosed with ADHD. The most common explanation of the higher rates of ADHD in boys is that girls are more likely to present with symptoms of inattention and boys are more likely to present with symptoms of hyperactivity, which tend to be more disruptive. It has also been shown that boys are more likely to annoy their teachers (Graetz et al., 2005) and that parents are more likely to see the more "masculine" hyperactive behaviors as being more problematic than the more "feminine" inattentive behaviors (Fresson et al., 2019; Ohan & Johnston, 2005). The study by Fresson et al. (2019) also indicated that, due to stereotyping of boys, psychology students rated boys more severely than they did girls.

The true prevalence of ADHD is thought to be comparable across racial and ethnic groups; however, some studies indicate lower rates in Black/African American (Bailey et al., 2010) or Latinx (Rothe, 2005) populations as compared to European American populations. The reason for this is likely due to lower rates of assessment and diagnosis in Black/African American and Latinx children. One study indicated that Black/African

American children actually displayed more symptoms of ADHD but were diagnosed less often, most likely due to lack of access to treatment (Miller et al., 2009).

Diagnosis and Assessment

Autism Spectrum Disorder

The symptoms of ASD are typically present by 3 years of age. However, some children experience much earlier patterns of symptoms, sometimes just after birth. Other children initially meet their developmental milestones and then experience a regression. Parents/caregivers tend to seek treatment between the ages of 1 and 3 years, when the obsessive behaviors, communication difficulties, and differences from their peers become more apparent. The more severe the symptoms, the earlier the child is brought to be evaluated by their parent, resulting in an earlier diagnosis. Parents sometimes report that the child had "normal" or "typical" development for a period of time and then experienced a regression; however, it could be that the parents simply do not recognize the earlier signs of the disorder (failure to reciprocate facial expressions, vocalization of sounds, and lack of response to stimuli). Although the majority of diagnoses of ASD are made by neurologists or developmental pediatricians, it is important for social workers to be familiar with the assessment process, including DSM criteria, direct observation, speech and language assessments, social skill assessments, medical evaluations, and a complete developmental history of the child.

Attention Deficit Hyperactivity Disorder

Historically, parents and caregivers who observed behavioral issues in their children would say the children were going through a phase. Indeed, some kids go through phases where they lag developmentally: they are not with their peers; they may act differently from their peers. Therefore, it is important to remember that almost a quarter of all children, for a period of time, are likely to meet the criteria for a disorder; this does not necessarily mean that a diagnosis is warranted. It is important to remember that what used to be called a phase may still be called a phase, but now we are quick to diagnosis it and develop a plan to fix it. Oftentimes, with careful investigation of the environment, patience, positive reinforcement, appropriate boundaries, and strong caregiving skills, the child will come out the other side, no worse for wear.

The assessment of ADHD must include both a comprehensive medical and psychosocial evaluation. The psychosocial evaluation should include interviews with the child, parents, and teachers. The combination of the medical and psychosocial evaluations will help to determine if the child meets the full DSM-5 criteria for inattention, hyperactivity/impulsivity, or both. In addition, the evaluation will determine whether the symptoms have been present for at least 6 months in multiple settings and impact functioning (of the child or the family or both). Unfortunately, children often underreport their symptoms and parent and teacher agreement has not been consistent (Tandon & Pergkika, 2017). Studies have indicated low to moderate agreement between parents and teachers on ADHD behaviors (Narad et al., 2015). Some studies have reported higher parent–teacher agreement for inattentive symptoms (Sibley et al., 2012; Wolraich et al., 2004), and others have reported higher agreement for hyperactive/impulsive symptoms (Mitsis et al., 2000; Sollie et al., 2013). Further studies indicate that ADHD symptom severity is reported at higher levels by parents, as compared to teachers (Murray et al., 2007; Papageorgiou et al., 2008). Assessment tools such as the Child Behavior Checklist (CBCL; Achenbach, 2019); Conner's Comprehensive Behavior Rating Scale; and the Swanson, Nolan, and Pelham IV Questionnaire (SNAP-IV) (Swanson et al., 2001) are often helpful in providing data from parents and teachers.

The prevalence of ADHD in toddlers is similar to that in school-age children with a male-to-female ratio of about 5:1 (Tandon & Pergika, 2017). Diagnosing a preschooler with ADHD is particularly difficult because they are undergoing significant developmental changes, including learning to control impulses, testing limits, and attempting to attain independence. As with older children, there has not been consistent agreement between teachers and parents in terms of observed ADHD behaviors. Global ADHD behaviors are reported at higher rates by parents, as compared to teachers. This discrepancy between the two may be, in part, due to a lack of understanding of age-appropriate behaviors or a difference in expectations. Preschool-age-specific assessments are available that can be helpful in determining whether a child's behavior is age appropriate. These scales include the ADHD Rating Scale IV, the CBCL/1.5-5, and the Conner's Comprehensive Behavior Ratings Scale.

Children with ADHD are typically treated with medications, behavioral therapy, and/or a combination of both. Research has indicated that the combination approach is the ideal treatment for ADHD (Barnard-Brak et al., 2020). There are several reasons for nonadherence, including concerns about the long-term impact of ADHD medications, the stigma of having ADHD, and refusal to take medication by older children. Over the past 30 years, nonadherence rates for ADHD medications have remained consistent at about 50% (Barnare-Brak et al., 2012). Another concern of parents are the side effects of the ADHD medications, which can include insomnia and loss of appetite. This loss of appetite can lead to weight loss and possible growth deficits (height and/or weight) (Schertz et al., 1996; Spencer et al., 1998). Most children, however, "catch up" with their peers upon ceasing the medication, with no effects into adulthood. Due to these concerns, some parents will put their children on "medication vacations" during the holidays or summer break. This practice is often seen as beneficial by the parent, particularly because the children typically experience a rebound phenomenon where they tend to gain twice as much weight as children who remain on their medications (Joshi, 2002). Medication vacations can interfere with the efficacy of the medication, however, leading to an increase in symptoms over the summer. While children are not in school during the medication vacations, they are still consistently learning and interacting socially. Without the medications and consequently, a return of symptoms, these children are at risk for social isolation and family conflict.

Sam

Sam is an 8-year-old White cisgender male who lives with his mother, stepfather, and two sisters, aged 10 and 13 years. Sam's mother, Vanessa, presented for the initial assessment, separate from Sam, to discuss the concerns she had for him. She had concerns about his behavior and wanted to know if counseling would be helpful. Sam is in the second grade in a faith-based private elementary school in an urban setting. Vanessa shared that Sam struggles in both the home and school settings. She is most concerned about his academics and how he interacts with his peers. Vanessa reported that, since she can remember, Sam has been "different from the other kids" with regard to what she perceived to be normal. She shared that he started speaking around the age of 2 years but used his words mainly to get what he wanted, rather than showing any emotion. Vanessa went on to share that Sam did not use words to express thoughts or feelings like her older two children.

Vanessa reported that Sam would often get easily frustrated and tantrum over minor things, such as any change in plans or not having a particular type of hairbrush. In addition, Sam never engaged with his peers unless he needed or wanted something. Vanessa shared that Sam has always been that child who played alone at parties or get-togethers. Despite being encouraged, Sam often resisted interacting with the other kids and did not seem interested in others' efforts to engage with him. Vanessa reported that, as Sam entered kindergarten, he appeared to become more interested in his peers; however, these interactions rarely ended well. Sam would often act bossy and was intolerant with the games the other kids "made up." He frequently got into arguments with peers and insisted that they were not playing "the right way."

From an early age, Sam had a fascination with the solar system, and Vanessa noted that he would talk about the planets continuously. As such, the topic has become a source of irritation to the family. Vanessa reports that Sam does not seem to recognize that others are not interested, despite their comments, and in fact will disregard the comments and continue to have one-sided conversations about the planets and galaxies. This frustrates Sam, because he does not seem to understand that others do not have the same interests. Vanessa shared that the family has encouraged Sam to expand his interests, but he resists all attempts to engage in other topics. Vanessa shared that the family dynamics have been challenging, as Sam is often demanding and bossy, frequently having meltdowns when things don't go his way, which impacts the family. Vanessa described the meltdowns as screaming, crying, and throwing objects at the slightest incitement. She also shared that when plans change or if there is a shift in routine, there is significant turmoil for Sam. Vanessa shared that they bought a new kitchen table last year with a different style of chair; when Sam lost his usual chair, his meltdown lasted until they recovered his old chair and added it to the new kitchen table set. She also shared that she cannot change brands of food, toothpaste, or other personal products without a similar reaction.

Recently, Sam has been having increased difficulty in school, particularly with his peers. Sam shares that he does not like the other kids in his class and does not appear to have any friends. Vanessa reports that Sam seems to be unhappy and shared concern about how his personality turns people off, and he is unable to make and keep friends.

Vanessa shared a recent report from Sam's teacher. The report states that he is often alone during recess and is frequently observed making awkward attempts to initiate interactions with others, which were described as off-putting, disruptive, or intrusive. Per the report, Sam's teacher made attempts to talk with Sam about his social interactions, but he did not seem to understand why the other kids would be upset with him when he is just trying to tell them how to do it "right." His teacher went on to share that Sam struggles with group work due to rigid ideas and attempts to tell the group how and what the group will do. Sam's teacher reported that his grades are suffering and that he frequently disagrees with her about the grades she gives on his assignments. She shared that he struggles to complete creative writing assignments, stating he cannot just "make things up." He is only willing to provide "real" and "right" information. Overall, Sam's teacher reports spending inordinate amounts of time with Sam and in helping his groups resolve conflicts for which he is responsible.

During the second session, Sam joined his mother. Sam said hello to the social worker but stated that he did not know why he had to come and that he is not the one with the "problem." During the interaction, Sam did not make eye contact and moved about the room, picking up and touching objects. He shared that the kids in his class are "mean and stupid." Sam reported that he would like to have friends, but there are not any good ones, and no one talks or plays with him. Sam was encouraged to play with various toys and games in the room with his mother; however, he took control, telling his mother how to play, saying things such as "That's not right," "No, not like that; like this," and "This is the right way." When Sam encountered something that he did not agree with or something that was not "right," he told his mother, "Don't you know anything?" When asked if he wonders how others may feel when he says these things, he responds that he does not know. The social worker pressed a bit further and asked how he would feel if someone talked to him like that, he stated that it never happened, so he does not know. When asked to guess, Sam became very irritated and told the social worker, "You're stupid; I'm not talking to you anymore."

Diagnostic Impression

Sam is demonstrating deficits in his social communication and interactions with others. This is happening in multiple contexts, including deficits in social–emotional reciprocity by history and continuing in the present, demonstrated by abnormal, often intrusive and disruptive, social approach; failure of normal back-and-forth conversation; failure to respond to social interactions; reduced sharing of interests and emotions; deficits in nonverbal communicative behaviors for social interaction— abnormalities in eye contact; deficits in developing, maintaining, and understanding relationships demonstrated by difficulties with adjusting behaviors to suit various social contexts; difficulties with imaginative play; and difficulties making friends. Sam also demonstrates highly restrictive, repetitive patterns of behavior, interests, and activities, demonstrated by insistence on sameness and inflexible adherence to routine, reflected in his "rule-following" and bossy behavior with peers and his history of strong preference for specific routine and objects. In addition, Sam's intense interest in planets and galaxies is a highly restricted and fixated interest that is abnormal in intensity and focus. His symptoms presented in the early developmental period and have created a clinically significant impairment in social and academic functioning in multiple settings.

Diagnostic Conclusion

Autism spectrum disorder (ASD), requiring support for deficits in both social communication and restricted repetitive behaviors, without accompanying intellectual impairment and without accompanying language impairment.

DIFFERENTIAL DIAGNOSIS I: RETT SYNDROME

Rationale: Sam has been presenting with autistic-like features since at least 2 years of age, and these features have continued to become more evident as he has grown up.

With Rett syndrome, these features would have decreased soon after turning 4 years of age, followed by a marked improvement in social communication skills, and thus autistic features would no longer be a major area of concern.

DIFFERENTIAL DIAGNOSIS II: ATTENTION DEFICIT HYPERACTIVITY DISORDER

Rationale: Sam presents with symptoms of irritability, being overly focused, and low frustration tolerance. These symptoms are common in individuals with ASD, as are hyperactivity. In this case, Sam is not presenting with hyperactivity or inattentiveness; therefore, further testing for ADHD is not recommended.

Note: When criteria for both ADHD and ASD are met, both diagnoses should be given. This same principle applies to concurrent diagnoses of ASD and developmental coordination disorder, anxiety disorders, depressive disorders, and other comorbid diagnoses.

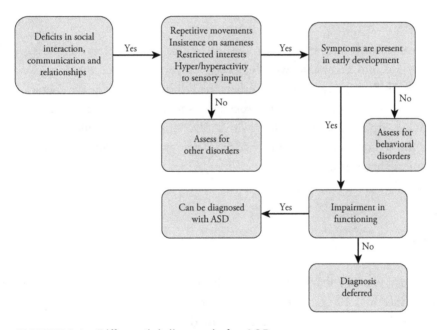

FIGURE 2.1   Differential diagnosis for ASD

Biopsychosocial
BIOLOGICAL

In the initial assessment, Sam's mother comes to the social worker with concerns over her son's behavior. Based on the case example, the social worker finds that his behavior is causing clinically significant impairment at school and at home. The social worker should refer the child to his pediatrician for a diagnosis. Sam's mother mentions that she compares her two older daughters to Sam, stating he did not begin speaking at the same age the girls did. During the initial assessment, the social worker can provide psychoeducation to the mother. It is important to mention that every child has a unique development, that some children reach developmental milestones before others, and that this is okay.

PSYCHOLOGICAL

Sam's mother shared that he struggles to complete creative writing assignments, stating he cannot just "make things up." The social worker can help Sam's mother advocate for an Individualized Education Plan (IEP) at Sam's school. This would allow Sam to have accommodations to assist him to be more successful in an adjusted school curriculum that is appropriate for his needs. An IEP would hopefully reduce Sam's stress and frustration with his classroom and assignments.

SOCIAL

Sam often resisted interacting with the other kids, would often act bossy, and frequently got into arguments with his peers. Sam was observed making awkward attempts to initiate interactions with others, had difficulty making eye contact, and had impulse control difficulties. The social worker should refer Sam to an agency that teaches social skills to children with ASD. Group work would be especially helpful in teaching Sam how to make friends, self-regulate his emotions, and better communicate his needs.

Jayden

Jayden is a 7-year-old Black/African American cisgender male who lives with his mother, father, and 10-year-old brother. At the initial assessment, Jayden presented with his mother, Olivia, and his brother Jordan, due to increased behavioral concerns in the classroom. Jayden is in the second grade at a public elementary school in a suburban neighborhood. Jayden presented as open, engaged, and very talkative. He walked around the office, exploring the space, as well as touching and picking up objects, and frequently interrupting his mom by putting the objects in her face, saying "Look, look!" As the social worker talked with Olivia, it was observed that Jayden did not sit down for the duration of the initial session. He moved from one activity to the next without engaging in any one for more than a few minutes. Jayden had to be redirected multiple times not to write on the dry erase board that was in the room. As his brother, Jordan, played on the floor, Jayden frequently intruded on his activity by grabbing objects from him. As Jordan grabbed the object back, Jayden became upset and whined to his mom that Jordan was not "sharing."

Olivia reports that she is often frustrated with Jayden, because he does not listen to her, even when she is speaking directly to him. She reports that Jayden has always struggled with following directions and completing his chores at home. She specifically reports that cleaning his room has become a constant battle. Olivia shared that Jayden knows how to clean his room but requires that either herself or Jayden's dad supervise and provide constant redirection with specific instructions. Olivia also states that Jayden often becomes excessively emotional over minor issues. She shared that he becomes upset when he learns that he is not going to the restaurant he likes or when his brother plays with something that belongs to him. Olivia described another situation in which Jayden was upset because he could not wear his favorite pajamas anymore, because he had outgrown them. He desperately tried to put them on, and when he could not, it took him 30 minutes to calm down and stop crying.

Olivia reports that Jayden has been "on the move" since he could crawl. She shared that he rarely sits still for long and constantly has something to say. After an incident in a restaurant where Jayden knocked over a tray of food when he was 5, Olivia stated that they had stopped going out to dine in restaurants and will only do drive through or carry-out. She continued to share that she had significant difficulty getting any tasks done when Jayden was younger, due to his requiring so much supervision and not being able to remain engaged in any activity for extended periods of time. Olivia shared that these issues have only intensified as Jayden has gotten older, and with the added demands of school, beginning when he started kindergarten.

Based on the reports from Jayden's teacher, Jayden has difficulty remaining in his seat and following the rules of the classroom. He is unable to follow specific directions and has difficulty completing his deskwork. Jayden is often observed fidgeting and playing with items in his desk and attempting to talk with his classmates during inappropriate times. He can also be observed simply staring off into space. Olivia added that getting Jayden to complete his homework is a constant struggle that can take several hours to finish. When he does finish his homework, he will still lose assignment points due to not following directions, such as putting his name in the top left corner, or simply forgetting to turn his homework in. Jayden's teacher reports that he has to continually remind Jayden to raise his hand if he wants to answer a question or if he needs to get his attention. Jayden's teacher continued to share additional areas of concern around impulse control. He shared that Jayden has difficulty with walking and/or waiting in line and will often step out of line to talk to peers, despite being told not to. Jayden has also been observed engaging in behaviors that his peers find intrusive. He will often interrupt games and will take others' belongings without asking. Olivia believes that it is these intrusive and impulsive behaviors that have made it difficult for Jayden to make or maintain friends. Despite the various concerns in the school setting, Jayden's teacher reported that when Jayden can pay attention he is able to avoid simple errors and can learn the material; however, the amount of time it takes to keep Jayden on task is more than what the teacher can do daily.

During the initial assessment, Jayden reported that he did not know why his mother brought him in to speak to the social worker. He shared that his parents are always yelling at him and that he does not understand why he is always getting into trouble. Jayden shared that he wants to do well in school but that his teacher does not like him. As Jayden shared his experiences, he expressed sadness and frustration at not having any close friends and reported that he tries to play with other boys at recess but that they ignore him and sometimes run away and hide from him.

Diagnostic Impressions

Based on what has been reported by both Olivia and Jayden's teacher, Jayden has demonstrated for more than six months a persistent pattern of inattention, hyperactivity, and impulsivity. The behaviors have been occurring since he was at least a toddler and have been observed in at least two settings (school and home). Jayden's inattentive symptoms include failing to give close attention to details by making careless mistakes in schoolwork, difficulty sustaining attention/focus during tasks, not seeming to listen when spoken to directly, often not following through on instructions, failing to finish schoolwork and chores, demonstrating difficulty organizing tasks and activities, being easily distracted by extraneous stimuli, and being forgetful in daily activities. As far as hyperactive symptoms, he is observed frequently fidgeting in his seat, leaving his seat when expected to remain, being unable to play or engage in leisure activities quietly, being often "on the go," talking excessively, blurting out answers, having difficulty awaiting his turn, and often interrupting or intruding on others. The difficulties that Jayden is experiencing have demonstrated a greater impact as academic expectations and the expectation of independence have increased.

Diagnostic Conclusion

Attention deficit hyperactivity disorder, combined presentation, moderate

DIFFERENTIAL DIAGNOSIS I: OPPOSITIONAL DEFIANT DISORDER

Rationale: Jayden's difficulty with completing school, chores, and other tasks is not due to his feeling controlled or needing to resist conforming to other's demands, which are consistent with a diagnosis of ODD. However, despite Jayden's normal feeling of sadness due to challenges with making and keeping friends, he does not present with negativity, hostility, or defiance. Jayden is struggling with sustaining mental effort, remembering instructions, and impulsivity. However, complicating the differential diagnosis is that some individuals with ADHD may develop secondary oppositional attitudes toward these tasks as they get older. ODD can co-occur with ADHD; however, in this case example, it does not at this time.

DIFFERENTIAL DIAGNOSIS II: INTERMITTENT EXPLOSIVE DISORDER

Rationale: Individuals with intermittent explosive disorder show serious aggression toward others, which is not characteristic of ADHD. In this case example, Jayden does present with impulse control issues, but he has not shown aggression toward others. In addition, intermittent explosive disorder is rare in childhood. However, intermittent explosive disorder can co-occur with ADHD, but more often as an adult.

DIFFERENTIAL DIAGNOSIS III: DEPRESSIVE DISORDER

Rationale: Individuals with depressive disorders may present with inability to concentrate, as Jayden appears to have; however, poor concentration in mood disorders becomes more prominent only during a depressive episode. In this case, Jayden is not exhibiting any other criteria that would warrant a depressive disorder diagnosis.

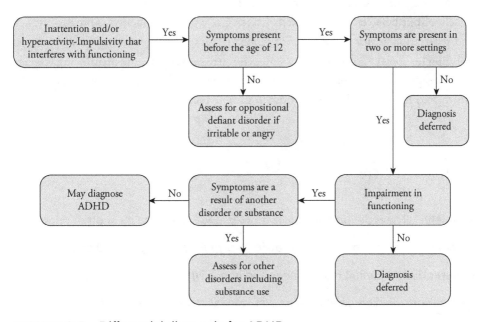

FIGURE 2.2   Differential diagnosis for ADHD

Biopsychosocial

BIOLOGICAL

The social worker should discuss with Jayden's parents whether he would benefit from pharmacotherapy. The social worker should provide psychotherapy to explain the benefits and risk factors associated with medications. If it is decided that medications will be introduced, the social worker can refer Jayden to see his pediatrician or a psychiatrist for pharmacotherapy.

PSYCHOLOGICAL

The social worker can help advocate for Jayden to have an IEP at his school. This could give Jayden more time on assignments provide an in-class teacher's aide, and adjust his learning to his specific needs. The social worker can suggest a reinforcement chart to improve behavior at home. Jayden can work toward more independence at home with small behaviors. For example, finishing his homework before dinner allots him a sticker on his behavior chart, and once he earns three stickers by the end of the day, he picks a fun activity to do before bed.

SOCIAL

Jayden appears to lack emotional regulation, evidenced by angry outbursts at his brother when having to share toys, not having his choice of dinner, and outgrowing his favorite pajamas. Jayden shared with the social worker that he wants to do well in school but believes that his teacher does not like him. He also expressed sadness and frustration at not having close friends. The social worker can support Jayden in building his social and communication skills. This would include identifying triggers, gaining appropriate coping tools, learning how to effectively express needs to his family and teacher, and learning how to initiate conversation with his peers.

TERMINOLOGY

echolalia   The repetition of vocalization or language made by another person.

elopement   To run or wander away from caregivers or supervised areas.

hyperactivity   Exhibit restlessness and impulsivity.

inattention   Exhibit careless mistakes and fail to attend to details.

pica   Ingestion of substances with no nutritional value.

REFLECTION QUESTIONS

1. What are risk factors for increased risk for ASD?

2. What are risk factors for lower rated and delayed diagnosis of ASD?

3. Which comorbid disorder with ASD causes higher rates of behavioral problems, such as aggression, self-injury, pica, and elopement?

4. What holistic approach to reducing the symptoms of ADHD began being researched in the 1980s?

5. Are ASD and ADHD more likely diagnosed in boys or girls?

CHAPTER 3

Schizophrenia Spectrum and Other Psychotic Disorders

LEARNING OBJECTIVES

1. Gain a basic understanding of the causes, prevalence, and comorbidities of schizophrenia spectrum and other psychotic disorders.

2. Become familiar with the criteria for schizophrenia spectrum and other psychotic disorders.

3. Be able to differentially diagnose schizophrenia spectrum and other psychotic disorders.

Characteristics of the Disorders

Schizophrenia is a complex mental health disorder characterized by hallucinations, delusions, and disorganized thoughts and behaviors. Schizophrenia is one of the most debilitating mental illnesses with no known single cause. The onset of schizophrenia is typically between the ages of 20 to 25 years. The disorder can have a significant impact on individual functioning, both socially and occupationally.

The disorders discussed in this chapter, often referred to as *psychotic disorders*, are characterized by what are referred to as positive and negative symptoms. However, does not mean that some symptoms are good and some are bad. Rather, *positive symptoms* refer to behaviors that are elevated (one way to remember this is that they are behaviors that are being *added*, +). Positive symptoms include hallucinations, delusions, and bizarre behavior and thinking.

Hallucinations may be:

- **Auditory:** Hearing sounds or voices that are not actually present.

- **Visual:** Seeing people or objects that no one else sees.

- **Tactile:** The impression that something is touching you when nothing is there, for example, bugs crawling in or on skin. Other examples of tactile sensations include the sensation of being kissed or having sex or that the internal organs are moving about on their own.

- **Olfactory:** Detecting smells that are not present in one's environment.

- **Gustatory:** Taste impairment or distortion.

Note that although hallucinations can be and often are a symptom of schizophrenia, they can also result from physical illness, trauma, neglect, and substance use or for unknown reasons. Most of us have felt something crawling on us only to see that there is nothing there. You may have smelled something earlier in the day and the smell stays with you even though no one else smells it, as though it is stuck in your nose. We all at one point have thought we have seen something out of the corner of our eyes only to find nothing is there. The difference between these types of experiences and hallucinations is insight; that is, the awareness that it was just a weird sensation and not an indication of a mental health problem.

The following are common types of delusions:

- **Persecutory:** The belief that people are out to get you.

- **Grandiose:** The belief that one has superior abilities or qualities despite no evidence of such abilities.

- **Somatic:** The belief that one has an illness or their body is impacted by a strange condition or entity despite there being no evidence.

- **Erotomanic:** The belief that another is in love with them despite no evidence. The delusion often involves a celebrity or person of power.

- **Referential (idea of reference):** Belief that a neutral event has special meaning, such as that a barking dog outside means that something bad is going to happen.

- **Nihilistic:** The belief of being dead or not existing as a person.

- **Delusions of control:** Belief that one's actions are being controlled by outside forces.

- **Thought broadcasting:** Belief that other people can hear one's thoughts.

- **Thought insertion:** Belief that one's thoughts are being inserted or implanted by an outside force or originating outside of one's mind.

- **Thought withdrawal:** Belief that one's thoughts are being taken.

Negative symptoms refer to those symptoms that involve a decrease in behaviors, emotions, or thought. It can be thought of as emotions or abilities being taken away (–). Examples include:

- **Alogia:** The inability to speak

- **Anhedonia:** An inability to experience pleasure.

- **Avolition:** A significant decrease or absence of the motivation to engage in tasks (e.g., paying bills, going out with friends).

- **Blunted or flat affect:** Diminished or absent emotional expression.

- **Catatonic symptoms:** Stupor (near unconsciousness), catalepsy (trancelike seizure with rigid body), waxy flexibility (limbs stay in place when moved by another), mutism (lack of verbal response).

- **Lack of motivation and socialization:** Decreased motivation and limited desire to socialize with others.

- **Speech poverty:** Extensive speech with little useful information.

- **Thought blocking:** Sudden cessation of speech mid-sentence without explanation.

History

In the mid to late 19th century, researchers sought to determine the cause of schizophrenia-type symptoms. At the time, a primary cause of these symptoms was late-stage syphilis. However, the researchers were unaware of the link between syphilis and schizophrenia-type symptoms. Today it is well known that the tertiary symptoms of syphilis overlap with the symptoms of schizophrenia. This was an important discovery, because it illustrates how a physical illness or infection can produce a psychological illness (Walker et al., 2004). It also led to the current assumption that the disorder we now call schizophrenia has multiple etiologies.

Schizophrenia, originally called *dementia praecox*, was first described by Emil Kraepelin (1896, as cited in Devylder, 2013) as a disorder of cognitive functioning caused by internal factors with deteriorating progression. He described in detail the chronic stages of the illness but did not offer much in the way of an etiological explanation other than to say it was caused by a biological source in which autointoxication from the sex glands caused a poisoning of the brain during puberty (DeVylder, 2013).

Adolf Meyer, a professor of psychiatry, is considered by many to have been one of the most influential psychiatrists in the United States during the first half of the 20th century. Meyer provided a strong opposing voice to the psychoanalytic and biomedical theories on the causes of schizophrenia. He was a proponent of psychology tailored toward the individuals and used a psychobiological approach to individual treatment. Treatment was considered in terms of biological, psychological, and social factors rather than biological dysfunction or maladaptive thought processes. This of course is the psychologically informed environment (PIE) approach social workers use today. Meyer's theory of the cause of dementia praecox was that it was the product of both biological and ecological influences that resulted in psychopathology in at-risk individuals (Meyer, 1910, as cited in Devylder, 2013). His theory was overshadowed by Freudian and biomedical theories that remain prevalent today. Meyer believed that it was not one symptom that led to a diagnosis, but rather that a diagnosis should be made based on the entire clinical picture. He also believed that people with dementia praecox deteriorated over time and had a poor prognosis, an assumption that is still widespread today.

The term *schizophrenia* was introduced by Eugen Bleuler in the beginning of the 20th century. The word is derived from two Greek words: *schizo* meaning "to tear or split" and *phren*, meaning "the mind" or emotional functioning. Therefore, the word *schizophrenia* describes a splitting of the mind and emotions. According to Bleuler, the fundamental symptoms of schizophrenia are ambivalence, disturbance of association and affect, and a preference for fantasy over reality (Walker et al., 2004). He thought that schizophrenia had a number of accessory symptoms, including delusions, hallucinations, motor (movement) disturbances, somatic (physical) symptoms, and manic and/or melancholic states. Bleuler noted that while these symptoms may occur in some patients with schizophrenia, they were not universal. What is interesting is that his reconceptualizing schizophrenia as a group of disorders rather than a single disorder is similar to today's conceptualization.

Changes in the diagnostic criteria of schizophrenia were offered by Kurt Schneider in the mid-20th century. Schneider assumed that a number of key symptoms, referred to as first-rank symptoms, were indicative of a diagnosis of schizophrenia, These first-rank symptoms include certain types of hallucinations and delusions (fixed false beliefs) that are signs of psychosis (Schneider, 1959 as cited in DeVylder, 2013).

The DSM-I (American Psychiatric Association [APA], 1952) had two classifications of mental health disorders: organic and psychogenic. Psychotic disorders were included in the latter category. The DSM-II (APA, 1968) also had two categories of mental illness: (1) psychoses and (2) neuroses, personality disorders, and other nonpsychotic disorders. *Psychoses* was defined as a mental health disorder in which the patient has an impairment in functioning. The ICD-9 (Medicode, 1996) adopted these two categories from the DSM-II; however, the ICD-9 made a distinction between organic and nonorganic psychoses. *Organic psychoses* referred to symptoms of impairment of memory, cognition, and judgment and disturbance in mood and personality. *Nonorganic psychoses* included delirium (i.e., confusion, disorientation, delusions, hallucinations) and dementia (i.e., psychoses that are chronic, progressive, and irreversible). The DSM-III (APA, 1980) had 15 categories of mental health disorders, one of which was psychotic disorders. In the DSM-III, the term *psychotic* is used to describe a mental disorder at which at some point, all patients with the disorder lack insight regarding their thoughts, perceptions, and external reality. Evidence of psychotic behavior involves hallucinations, delusions, disorganized behaviors, and/or thoughts and a lack of insight and reality testing is severely impacted. The DSM-III-TR (1987) replaced the term *schizophrenic disorders* with *schizophrenia*. In the DSM-IV (APA, 1994), a diagnosis of psychosis was no longer based on the severity of the impairment in functioning but rather on the presence of hallucinations, delusions, disorganized speech, or catatonic behaviors. The DSM-IV-TR (APA, 2000) had four categories of schizophrenia: paranoid, undifferentiated, catatonic, and residual. Oftentimes it was difficult to fit a client's symptoms into a specific category. The DSM-5 (APA, 2013) removed the four categories and provided a new title for this class of disorders: schizophrenia spectrum and other psychotic disorders. Specifiers were added for course and severity.

Psychotic symptoms do not necessarily mean that an individual has schizophrenia. Psychosis is just one symptom of schizophrenia. The term *psychotic symptoms* refers to hallucinations, delusions, and/or disorganized thinking and behavior. Several medical conditions can cause psychosis or psychotic symptoms (diagnosed as psychotic disorder due to another medical condition). These include organ failure (kidney, liver), hypoxia, hypoglycemia, vitamin deficiencies, electrolyte imbalance, infections, head injury, epilepsy, dementias, and other degenerative diseases (just to name a few). People who are intoxicated or withdrawing from medications may also suffer from psychotic symptoms.

Etiology

Neurobiological

GENETIC

Research has consistently indicated that the vulnerability to schizophrenia can be inherited (Walker et al., 2004). Twin, adoption, and family history studies indicate that the genetic risk of schizophrenia is elevated in individuals who have biological relatives with the disorder. The closer the relative with schizophrenia, the higher the risk. Monozygotic twins share nearly 100% of their genes. A monozygotic twin has a 50% to 90% likelihood of developing schizophrenia if their twin has a diagnosis (Walker et al., 2004; Zwicker et al., 2018). Dizygotic twins who share approximately 50% of their genes have about a 10% to 20% likelihood of developing schizophrenia if their twin has a diagnosis (Gottesman, 1991, as cited in Walker et al., 2004). Early adoption studies have indicated that among individuals with schizophrenia diagnoses who were adopted at birth, increased rates of schizophrenia were found among biological relatives but not within their adoptive families (Heston, 1966; Kety, 1988). More recent studies have revealed that genetic and environmental influences act in concert with each other (see Baumeister et al., 2016; Uher & Zwicker, 2017; Wolke et al., 2014). A study conducted in 2014 found that family disruptions are elevated in families with first degree relatives with schizophrenia. This indicates that the susceptibility to psychosis is dependent upon the interaction of biological and soical environmental influences across developmental periods (Walder et al., 2014)

The strongest predictor of risk of schizophrenia or psychosis is having a close biological relative who has a psychotic disorder (Gottesman et al., 2010). Family studies indicate that a child with one parent with schizophrenia has about a 7% chance of developing the disorder. Children with two parents with schizophrenia have approximately a 27% chance developing the disorder (Gottesman et al., 2010).

NEUROTRANSMITTERS

The fact that antipsychotic medications that block dopamine receptors are effective in treating schizophrenia has led to theories that schizophrenia is a result of elevated dopamine levels. However, this theory has been challenged due to the lag time (time it takes for the drug to take effect) of the medications used, which is typically 2 to 4 weeks. This may indicate that the effect of the antipsychotic medication may be a neurochemical adaptation in the brain, rather than a straight decrease in dopamine transmission (Marder & Cannon, 2019). Although the dopamine theory states that there is an increase in dopamine in people who have schizophrenia, it does not state whether this increased level is due to too much release, too many receptors, hypersensitive receptors, or a combination of all three. In addition, dopamine interacts with gamma-aminobutyric acid (GABA) and glutamate in terms of the excitation of neurons. Research has indicated that a loss of neurons that inhibit GABA could lead to hyperactive dopamine neurons. Interestingly, the neurotransmitter glutamate has been implicated in the etiology of schizophrenia due to observations of people who have ingested phencyclidine (PCP). PCP is a glutamate antagonist and produces acute symptoms that are similar to schizophrenia (Shameer Nijam et al., 2019).

Environment

Evidence suggests that certain environmental exposures are involved in the onset of schizophrenia. One such exposure is low socioeconomic status and income inequality (Zwicker et al., 2018). Low socioeconomic status and income inequality have wide-reaching implications for health and mental health. Studies have indicated that people with low incomes have higher rates of schizophrenia as compared to those of a higher income (Lee, 2018).

Interestingly, a disproportionate number of people with schizophrenia were born in the winter months. This timing coincides with exposure to viral infections (such as the flu), which are most common in late and early winter, exposing the fetus in the second trimester (Walker et al., 2004). Other prenatal complications associated with schizophrenia include toxemia, preeclampsia, and hypoxia. Evidence also indicates that stressful life events (death of a spouse, military invasions) during pregnancy are also involved in the onset of schizophrenia (Khashan et al., 2008; Malaspina et al., 2008).

Prevalence and Comorbidities

In the United States, the lifetime prevalence of schizophrenia is approximately between .6 and 1.9%, (Van Os & Kapur, 2009). Globally, schizophrenia affects approximately 1% of the population, 51 million individuals over the age of 18 (Vyas et al., 2011). Up to 69% of people with schizophrenia are not receiving appropriate care with 90% of those who are untreated living in low- or middle-income countries (Lora et al., 2012).

Approximately 50% of individuals with schizophrenia have comorbid diagnoses (Tsai & Rosenheck, 2013). Anxiety and depressive disorders are common comorbid conditions in people with schizophrenia. It is estimated that 50% of people with schizophrenia will have a diagnosis of depression, 15% panic disorder, 29% post-traumatic stress disorder (PTSD), and 23% obsessive compulsive disorder (OCD) (Buckley et al., 2009). It is also estimated that 50% will have a comorbid substance use disorder (Kerner, 2015).

Course and Prognosis

Schizophrenia is characterized by symptom presentations and remissions. After the first episode of psychosis, the patient typically recovers and may function normally. Individuals are likely to relapse, and the pattern of illness during the first 5 years typically indicates the patient's future course with the disorder (Sadock et al., 2015). With each psychotic episode the patient will likely experience a deterioration in functioning. As time passes the positive symptoms tend to become less severe and the negative symptoms tend to become more pronounced.

The standard treatment for schizophrenia is medication. Patient response to antipsychotic medications varies widely. Between 10% and 30% of patients will experience limited benefit from medications and at least 30% will show improvement but still have persistent symptoms that impact their quality of life (Marder & Cannon, 2019). Although approximately one-third of those with schizophrenia have an integrated social life, the majority experience factors associated with decreased quality of life. These factors include homelessness, unemployment, poverty, frequent hospitalizations, and inactivity. In addition, a diagnosis of schizophrenia is associated with a reduced life expectancy of 10 to 20 years. One study that evaluated more than 1 million participants found that the increased mortality rates were related to alcohol and/or tobacco use (Oakley et al., 2018). A similar study found that the increased mortality rates were due at least, in part, to metabolic syndromes that resulted from the medications (Mitchell et al., 2013). Suicide rates for individuals with schizophrenia are significantly higher than in the general population. It is estimated that the lifetime suicide risk of suicide risk is 4.9% for individuals with schizophrenia (Palmer et al., 2005). Studies have also found that individuals who were discharged from the hospital after a first episode and were not taking regular doses of antipsychotic medication had a 37 fold increase in death by suicide (Tiihonen et al., 2006).

Schizophrenia is a chronic disorder and full recovery is not likely. In fact research indicates that only 13.5% of patients achieve recovery (Jaaskelainen et al., 2013). However, a number of protective factors can indicate a good prognosis. Some of these factors include a later onset (Rabinowitz et al., 2006), a strong social support system (Norman et al., 2005), more positive symptoms as opposed to negative symptoms (Rabinowitz et al., 2012), and good premorbid functioning (Addington & Addington, 2005).

Cultural and Gender-Related Considerations

Black/African Americans are disproportionately diagnosed with schizophrenia and experience worse outcomes than their White counterparts (Nagendra et al., 2020). A meta-analysis of 55 studies found that Black/African Americans are 2.4 times more likely to be diagnoses with schizophrenia than their White counterparts (Olbert et al., 2018). In addition, Black/African Americans with schizophrenia are more likely to be hospitalized (Rost et al., 2011), be incarcerated (Baillargeon et al., 2009), have difficulty finding employment (Salkever et al., 2007), and experience homelessness (Folsom et al., 2005).

Although rates of schizophrenia are similar in males and females, males tend to develop symptoms earlier (early 20s) as compared to females (early 30s). In addition, males are more likely to have poorer premorbid functioning, worse prognosis, and exhibit more negative symptoms (Leung & Chue, 2000). Females are more likely to display more affective symptoms and more positive symptoms. Females are also more likely to respond to antipsychotic medication (Hsu et al., 2019).

Diagnosing and Assessment

Eight disorders that include primary psychosis (psychosis not caused by a medical condition) fall on the schizophrenia spectrum: schizophrenia, schizoaffective disorder, brief psychotic disorder, schizophreniform disorder, other specified schizophrenia spectrum and other psychotic disorders, delusional disorder, major depressive disorder with psychotic features (discussed in a subsequent chapter), and bipolar manic with psychotic features (discussed in a subsequent chapter). A number of factors should be considered when assessing clients for schizophrenia. These factors include duration of symptoms, use of any medications or drugs, current stressors, any underlying depression or anxiety symptoms, and history of psychotic symptoms, either personal or familial.

Schizophrenia

The symptoms of schizophrenia include hallucinations, delusions, disorganized speech, disorganized behavior, and/or negative symptoms for between 1 and 6 months. The DSM-5 (APA, 2013) divides the course of schizophrenia into three phases: prodromal, active, and residual. The prodromal phase indicates that the individual has a decline in functioning but does not have any active psychotic symptoms. In this phase, negative symptoms may be present, and there may be a dramatic decline in school, work, or social performance. In the active phase, the client is actively psychotic and experiencing hallucinations, delusions, and disorganized thoughts and behaviors. In the residual phase, the client still has impairment, typically negative symptoms, but is no longer experiencing positive symptoms. For a diagnosis of schizophrenia, the symptoms (negative, positive, disorganized behavior/thinking or speech) must be present for at least 6 months and not be present only during mood episodes, movement disorder, or during the use or withdrawal of substances (APA, 2013). Of course, as with all disorders, in order to make a diagnosis there needs to be impairment in functioning occupationally, socially, and/or academically.

Schizophreniform Disorder

The diagnostic criteria of schizophreniform disorder are identical to those of schizophrenia (positive or negative symptoms, disorganized behavior or speech, or catatonic behaviors) except for duration of illness. For a diagnosis of schizophreniform disorder the total duration of the illness, including all phases, is 1 month but fewer than 6 months. This diagnosis would be made if the individual had symptoms for 1 to 6 months and then recovered or the individual meets criteria for the disorder but the symptoms have not lasted for 6 months or more (APA, 2013). If the symptoms persist for longer than 6 months, a diagnosis of schizophrenia is warranted. Again, as with schizophrenia, the symptoms must not be present only during mood episodes, movement disorders, or during the use or withdrawal of substances. A diagnosis of schizophreniform disorder requires a prognostic specifier. A specifier of "good prognostic features" is warranted if two of the following are present: the psychotic symptoms occurred within 4 weeks of the first noticeable change in behavior (rapid onset), the individual is confused by the symptoms (insight is present), there was a high level of functioning prior to the onset of symptoms, and there is no blunt or flat affect (APA, 2013). A specifier of poor insight is warranted if at least two of the aforementioned criteria are not met. This would indicate that a future diagnosis of schizophrenia is likely.

Brief Psychotic Disorder

Brief psychotic disorder is the sudden onset (within 2 weeks) of positive symptoms or catatonia (APA, 2013). The episode lasts at least 1 day but less than 1 month. The symptoms must not be present only during a mood episode, movement disorder, other psychotic disorder, or the presence of or withdrawal from substances. An onset specifier must be indicated when diagnosing brief psychotic disorder. A specifier of "with marked stressors" would be indicated if the onset of symptoms occurred in response to a stressful event. A specifier of "without marked specifiers" would be indicated if there was no stressful event prior to the onset of symptoms. A specifier of post-partum onset is warranted of the onset is during pregnancy or four weeks post-partum (APA, 2013). If this is the case it is important to refer the individual to a medical doctor for an immediate evaluation.

Schizoaffective Disorder

Schizoaffective disorder is characterized by an uninterrupted mood episode, either depressive or manic and criteria A of schizophrenia (positive symptoms, disorganized speech or behavior, catatonic behavior and/or negative symptoms) (APA, 2013). In addition, the positive symptoms (hallucinations and delusions) must be present for two or more weeks *in absence of* the mood episodes at some point during the duration of the illness. This is the key feature that distinguishes schizoaffective disorder from bipolar or major depressive disorder with psychotic features. When making a diagnosis, it is important to specify if the schizoaffective disorder is bipolar type (meaning that there have been manic or hypomanic episodes) or depressive type (only depressive episodes are present).

Delusional Disorder

Delusional disorder is characterized by the presence of at least one delusion for a duration of 1 month or longer. If the individual meets criteria for schizophrenia a diagnosis of delusional disorder cannot be given. If the individual has hallucinations, they cannot be prominent and the must relate to the delusion (APA, 2013). For example, an individual who believes that they process great abilities may hear the voice of a great leader.

Janice

Janice is a 20-year-old Asian American undergraduate student who was brought to the emergency room by ambulance. Her best friend and roommate had called her parents when she came back from class crying hysterically and stating that someone was following her and that she thinks the campus is "bugged" and her professors are really FBI agents who are trying to take her away. When the social worker met Janice in the ER, she noted that she seemed very preoccupied looking off into the corner and listening to something that no one else could hear. Her hair was matted on one side, and her shirt and blue jeans were dirty. Janice's roommate reported that she has mentioned on more than one occasion that television shows and commercials are signs and signals for tasks that she is to perform. She has not been eating for the past few months, as she believes that someone is poisoning her food. She has lost quite a bit of weight. Janice is no longer meeting up with friends and she has not been going to class or any club meetings. She rarely does her laundry, and her hygiene is poor, because she rarely showers. Her roommate states that Janice was a straight-A student in high school and very social. She was a member of numerous clubs and always seemed to have a boyfriend. Over the past 6 to 7 months (since this behavior began) Janice has spent much of her time in her room and rarely comes out except to use the bathroom and yell at her roommate. She can often be heard carrying on conversations with someone in her head (in the absence of earbuds or a mobile device). Janice occasionally went to parties and would drink alcohol but has no history of drug use, and her toxicology screens in the ER came back negative. Her parents confirmed that during her childhood and high school Janice seemed like a "normal kid." It is "just since she went to college" that she has become "odd." Her parents did report that Janice's grandfather "went insane" in his 20s and was never heard from again.

Diagnostic Impression

Based on what has been reported by Janice's roommate and parents, Janice has demonstrated 6 months of grossly disorganized or catatonic behavior, as evidenced by her lack of personal hygiene and remaining in her room, as well as delusions, as evidenced by believing her food is being poisoned, her professors are FBI agents, and the television is giving her signs. It also appears that she is having auditory hallucinations, as evidenced by her having conversations when no one else is there. She also seems to be experiencing negative symptoms, as evidenced by her lack of avolition. Her level of functioning is significantly impaired, as she has not been attending classes or social events and she has stopped eating. There is no history of alcohol or other drug use, and her parents have stated that she had a normal childhood.

Diagnostic Conclusion

Schizophrenia first episode, currently in an acute episode

DIFFERENTIAL DIAGNOSIS I: SCHIZOAFFECTIVE DISORDER

Rationale: A diagnosis of schizoaffective disorder depressive type can be ruled out. The criteria for schizoaffective disorder requires mood episodes. Janice does not meet the criteria for depressed mood or hypomania or mania.

DIFFERENTIAL DIAGNOSIS II: MAJOR DEPRESSIVE DISORDER WITH PSYCHOTIC FEATURES

Rationale: Although Janice is experiencing some symptoms that are consistent with depression (weight loss, psychomotor agitation), she does not meet the full criteria for depression and her psychosis is clearly prominent.

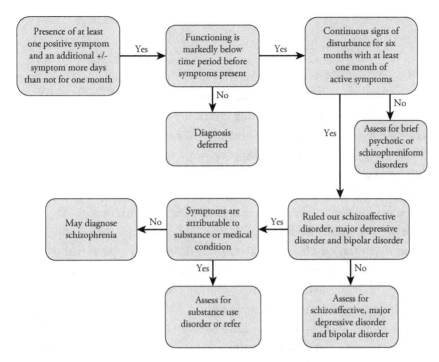

FIGURE 3.1   Differential diagnosis for schizophrenia

Biopsychosocial

BIOLOGICAL

Biological considerations include Janice's hygiene and lack of nutritional intake. The social worker may want to further assess why Janice's hair is matted and why her jeans were dirty and other activities of daily diving (ADLs) that may not be met. Teaching Janice life skills such as proper hygiene, dressing, toileting, and eating may be important aspects of the treatment plan.

PSYCHOLOGICAL

Janice's parents report that Janice's grandfather "went insane" in his 20s, with the family losing touch with him. This suggests that there may be a family history of schizophrenia or other psychotic disorders.

SOCIAL

According to this case example, Janice has always been very social and involved in extracurricular activities, and it wasn't until 6 months ago that this shifted to a more isolated lifestyle. More assessment is needed on the positive symptoms that Janice is experiencing and possible triggers to her hallucinations and delusions.

Joseph

Joseph is a 40-year-old European American, Jewish man who is currently in an inpatient facility. He was admitted 4 days ago because when he was pulled over for speeding the officer stated he was acting erratically and not making any sense when she was asking him questions about where he lived and where he was driving to. When he was brought to the facility, the admitting nurse was able to access the contacts in his phone and contacted his mother. Joseph's mother then contacted Joseph's ex-wife, and they both came to the facility. Joseph's ex-wife, Aviva, reported that she and Joseph had been divorced for just over a year. They were married for 15 years when things got so "bad" she "had to leave." Joseph and Aviva met their freshman year in college and were married a few years after graduation. Aviva reports that over the past 5 years Joseph has been experiencing periods of weeks at a time where "pretty much every day" he "just seemed really down." During these periods he could not seem to fall asleep and would pace the halls until around 3 a.m. when he would finally go to sleep. In the morning he would wake early but stay in all day if he was not working. If he did have to go to work, he would dress, drink some coffee, and head off to work. He reported on more than one occasion that his boss threatened to fire him because he is "moving like a turtle stuck in molasses" and not getting his work completed on time. Joseph would say he just "couldn't get his head in the game." He would often say that he wishes "things would just end." He and Aviva had a standing double-date with friends every Saturday evening, during these episodes Joseph was uninterested in spending time with them, and he refused to play golf with his buddies. If Aviva tried to discuss his mood with him, he would get angry. About 2 years ago Aviva became increasingly concerned when Joseph started "getting paranoid." He thought their friends were talking about them behind their backs and was convinced that their dog walker was stealing from them (there was nothing missing). She would try to explain to him that their friends were likely not talking about them and the dog walker was not stealing from them, but he would not believe her. He had the paranoia "pretty much constantly," but it seemed much worse when he was feeling down. Aviva consistently encouraged Joseph to get help, but he always refused. Joseph now lives alone in a one-bedroom apartment. She reports that she attempts to keep in touch with him, but he has accused her of trying to turn their dog against him and has even accused her of trying to hurt the dog. Joseph's parents say that when he was in high school he went through periods like this. The sadness would last a few weeks. They did report that he would say that he thought his teachers hated him, but they just assumed he was being "silly." Aviva has reported that Joseph is physically healthy, and his parents stated that he had no health issues as a child other than chicken pox and the flu.

Diagnostic Impression

Based on reports from Joseph's ex-wife Aviva and his parents, Joseph has demonstrated a persistent pattern of episodes of sadness, psychomotor retardation ("moving like a turtle"), sleep issues, diminished ability to think ("can't get his head in the game"), reduced interest in activities he enjoyed (golf and date night), thoughts of death ("wish things would just end"). In addition, he has been demonstrating symptoms of psychosis, more specifically paranoid delusions as evidenced by feeling that his friends were talking about him, the dog walker was stealing from them, and his ex-wife trying to hurt the dog or turn the dog against him. The paranoid delusions occur both during and in between his depressive episodes. These depressive episodes and the accompanying psychosis have been observed by his ex-wife for over 5 years, and his parents report that he had similar episodes when he was in high school.

Diagnostic Conclusion

Schizoaffective disorder depressive type, multiple episodes, currently in acute episode

DIFFERENTIAL DIAGNOSIS I: MAJOR DEPRESSIVE DISORDER WITH PSYCHOTIC FEATURES

Rationale: This is the most difficult differential diagnosis. It is clear that Joseph is suffering from major depressive disorder and psychosis, which is consistent with major depressive disorder with psychotic features. However, his psychosis continues (for more than 2 weeks) when he is not in a mood episode. Therefore, the best diagnosis is schizoaffective disorder, depressive type.

DIFFERENTIAL DIAGNOSIS II: SCHIZOPHRENIA

Rationale: Although Joseph clearly meets the criteria for schizophrenia, he also has the additional symptoms that are consistent with major depressive disorder. Therefore, the best diagnosis is schizoaffective disorder, depressive type.

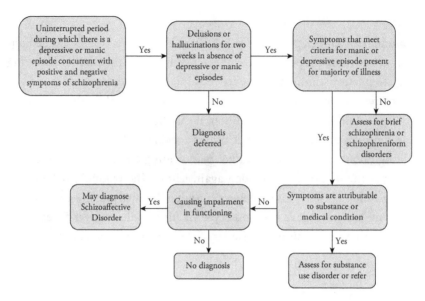

FIGURE 3.2   Differential diagnosis for schizoaffective disorder

Biopsychosocial

BIOLOGICAL

Joseph is physically healthy and young with no known health issues. It is important given his cognitive symptoms that he be evaluated by a neurologist to determine if there is a physical cause for his symptoms. It is also important for a blood test to be conducted to determine if he has used any substance that may have caused or exacerbated his current condition.

PSYCHOLOGICAL

Joseph presents with a number of symptoms consistent with both depression and psychosis. Joseph's parents reported that when he was young he did have episodes of sadness, indicating that his depression has likely been occurring since childhood. It was only in adulthood that Joseph started developing psychotic symptoms. By saying that he wishes "things would just end," Joseph indicates that he is experiencing suicidal ideation. It is critical that Joseph be strictly monitored and continuously assessed for worsening ideation.

SOCIAL

Joseph has an established support system with his ex-wife and his parents. This support will be important in Joseph's recovery both psychologically and in terms of medication adherence (should he be prescribed medications). Individuals with a strong support system have a better long term prognosis than those individuals without a strong support system.

TERMINOLOGY

dizygotic twins   Fraternal twins that share about 50% of their genes.

lag time   Time frame of how long it takes for a drug to be absorbed and affect the body.

monozygotic twins   Identical twins that share 100% of their genes.

REFLECTION QUESTIONS

1. What are hallucinations, delusions, bizarre behavior, and disordered thinking examples of?

2. Can other pathologies cause psychosis or psychotic symptoms?

3. What is the likely prognosis for schizophrenia?

CHAPTER 4

Bipolar and Related Disorders

with Celine Rodriguez

LEARNING OBJECTIVES

1. Have a basic understanding of the causes, prevalence, and comorbidities of the bipolar disorders.

2. Become familiar with the criteria for the bipolar disorders.

3. Be able to differentially diagnose the bipolar disorders.

Characteristics of the Disorders

Bipolar disorder is a serious mental health disorder that is characterized by mood episodes, including depression and mania or hypomania. Three primary diagnoses are included under bipolar: bipolar I, bipolar II, and cyclothymia. Each disorder is characterized by a combination of depressive episodes and manic or hypomanic episodes. What do these episodes look like?

- *Depressive episode*: Depressive episodes include symptoms such as depressed mood, lack of interest in pleasurable activities, negative thinking, emotional reactiveness, loss of energy and/or motivation, irritability, and low self-esteem. The individual must meet five criteria, and symptoms must last for at least 2 weeks (APA, 2013).

- *Manic episode*: A manic episode is a discrete period (at least 1 week) in which the individual's mood is dramatically elevated and expansive. These episodes may include inflated self-esteem, grandiosity, pressured speech, a decreased need for sleep, racing thoughts, and/or increased goal-directed activity and distractibility. At least three of these symptoms must be present and last for days or months (1 week is required for diagnosis of bipolar, as discussed later in chapter) (APA, 2013).

- *Hypomanic episode*: A hypomanic episode is essentially a less severe form of mania, in which, for a discrete period (at least 4 days), the individual experiences inflated self-esteem, grandiosity, pressured speech, a decreased need for sleep, racing thoughts, and/or increased goal-directed activity and distractibility (APA, 2013).

You have likely noticed that mania and hypomania have the same criteria. The primary difference between manic and hypomanic episodes is the level of severity. It is important to remember that a hypomanic episode is characterized by symptoms that occur during a discrete period of time. The symptoms must be a change from the individual's "normal" level of functioning. Some individuals are just naturally a bit more elevated than others. If there is no significant impact in functioning, then there is no diagnosis.

Cyclothymia is characterized by subclinical depression, which means that the individual has depressive symptoms that do not meet the required criteria for major depressive episode (they meet fewer than five criteria). They have subclinical hypomania symptoms, but they do not meet criteria for hypomanic episode (three symptoms). In addition, the duration of cyclothymia is 2 years. What this means is that the individual must meet criteria on most days for at least 2 years.

History

The term *bipolar* means "two poles," referring to the polar opposites of mania and depression. Prior to being termed *bipolar*, the disorder was referred to as *manic depression*, and first appeared in the DSM-I as *manic depressive reactions* (APA, 1952). It was classified as a psychotic disorder characterized by varying degrees of personality integration and a lack of reality testing. In the DSM-I, hallucination and delusions were listed as possible symptoms, but today they make up a small component of the diagnosis. The DSM-I listed three types of manic depression: depressed, manic, and other. The depressed type was characterized by depressed mood with moments of mania. The manic type was characterized by what we now call mania with depression in fleeting moments. The "other" type of manic depression was characterized by a combination of both depressive periods and manic periods. The DSM-II (APA, 1968) characterized the disorder as manic depressive illness under the category of affective disorders. It was characterized by mood swings that tended to remit and recur. It had three subtypes: manic, depressed, and circular. The manic and depressed types were basically the same as those in the DSM-I, and the circular subtype was characterized by cycling of at least one episode of both depression and mania. The DSM-III (1980) renamed the disorder as *bipolar disorder* and listed specific criteria that were included in the manic and depressive episodes. The possibility of mixed episodes was also introduced at this time, as was the specifier "with psychotic features," which will be discussed later in the chapter. The DSM-II also added in the rule out of separate causes, such as disease or drugs. The DSM-IV (APA, 1994) further described the diagnosis of a mixed episode and added hypomanic episodes. The current edition of the DSM, the DSM-5, has retained the criteria for episodes of depression and mania, but the mixed episode has been removed and replaced with specifier of "with mixed features," which can apply to either the depressive or manic episode.

Etiology

The causes of bipolar disorder are determined by both environmental and biological factors.

Environmental Factors

Evidence has suggested a link between maternal influenza exposure and an increased risk of bipolar disorder. Canetta et al. (2014) and Parboosing et al (2013) found that maternal exposure to influenza resulted in an increased risk of bipolar disorder. Maternal exposure to influenza may increase the likelihood of psychotic features associated with bipolar disorder (Canetta et al., 2014), but not necessarily the onset of the disorder. Childhood trauma has been associated with the development of psychiatric disorders, including bipolar disorder. However, there is evidence to suggest that those individuals who are genetically vulnerable to bipolar disorder are more likely to develop the disorder if exposed to trauma (Goldberg & Garno, 2009). A more recent meta-analysis indicated that childhood adversity is a strong risk factor for bipolar disorder (Bortalato et al., 2017).

Biological Factors

Approximately 50% of patients with bipolar disorder have a family history of the disorder, with some studies finding the heritability risk to be as high as 85% (McGuffin et al., 2003). In some families, known as *multiplex families*, there are many members with the disorder across generations (Belmaker, 2004). Studies of twins have suggested a concordance of bipolar disorder of 40% to 80% in monozygotic (identical) twins and 10% to 20% in dizygotic (fraternal) twins (Bertelsen et al., 1997; Smoller & Finn, 2003).

Neuroimaging studies have indicated brain abnormalities in patients affected by bipolar disorder (Squarcina et al., 2016). More specifically, those with bipolar disorder have reduced grey matter in the temporal cortex, prefrontal cortex, and the claustrum. Research also suggests more pronounced age-related grey matter decline in those with bipolar disorder as opposed to those without bipolar disorder (Serap Monkul et al., 2005). Further studies have indicated that there is evidence of white matter inflammation, tissue loss, and altered metabolism in those who have bipolar disorder (Johnson et al., 2015).

Prevalence and Comorbidity

In the United States, bipolar disorder has a prevalence rate of approximately 1.5% to 2% (Merikangas et al., 2011). The World Health Organization (WHO) has indicated that bipolar disorder is the second most common reason for taking off work (Alonso et al., 2011). In 2009, the economic cost of bipolar disorders was estimated to be $151 billion, with 79% of this cost being from lost productivity (Dilsaver, 2011). The average age of onset of bipolar disorder is slightly younger for women at 21.5 years, as compared to 23 years for men (Blanco et al., 2017).

At a global level, the highest number of cases are found in China, Brazil, the United States and Indonesia, which also happen to be the most populous countries. The countries with the lowest number of cases were Bermuda, Tonga, Greenland, American Samoa, the Marshall Islands, and Northern Mariana Islands. A study comparing cases from 1990 to 2017 found that the largest increase in cases occurred in Qatar (495.5%) and the United Arab Emirates (440%). This increase is likely due to population surges in both countries. Among the most populous countries, India had the largest increase at approximately 67.5% (He et al., 2020).

The diagnosis of bipolar disorder in children is controversial. In 1994, researchers determined that bipolar presented differently in children than in adults, with mania in children presenting as irritability, temper tantrums, poor concentration, and impulsivity (Parry et al., 2018). By 2004, bipolar disorder had become the most common diagnosis among preteen inpatients (Blader & Carlson, 2007) with a 40-fold increase between 1994 and 2003 (Moreno, 2007). Several reasons have been offered for the dramatic increase in diagnoses. One explanation may be the change in symptom interpretation by clinicians based on the research conducted in 1994. Other possible reasons include children being included multiple times in statistics due to repeat visits and "up-coding" to ensure services from insurance providers (Goldstein & Birmaher, 2016). Bipolar diagnoses in children are much higher in the United States as compared to European and Australasian countries. For example, Clacey et al., (2015) found that rates of diagnosis for children 5 to 9 years were 100- to 1,000-fold greater in the United States. For example, rates in clinical settings per 100,000 in the United States were 27, as compared to New Zealand at .22, England at .00, Germany at .03, and Australia at .14.

Bipolar disorder is highly comorbid with a number of other mental health disorders. Individuals with a diagnosis of bipolar disorder are 5 times more likely to have a substance use disorder and 7.5 times more likely to have any anxiety disorder (Blanco et al., 2017). Panic disorder is the most commonly comorbid anxiety disorder. The comorbidity of posttraumatic stress disorder (PTSD) and bipolar disorder ranges from 16% to 32% (Etain et al., 2008; Otto et al., 2004). Childhood trauma in general (either with or without a diagnosis of PTSD) is found in approximately 50% of those diagnosed with bipolar disorder (Garno et al., 2005).

Course and Prognosis

Bipolar is a chronic lifetime disorder. Studies have indicated that 71% of people with a diagnosis with bipolar disorder will have a 12-month to lifetime prevalence (Blanco et al., 2017). What is concerning is that despite the fact that bipolar disorder is a chronic disorder and causes a significant decrease in quality of life, less than half of individuals diagnosed will seek treatment. There are a number of reasons individuals with bipolar disorder will not seek treatment (Blanco et al., 2017), including, but not limited to, lack of insurance or other financial barriers, lack of insight on the part of the patient, incorrect assessment, and stigma (Carvalho, et al., 2014).

The rate of suicide in individuals with bipolar disorder is 20-30 times higher than individuals in the general population (Pompeii et al., 2013). Several factors are predictive of suicide in bipolar disorder. Previous suicide attempts are considered to be the strongest predictor of future attempts. A recent discharge from inpatient treatment is also considered to be correlated with a significant elevated risk of suicide attempts.

Forte et al. (2019) found that over 25% of suicide attempts occurred within the first 4 weeks following discharge and 40% within the first 3 months. A more recent study of over 22,000 patients by Iliachenko et al. (2020) revealed a total of 596 suicide deaths, and of these 213 (35.7%) occurred within 120 days of discharge.

Women with bipolar disorder are significantly more likely to attempt suicide (Antypa et al., 2013) but are significantly less likely to use violent or highly lethal methods (Perroud et al., 2007). Men are more likely to have higher rates of suicide deaths due to use of more lethal methods (Gonda et al., 2012). People who are in depressed or mixed episodes have a greater likelihood of suicide attempt as opposed to those in manic or hypomanic states (Illiachenko et al., 2020).

Cultural and Gender-Related Considerations

Black/African Americans are less likely to be diagnosed with bipolar disorders when presenting with other medical problems. This could be due to mistrust in medical professionals, cultural barriers between patients and healthcare providers, and the tendency to emphasize physical problems over mental health issues (Satcher, 2013, as cited in Paniagua, 2014). The prevalence of bipolar disorder is lowest among Asian Americans than all other racial/ethnic groups (Corcoran & Walsh, 2015).

Unlike major depressive disorder, which is almost twice as common in women, bipolar disorder has an equal prevalence in men and women. Men are more likely to have manic episodes, and women are more likely to have depressive episodes. When women have manic episodes they are more likely to have a mixed presentation (depression and mania simultaneously). Women are also more likely to experience rapid cycling, meaning they have four or more episodes (mania, hypomania, or depression) in 1 year. The most distinctive difference that the research reveals is the impact that women diagnosed with bipolar experience, most likely because of biological differences and the experience of life events related to reproduction: hormonal changes surrounding menstruation, pregnancy, childbirth, and menopause (Diflorio & Jones, 2010; Hilty et al., 1999).

Diagnosis and Assessment

As mentioned earlier, the bipolar disorders are characterized by depressive episodes and hypomanic or manic episodes. The three major bipolar disorders are bipolar I, bipolar II, and cyclothymia.

Bipolar I is characterized by at least one manic episode that lasts at least 1 week and at least one depressive episode that lasts at least 2 weeks. Bipolar II is characterized by at least one hypomanic episode that lasts at least 4 days and at least one depressive episode that lasts at least 2 weeks. Cyclothymia is characterized by subclinical depressive episodes (does not meet full criteria for depressive episode) and subclinical hypomania (does not meet full criteria for hypomanic episodes). This means that the individual experiences symptoms of both depression and hypomania but not enough to meet the full criteria, which are five and three symptoms, respectively. What makes cyclothymia significantly different than bipolar I and bipolar II is the duration of the symptoms. The individual has symptoms of either hypomania or symptoms of depression at least half the time for *two years* and has not been without symptoms for more than 2 months. When diagnosing one of the bipolar disorders, it is important to record the current/most recent episode (depressive, manic, hypomanic) and the severity (mild, moderate, severe, with psychotic features).

Paresh

Paresh is a 28-year-old cisgender first-generation Indian male who has presented for an evaluation at the urging of his wife, Sarah. Sarah reports that she could barely get Paresh out of the house to come to the clinic. He has been "barely functioning" for the past month. He spends all of his time in bed either watching TV or sleeping. He sleeps most of the day, and she can hear him wandering around the house at night. His friends have stopped calling because he does not answer when they do. He has no interest in sex and must be coaxed to eat anything. He has lost 15 pounds. The "final straw" for Sarah was when Paresh began talking about how life would be better for her if he were not around anymore.

Paresh grew up in an upper-middle-class neighborhood in the suburbs of Cleveland. He reports that he had a "normal" childhood. He lived with both of his parents who are of Indian descent and came to the United States in their 20s. Paresh has two siblings, both of whom live in Cleveland. He has remained close with both. Paresh earned "good grades" and his parents were supportive. He attended college in South Florida, where he met Sarah and currently still resides. Until his recent termination, he worked at the same accounting firm that hired him when he graduated from college. Sarah and Paresh have no children but have talked about starting a family.

Sarah states that when she and Paresh were in college he would have bouts (about 2 to 3 weeks) of what she thought was "normal depression." He would skip classes and sleep all day and would seem to be moving in slow motion. During these times he would not want to "hang out with friends," and when they did, he would bring up depressing topics of conversation. He would also start apologizing for things she did not even remember him doing in the past. Sarah said she just figured the stress of school was "getting to him." She was not particularly worried because at other times he was "a blast." He would be the life of the party. He would want to stay out all night and didn't need more than 4 hours of sleep (when his norm was to get 8 hours). He would seem to have a "ton" of energy (more than usual), and would talk about starting his own accounting firm before he even graduated. He would get all of his work done and even turn assignments in early. Sarah reported that when he would have one of these bouts, he would want to have sex constantly and was "super" talkative. She said that over the years he has had a couple of these episodes and that they last about 4 or 5 days. Sarah reports that he has long periods of time (months) where he is just "normal Paresh." She said this last episode has her very concerned.

Diagnostic Impression

Paresh presents with episodes of both depression and hypomania. His depressive symptoms include depressed mood most of the day, diminished interest in activities (sex and friends), significant weight loss, hypersomnia, and thoughts of death. His hypomanic symptoms include decreased need for sleep, more talkative, an increase in goal-directed activity, and inflated self-esteem.

Diagnostic Conclusion

Bipolar I disorder, most recent episode depressed, severe

DIFFERENTIAL DIAGNOSIS I: BIPOLAR I

Rationale: Paresh meets full criteria for major depressive episodes and hypomanic episodes. Although he has an elated mood, which is a change from his functioning level, the episodes are not severe enough to cause an impact in functioning. This is what differentiates hypomania from mania.

DIFFERENTIAL DIAGNOSIS II: ATTENTION DEFICIT HYPERACTIVITY
DISORDER (ADHD)

Rationale: While in a hypomanic episode, individuals may seem hyperactive. In the case of Paresh, he has *episodes* of elated behavior. ADHD is not an episodic disorder; the symptoms are present the majority of the time. The hyperactive symptoms of ADHD would also cause impairment in functioning, whereas hypomanic symptoms do not. The major primary differential between the two disorders is that bipolar disorder is episodic and the manic must last 4 or more days, whereas ADHD presents with constant symptoms.

DIFFERENTIAL DIAGNOSIS III: MAJOR DEPRESSIVE DISORDER (MDD)

Rationale: Because Paresh has a history of manic episodes, major depression cannot be diagnosed.

Biopsychosocial

BIOLOGICAL

There is no indication of a history of mental health issues in Paresh's family. He seems to be in good health physically; however, it is important that he be seen by a health professional for a physical examination to determine if there is a physiological cause for his mood episodes.

PSYCHOLOGICAL

Paresh is currently reporting suicidal ideation. It is critical to determine whether he has a current plan to assess for his safety. Paresh has lost his job due to his depressive episodes.

SOCIAL

Paresh has a support system in both his wife and his social circle. Although he has been isolated from his friends, and trying to isolate from his wife, she remains supportive. Growing up his parents were supportive of him and there is no indication of any significant family issues. It will be important to involve Sarah in the recovery process.

Karen

Karen is a 55-year-old White cisgender woman who was brought to the emergency room by her son, Bob. Karen lives alone in an apartment downtown. She has been divorced for 15 years and no longer has any contact with her ex-husband. She has two children, her son Bob and a daughter Olivia, and two grandchildren. Karen is observed by the social worker as being very disheveled. She is wearing two different shoes; her shirt is buttoned incorrectly, and her hair is tangled and stuck to the side of her head. She is wearing makeup that is smeared under her eyes. Karen is hunched over and slowly rocking back and forth and seems to be having a conversation with someone who is not there. She is not able to respond to any questions asked by the social worker or the physician and is becoming increasingly agitated with each question that is asked. Her son Bob reports that over the past month Karen has seemed "really down in the dumps." She refuses to visit her children and grandchildren, whom she previously had enjoyed spending time with. Bob has become increasingly worried over the past couple of weeks because her sadness has gotten worse, and when he calls her on the phone she seems to be talking very slowly and will start rambling nonsensically.

Bob went over to Karen's house to check on her after she failed to come to a birthday party and he was not able to reach her by phone. When he arrived at her apartment, he was shocked by what he saw. His mother was sitting in a chair crying and mumbling to herself. The apartment was a mess with garbage all over the counters and the floor and dishes piled in the sink. This was very unusual, because his mother is a very neat, organized individual. Bob noticed that his mother had lost quite a bit of weight, because her shirt looked as though it was two sizes too big for her. When he tried to ask her how she was feeling she just stared at him.

While Bob was in the apartment, Karen's neighbor, Dawn, stopped by. Dawn has lived next door for 10 years and she and Karen have dinner and play backgammon on a regular basis. Dawn stated that Karen has said that she has been unable to sleep lately and has seemed "super spacey." Karen was not able to play backgammon last week because her mind "kept going blank." Dawn also said that about 6 weeks ago (she remembered because it was around the time of her birthday) Karen was pounding on her door at 6 a.m. saying that they needed to start celebrating with a mimosa and then a hike. Dawn found this strange because Karen is not a morning person and they had been out late the night before, and hiking was not something they normally do together. Dawn said that it seemed as though Karen had not gone to bed. Karen confirmed she was "pulling an all-nighter," because she "can sleep when she is dead." Dawn said that for the next 5 days or so she could not "keep up with Karen"; she was talking nonstop and "always on the go." She wanted to be doing "fun things" at all times. Dawn reported that Karen has been bringing home a different man every evening, which is very out of character because Karen rarely dates. Karen also has been shopping every day and has bought herself a new wardrobe. Karen has started wearing her hair differently and wearing more makeup. She said that when she asked Karen about her behaviors, she replied, "I am a really great person, I am smart, I am fun, and everyone needs to see that!"

After seeing the condition of his mother and hearing Dawn's account of the past couple of months, Bob decided to bring his mom to the ER. Bob reported to the social worker that he is not aware of any history of mental illness in his mother's family.

Diagnostic Impression

Karen is currently exhibiting symptoms of major depressive episode. Over the past 5 weeks she has been sad ("down in the dumps"), has lost a significant amount of weight, has not been participating in activities she once enjoyed (spending time with grandchildren), is unable to concentrate ("mind going blank"), and is experiencing psychomotor retardation (talking slowly, not responding). She is also currently exhibiting signs of psychosis (auditory hallucinations), as evidenced by her having a conversation with someone who is not there. It has also been reported by the neighbor that Karen had a period of 5 days where she was showing signs of mania. She had an inflated self-esteem, a decreased need for sleep, and excessive involvement in pleasurable activities.

Diagnostic Conclusion

Bipolar I, current episode depressed, severe with psychotic features

DIFFERENTIAL DIAGNOSIS I: SCHIZOAFFECTIVE DISORDER
Rationale: Although Karen meets the criteria for bipolar and also has psychotic features, there is no evidence of psychosis in the absence of the mood episodes. Interepisodic psychosis is required for a diagnosis of schizoaffective disorder.

DIFFERENTIAL DIAGNOSIS II: BIPOLAR II
Rationale: Karen meets all the criteria for a manic episode, therefore bipolar II (which is characterized by hypomanic episodes) can be ruled out.

DIFFERENTIAL DIAGNOSIS III: SCHIZOPHRENIA
Rationale: Although Karen is clearly having auditory hallucinations, they seem to occur only when she is experiencing a mood episode. Therefore, a diagnosis of schizophrenia can be ruled out.

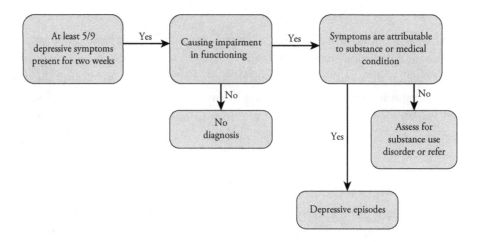

FIGURE 4.1   Depressive episode

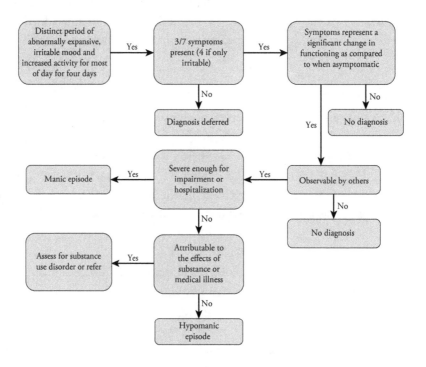

FIGURE 4.2   Hypomanic episode

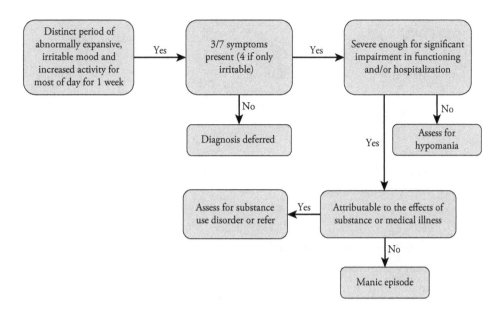

FIGURE 4.3   Manic episode

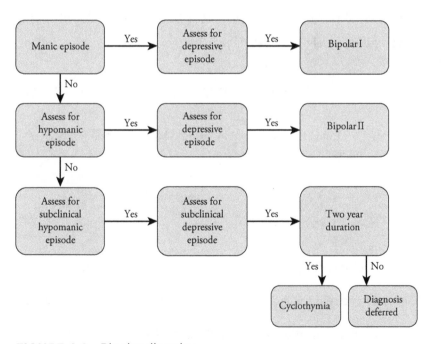

FIGURE 4.4   Bipolar disorder

Biopsychosocial

BIOLOGICAL

Because Karen is neglecting her self-care, it is important for her to have a thorough physical exam. In addition, a neurological examination is recommended to rule out any organic causes for her behaviors.

PSYCHOLOGICAL

There is no known history of mental illness in Karen or her family, which typically indicates a better prognosis.

SOCIAL

Karen has a supportive support system both with her family and her neighbor Dawn. It is important that throughout her treatment her family and Dawn are involved to lend support.

TERMINOLOGY

hallucinations   Altered sensations that appear real but are not actually there.

delusions   Altered reality and beliefs that are strongly held despite evidence to the contrary.

mixed presentation   An individual displaying symptoms of mania and depression simultaneously.

rapid cycling   An individual experiencing at least four episodes of depression, mania, or hypomania in a 1-year period.

REFLECTION QUESTIONS

1.   Which symptoms of bipolar disorder are more common in women?

2.   What are some reasons individuals with bipolar disorder remain untreated?

3.   When is an individual more at risk for suicidal ideation and attempt?

CHAPTER 5

Depressive Disorders

with Celine Rodriguez

LEARNING OBJECTIVES

1. Gain a basic understanding of the causes, prevalence, and comorbidities of the depressive disorders.

2. Become familiar with the criteria for the depressive disorders.

3. Be able to differentially diagnose the depressive disorders.

Characteristics of the Disorders

Depressive disorders, formerly referred to as mood disorders or affective disorders, are a group of disorders with the primary feature of sadness (irritability in adolescents). What is important to remember is that at some point in life, most, if not all, individuals will experience depressive symptoms. These symptoms are not pleasant but are unfortunately a part of life. What distinguishes normal sadness from depression is the level of impairment and duration of the symptoms. If the symptoms do not cause enough distress to result in impairment in functioning at work, home, or school, then a diagnosis is not warranted. The depressive disorders consist of disruptive mood dysregulation disorder (new to the DSM-5; American Psychiatric Association [APA], 2013), major depressive disorder, persistent depressive disorder (also called dysthymia), and premenstrual dysphoric disorder (also new to the DSM-5, and which is diagnosed only by medical professionals).

Disruptive Mood Dysregulation Disorder

There has been much debate over how to appropriately diagnose children who exhibit emotional dysregulation, including irritability and severe temper tantrums. In response to this debate, and in attempt to reduce the overdiagnosing of bipolar disorder in children, a new disorder, disruptive mood dysregulation disorder (DMDD) was created for inclusion in the DSM-5. DMDD is characterized by intense, recurrent angry outbursts (three or more times a week) that are out of proportion to the situation and the child's developmental level. The child will exhibit irritability on most days, and the symptoms are present both at home and external settings. These symptoms are present over the course of 12 months and cause impairment that requires clinical attention. It is important to note that tantrums, bad moods, and outbursts are a normal part of childhood development. Although these episodes are stressful, and sometimes even embarrassing for the family, the episodes are typically manageable and/or infrequent. These behaviors become a diagnosis when the family unit becomes impaired.

Major Depressive Disorder

Major depressive disorder (MDD; sometimes referred to as unipolar depression) is a major mental health disorder that causes significant impairment in psychosocial functioning (Perocco Zanatta et al., 2019). In fact, it is one of the most prevalent and disabling forms of mental health disorders (Kessler, 2005).

MDD can occur at any age, but is most likely to occur after the onset of puberty. The disorder seems to peak among those in their mid-20s. An onset of depression later in life is also quite common.

MDD is characterized by 2 weeks of depressed mood, lack of interest in pleasurable activities, negative thinking, emotional reactiveness, loss of energy and/or motivation, irritability, and low self-esteem. Some individuals will experience significant weight issues (loss or gain). Research suggests that the relationship between depression and weight gain or obesity is a complicated one. The obvious assumption is that people who are experiencing depression crave and consequently eat unhealthy foods (let's face it, when we are experiencing strong emotions, we tend not to crave broccoli). However, a number of biopsychosocial variables contribute to weight gain in depression. People experiencing depressive disorders often experience hopelessness, aggression, rumination, anxiety, and worry. In addition, they may experience cognitive reactivity, which is the triggering of negative thinking patterns with minor triggers that ultimately manifest in negative thoughts (Paans et al., 2017). Research has indicated associations between higher cognitive reactivity and higher body mass index (BMI). Chronic psychosocial stress has been associated not only with depression but also with weight gain and the development of obesity (Horesh & Iancu, 2010). Studies also indicate that consequences of low socioeconomic status (SES), such as poverty, social isolation, lack of social support, and low education levels, are implicated in both obesity and the development of obesity (Devaux & Sassi, 2013).

MDD is often referred to as either endogenous (biological) or reactive (sometimes referred to as exogenous). Although these categories are not utilized for diagnostic purposes, they are helpful clinically in terms of treatment. Endogenous depression is characterized by depressive symptoms that happen seemingly without reason. They are seen as a result of one more biological condition, such as medical illness, hormone fluctuations in women, genetics, brain or neurotransmitter abnormalities, or medications. Endogenous depression is associated with psychomotor disturbances, disturbances in affect, cognitive impairment, and vegetative dysfunction (interrupted sleep, loss of appetite, reduced sex drive, and loss of energy in morning hours), and sometimes psychosis (Parker et al., 2010). Endogenous depression seems to manifest suddenly—in the absence of a stressor—for no apparent reason. Oftentimes endogenous depression is the result of medical illness (e.g., hypothyroidism), hormonal issues, medications, or recreational drug use. People with endogenous depression are more likely to experience physiological symptoms of depression, including fatigue, decreased sex drive, restlessness, impaired coordination, and sleep disturbance.

Reactive depression, in contrast, manifests as a result of psychosocial stressors such as death of a loved one, relationship problems, or major life changes. Individuals with endogenous depression are more likely to respond to antidepressants than those with reactive depression (Ghaemi & Vohringer, 2011), and those with reactive depression are more likely to benefit from psychotherapy. A study of Japanese psychiatrists indicated that despite the debate as to whether there are indeed two different types of depression, the psychiatrists chose different treatments based on whether their patients' depression was reactive or endogenous (Mizushima et al., 2013). The vast majority of individuals have a combination of both types of depression, and therefore a combined approach of medications and psychotherapy is often warranted. For diagnostic purposes, there is only one major depressive disorder, but from a clinical perspective determining the root cause (if possible) can help with the treatment aspect of the disorder.

Persistent Depressive Disorder (Dysthymia)

Persistent depressive disorder (PDD) is sometimes categorized as a minor depressive disorder, meaning that the symptoms do not rise to the level of those of MDD. Although the symptoms of PDD may not be as severe, they tend to be very long term and begin earlier in life, often in childhood or adolescence. The long-term impact of the disorder on quality of life and productivity can be significant. The term *minor depression* therefore is not an accurate description of PDD. PDD is characterized by 2 years or more (with symptoms on most days) of chronic sadness, irritability, negativity, low self-esteem, low motivation and energy, and/or lack of enthusiasm for pleasurable activities. Most individuals with PDD will experience a major depressive episode. This means that in addition to their low-grade depressive symptoms, they will have 2-week (or longer) periods in which their symptoms escalate to the level of full clinical depression. When the patient recovers from the major depressive episode, they return to their "normal" of PDD. This is often referred to as double depression.

Historically, mental health professionals have viewed PDD as being part of one's character, and therefore difficult to treat. However, some patients do respond to antidepressants, which suggests that these individuals may in fact be suffering from a low-grade biological depression rather than a character-based depression. Because of the tendency of those individuals with PDD to experience major depressive episodes, often an emotional response to being low energy and lacking enthusiasm, the integration of psychotherapy in conjunction with psychotropic medications is important.

History

Although there have been references to depression throughout history, there was no formal definition of the disorder until the DSM-III (APA, 1980). Prior to the classification in the DSM-III, depressive symptoms were referred to as melancholia or reactive depression. Melancholia was described as a severe disabling depression that had no known cause and often resulted in suicidal ideation and somatic symptoms. The earliest accounts of melancholia are found in ancient Mesopotamian texts and discussions of it appear throughout history. In the 1950s, researchers began to make the distinction between neurotic depression (melancholic) and reactive depression. Reactive depression was referred to a depression that could be linked to a life event. It typically had milder symptoms such as sadness and guilt and unworthiness. The DSM-III had three severity categories: mild, moderate, and severe. It also had subtypes: known cause, psychotic symptoms, and melancholic. The DSM-III also included dysthymic disorder, a form of chronic clinical depression with a duration of 2 years or more (APA, 1987). The DSM-IV listed nine criteria of which five had to be met for a diagnosis of major depressive episode. The individual also had to exhibit depressed mood or loss of interest in pleasure, the symptoms had to cause impairment, and the person had to have no history of mania or hypomania. The DSM-IV-TR (APA, 2000) kept the same criteria; however, the new version added associated features of the disorder, the course of the disorder, and updated prevalence rates. The DSM-5 (APA, 2013) has the same criteria as in the DSM IV-TR; however, the DSM-5 has added a specifier of "with mixed features," which is comorbid manic symptoms (fewer than three). The DSM-IV had a bereavement exclusion, which meant that if someone had suffered a loss within 2 months, then MDD could not be diagnosed. The DSM-5 has omitted this exclusion.

Etiology

The DSM-5 includes one type of depression—major depressive disorder—the diagnosis of which varies only by severity. Depression is diagnosed based on a list of criteria or symptoms; a greater number of symptoms or a higher impact on functioning results in a more severe diagnosis. The problem, however, is that people are heterogenous and often present with different symptoms. Despite decades of research, there is no consensus as to what causes depression. Several theories from biological, psychological and lifestyle perspectives have been proposed. What is largely agreed upon is that most mental health disorders are caused by a combination of biological, psychological, and sociological factors, a biopsychosocial model.

Biological theories have explored the role of genetics, neurotransmitter abnormalities, physical illness or disease, medications, lack of sunlight or bright light, and/or nutrition.

Determining the genetic risk or heritability of depressive disorders is challenging for several reasons. Although there are several diagnoses under the umbrella of depressive disorders, the disorders differ primarily only in severity and duration. *Genetic studies,* primarily from family, twin, and genome studies, indicate an overall heredity rate of MDD of 10% to 44% (Corfield, et al., 2017). Family data indicate that if one parent has depression or bipolar disorder there is a 10% to 25% chance the child will develop the disorder. The rate doubles if both parents have the disorder. The greater the number of family members who have depression or bipolar disorder, the greater the risk to the child. A study of 130,620 individuals with a diagnosis of depression found a 46% heritability rate of major depression in older adults and 40% in a cohort of younger adults (aged 23 to 38 years) (Corfield et al., 2017). Twin studies have provided the most powerful data in terms of separating nurture from nature. Data indicates that genetics explains only 30% to 50% (depending on the study) of the heritability of depression, the rest being likely explained by environmental or other factors (Kendler et al., 2018;. It is difficult to isolate the actual heritability of depression because it may be multiple disorders with similar symptoms that may have different genetic risks. These differences are based on a variety of factors, including, but not limited to, age, gender, culture, environment, nutrition, and so on. The stress diathesis model (Zuckerman, 1999) focuses on the relationship between the environment and genetics in mental health disorders (particularly schizophrenia). The model posits that mental health disorders result from a combination of genetics and biology and environmental factors. The likelihood of two individuals with the same genetic vulnerability being diagnosed with depression is largely dependent upon the environment. For example, with genetic risk being equal, and individual who is homeless and lacks emotional and physical resources is more likely to manifest with a disorder than an individual who has their physical and emotional needs met.

Neurotransmitters

Serotonin is the neurotransmitter that is most often associated with depressive disorders, largely due to the effectiveness of medications known as selective serotonin reuptake inhibitors (SSRIs) (e.g., fluoxetine [Prozac] and sertraline [Zoloft]) in treating them. Studies have demonstrated that serotonin has a role in the modulation of depression and that specific serotonin receptors can be linked with various symptoms (Nautiyal & Hen, 2017). Research has also found a link between suicide and serotonin. For example, Underwood et al. (2018) found that people who have attempted suicide have altered serotonin receptors in the prefrontal cortex of the brain. Norepinephrine has also been associated with depression, both through the effectiveness of medications with noradrenergic effects and brain studies. Studies of the brain have indicated that norepinephrine neurons project into parts of the brain that regulate emotion and cognition. Postmortem studies have indicated numerous norepinephrine differences in brains from depressed patients compared to people without depression (Moret, & Briley, 2011).

Physical/Medical Illness

Physiological illness can often lead to endogenous or biological depression. Several medical illnesses can lead to depression. Therefore, it is important that clients who present with depressive symptoms be referred to their medical doctor for a physical examination and bloodwork. Approximately 15-20% of individuals with heart disease also have comorbid depression (Freedland et al., 2003; Jiang et al., 2005; Lichtman et al. 2008). Individuals with heart disease and depressive symptoms are often slower to recover from illness, are more likely to have future complications from their heart disease and are at higher risk of dying. One study found that depression is the strongest predictor of death in the first decade after a diagnosis of heart disease (May et al., 2017). In terms of treatment, it is important to consider whether heart disease leads to depression (either biologically or emotionally) or whether the depression came first. If the heart disease has triggered a stressful reaction leading to the depression, once the symptoms of heart disease are managed, the depression should remit. However, if the depression was present prior to the diagnosis of heart disease, then treatment specifically for the depressive symptoms is warranted. Research has indicated that regardless of which disorder comes first, there is a higher risk of death with a comorbid diagnosis of depression and heart disease. Anada et al. (1993) found those individuals with a diagnosis of depression are 2–4 times more likely to be diagnosed with heart disease. More recently, May et al., (2017) found that a depression diagnosis at any time following a diagnosis of coronary artery disease is associated with a two fold higher risk of death than those without a depression diagnosis.

There is evidence that a number of medical disorders are associated with depression and that the relationship may be bidirectional. These disorders include: HIV/AIDS, asthma, chronic infection and/or pain, influenza, hepatitis, diabetes, multiple sclerosis, and Parkinson's disease (Jones et al., 2004; Lemke 2008; Walker, 2015), to name just a few. It is important to remember in most cases, individuals with these disorders are typically taking medications to treat the disorder. It is possible (often likely) that the medications are causing or contributing to the depressive symptoms (Celano et al., 2011).

Medications/Drugs

Several medications can either cause symptoms of depression or exacerbate existing symptoms. Antihypertensives such as beta blockers (eg. propranolol [Inderal]), calcium channel blockers, (eg. Amlodipine [Norvasc]) and ACE Inhibitors (eg. Benazepril [Lotensin]) have long been thought to cause depressive symptoms (Rogers & Pies, 2008). Antihypertensives such as beta and calcium channel blockers are not only used to treat hypertension, but also to treat the physiological symptoms of anxiety. The data surrounding the association between the antihypertensive medications is limited and indicate mixed results. Some studies have found that depressive symptoms occur in high doses of beta blockers and remit when doses are lowered (Steffensmeier et al., 2006), others found a positive relationship between beta and channel blockers and depressive symptoms (Lindberg et al., 1998). While other studies have found that the link between the two is much smaller than original thought (Rogers & Pies, 2008) or that there was no significant association between depression and antihypertensives (Hertzman et al., 2005). Studies indicate a positive association between ACE inhibitors and depressive symptoms (Hallas, 1996). It is important to remember that (as mentioned above) there is a strong link between heart disease and depression. A comprehensive psychosocial assessment is very important to determine the source(s) of the depressive symptoms and choose the best possible intervention.

Benzodiazepines (diazepam [Valium], alprazolam [Xanax], and lorazepam [Ativan]), which are used to treat anxiety have also been linked to depression. However, it is unclear as to whether the pills themselves are causing depressive symptoms or if the benzodiazepines reduce the symptoms of anxiety causing the depressive symptoms to become more prominent (Baldwin et al., 2013). People who are elderly have an increased risk of depression. A study by van Vliet et al. (2009) found a significant association between the use of benzodiazepines and depressive symptoms in older adults and the use of benzodiazepines preceding the depressive symptoms.

Anticonvulsants (antiseizure) have also been liked with the development of depression in a small number of individuals (Miller, 2008; Mula, 2007). There are three (barbiturates, vigabatrin and topiramate) that are thought to have more of a depressive effect than the other types of anticonvulsants. These medications impact the neurotransmitter GABA and may cause sedation, fatigue and/or symptoms of depression (Miller, 2008).

Long term corticosteroids have commonly been associated with the development of depressive symptoms. Corticosteroids are used to treat a number of medical issues including but not limited to neurological, gastrointestinal, respiratory issues and inflammation. They are also used to treat the side effects of chemotherapy. A study by Bolano et al., (2004) found that there was a 60% lifetime risk for mood or anxiety disorders with corticosteroid use. Another study found an increase of depressive disorder was associated with high dose corticosteroid use but found that stress levels increased as the dose was tapered down. Therefore, it was difficult to determine if the symptoms were from the steroid exposure or the dose reduction (Breitbart et al., 1993).

This section discussed just a few of the many medications that may cause or exacerbate depressive symptoms. When a client reports symptoms of depression It is very important to get a full list of medications the individual is taking. This list should include prescribed and non-prescribed medications. Oftentimes individuals will take medications that are prescribed to others and may be afraid to disclose this information. It is important that the client feels safe to do so. It is also important to ask about any herbal medications (including marijuana and CBD) or remedies and of course illicit drugs.

Lifestyle

Research has indicated an association between diet and depressive symptoms. One study found that individuals who had a "whole" diet consisting of fruits vegetables and fish were significantly less likely to be depressed than those individuals who had a high intake of processed foods, such as sweets, processed meats, and refined grains (Akbaraly et al., 2009). A study by Sanchez-Villeges et al. (2007) found that those who adhered to a Mediterranean diet (a diet high in fruits, nuts, fish, and legumes) were less likely to have a diagnosis of depression than those who did not adhere to the diet. The consumption of meat and/or high-fat dairy products was associated with higher levels of depression.

Studies have indicated an association between obesity and depression, with the relationship between the two being reciprocal. Longitudinal research has indicated that a high BMI (particularly in those individuals who are classified as obese) is associated with an increased risk of depression and that depression is associated with a higher risk of developing obesity (Luppino et al., 2010). People with obesity are found to have a 1.5–two times higher risk of developing depression (Faith et al., 2011; Luppino et al., 2010) The mechanism for the association between the two disorders is complicated. In societies that value "thinness" and have an emphasis on physical beauty, such as the United States, Europe, and parts of Asia, being overweight may lead to overall body dissatisfaction, low self-esteem, and ultimately depression (Hoek et al., 2005).

Psychological Perspective

Behaviorism posits that the environment shapes behavior, focusing on the observable and how individuals learn behaviors. Depression is the result of a person's interaction with the environment. Individuals learn behaviors through classical conditioning (often called Pavlovian conditioning), operant conditioning, and through observation, imitation, and reinforcement (social learning theory) (Bandura, 1971). In terms of depression, classical conditioning proposes that depression is learned through the association of certain stimuli with negative emotional states. If a child experiences negative experiences repeatedly in the classroom, exposure to the classroom becomes a cue for negativity. In terms of operant conditioning, depression is caused by the removal of positive reinforcement (Lewinsohn, 1974). For example, a breakup with a significant other could induce depression because the person is losing a source of positive reinforcement (from both the significant other and the social group that came along with that individual). People who are depressed often become inactive and withdrawn. An individual's friends become a sounding board and source of sympathy, providing attention, and thus further reinforcing the depressive behaviors. The constant complaining, feeling sorry for themselves, and negativity may alienate their friends, leading to further loss and sadness, thereby creating a cycle of depression.

Prevalence and Comorbidities

Major depressive disorder is the most common mental health disorder, with a lifetime prevalence of 20.6% of U.S. adults (Hasin et al., 2018). It is the largest contributor to disability worldwide, with an estimated 4.4% of the population (322 million people) suffering from the disorder (World Health Organization [WHO], 2017). Nearly half of those suffering from depression live in Southeast Asia and the Western Pacific, areas that are highly populated. Rates are highest among older adults, at 7.5% for females and 5.5% for males. The number of people living with depression increased by more than 18% between 2005 and 2015. This is due, in part, to the overall growth of the population and an increase in population in the age groups in which depression is more common (i.e., older adults).

The most common comorbid disorder with depression is substance use disorder (57.9%), with alcohol use disorder being the most prevalent (40.8%) (Hasin et al., 2018). Individuals tend to use mood-congruent drugs, or drugs that "match" the mood that they are in. For example, someone who is feeling down is likely to use alcohol or a benzodiazepine. The opposite is true for someone in a good mood or in a manic episode. The goal would be to feel even better, often by using a drug such as cocaine or an amphetamine (either illicit, such as crystal methamphetamine, or prescription, such as Adderall or Ritalin). Using a substance that is considered a "downer" is likely to make the symptoms of depression worse. Using a mood-congruent drug sounds counterintuitive, and it is; however, oftentimes people who are feeling down are not necessarily looking to feel better, some are looking to not feel at all, and some prefer to wallow. Someone who is feeling down is likely to listen to more mellow (or even depressing) music and/or watch something sad on TV.

Anxiety disorders are diagnosed in approximately 37% to 67% of individuals with a diagnosis of MDD (Hasin et al., 2018; Lamers et al., 2012). Lamers et al. (2012) found that the lifetime comorbidity rate of depression and social phobia is 41%; panic disorder, 42%; and generalized anxiety disorder, 38%.

Because DMDD is a relatively new diagnosis, little is known about its prevalence or comorbidities. Evidence suggests that the creation of the diagnosis of DMDD may actually be complicating diagnosis rather than simplifying it. The symptoms of irritable or angry mood and outbursts overlap with criteria of oppositional defiant disorder (ODD). In a community sample of 6-year-old children (Dougherty et al., 2014) found that 8% met the criteria for DMDD; however, 55% had comorbid ODD. A study of 6- to 12-year-olds with psychiatric histories found that 26% met criteria for DMDD, and 96% of those had a comorbid diagnosis of ODD or conduct disorder (CD) (Axelson et al., 2012). In an epidemiological study of 6- to 12-year-old children, the prevalence of DMDD symptoms was 9% (Mayes et al., 2016). Interestingly, 92%

of the children with DMDD symptoms had ODD and 66% of children with ODD had DMDD symptoms. This indicates that it is unlikely to have a DMDD without ODD, but ODD can and often does occur without DMDD symptoms (Mayes et al., 2016). Thus, differential diagnosing of DMDD from ODD is difficult.

In response to the lack of differentiation from the disruptive disorders, a lack of peer-reviewed research surrounding DMDD, and limited reliability of the diagnosis, the World Health Organization's (WHO) International Classification of Diseases, 11th Revision (ICD-11) task group "recommended that WHO not accept DMDD as a diagnostic category in ICD-11" (Lochman et al., 2015, pp. 31–32). The task group recommends that the criteria of ODD include a specifier as to whether irritability and anger are present.

Course and Prognosis

Despite the effectiveness of medications and psychosocial intervention, many people with depression remain untreated. Of those who are treated nearly 50% will discontinue their medications within six months (Hung, 2014). 20–35% of all patients will develop a chronic depressive disorder that lasts two years or more (Rubio et al., 2011). There are a number of factors that may predict the course of MDD such as early age of onset (Rhebergen, et al., 2012) and trauma (Wiersma et al., 2009). Studies indicate that a perceived lack of social support has been related to poor recovery from depression (Bosworth et al., 2008; Joseph et al., 2011). This relationship has been noted more so in younger adults as opposed to older adults. Loneliness has been shown to adversely affect the prognosis of depressive disorder in both younger and older adults. Individuals with comorbid anxiety disorders are more likely to have a poorer prognosis, poorer quality of life, and impaired social and occupational functioning (Bosworth et al., 2008; Joseph et al., 2011).

Cultural and Gender-Related Considerations

The prevalence of MDD is similar among Whites, Hispanics/Latinx, and Black/African Americans (Walton & Shepard Payne, 2016); however, data indicate that MDD is underdiagnosed in most racial and ethnically diverse groups (Kirmayer et al., 2017) and that depression is underdiagnosed in Black/African Americans (Walton & Shepard Payne, 2016). Some possible explanations include bias and stigmatization in treatment seeking and referrals and discrimination by healthcare professionals. People who are members of ethnically diverse groups are less likely to seek treatment for MDD. The lack of treatment-seeking among Asian Americans, Black/African Americans, Latinx/Hispanics, and American Indians/Alaskan Natives results in their being less likely to receive adequate mental health care, as compared to White Americans. This also means that these groups are more likely to have greater severity in symptoms and more disabling conditions than Whites. For example, Walton and Shepard Payne (2016) found that Black/African Americans have lower reported prevalence rates of depression and that they are more likely to experience more severe psychological distress and disabling symptoms and present with more somatic complaints. Racial and ethnically diverse groups are most often seen for mental health issues in primary care settings and are more likely to report somatic symptoms (i.e., headaches, insomnia, loss of energy) as the presenting complaints, and are more likely to attribute these symptoms to physical exhaustion rather than to depression (Walton & Shepard Payne, 2016). Some Asian may be more likely to report somatic symptoms such as report weakness or tiredness, or imbalance rather than the "traditional" symptoms of depression (Novick et al., 2013). American Indians/Alaskan Natives have the highest rate of suicide among those aged 15 to 24 years and 25 to 44 years (Centers for Disease Control and Depression [CDC], 2019). It might be argued that depression is a likely precedent of suicide, but not enough studies have been done to rule definitively.

Mental health clinicians need to be aware of cultural differences in depression among racial and ethnic cultural groups, along with other factors that contribute to this underdiagnosis. Underdiagnosis among these groups is likely explained through a variety of factors, such as implicit bias by mental health professionals, race-based mental health disparities, a lack of training and experience working with diverse groups, lack of cultural understanding in diagnosing, and cultural stigma surrounding help-seeking (Jones, 2018; Paniagua, 2014; Williams et al., 2018). Cultural beliefs and customs can shape the way mental illness is experienced, the ways in which behaviors are perceived, and the ways mental health practitioners understand and interpret those behaviors and subsequent symptoms.

Surveys of MDD across diverse cultures have shown differences in prevalence rate, age at onset, and the likelihood of comorbid substance use. While these findings suggest substantial cultural differences, the study samples are too small to develop statistically significant linkages among particular cultures with regard to the likelihood of specific symptoms. Additionally, the cultural expression of MDD is different among groups (APA, 2013; Paniagua, 2014).

The criteria for MDD are based off of European and American psychiatry (Kirmayer et al., 2017). Individuals interpret what is happening with their body and mind through their cultural lens. There are cultural norms that impact the threshold at which individuals will report the symptoms of mental health issues. Their experiences that may lead to lowering the threshold include the willingness to pathologize certain experiences; expression of suffering rather than coping or becoming more resilient, which can lead to demoralization; and finally the act of labeling. All of these experiences (behaviors) can lead to an overdiagnosis of depression.

Worldwide, MDD is twice as common among women (Salk et al., 2017). In fact, by one estimate women are thought to be 70% more likely to experience depression than men within their lifetime (Kessler, 2001). These numbers raise an important question— why? Earlier research indicated that gender differences tend to emerge between the ages of 13 and 15 years and become even more pronounced between 15 to 18 years (Hankin, 1998; Salk et al., 2017). However, recent meta-analyses indicate that gender differences in depression emerge by the age of 12, if not sooner (Salk et al., 2017). This may be, in part, due to the convergence of hormonal and neurodevelopmental changes that occur during puberty (Salk et al., 2017). Girls who go through puberty early may be at an increased risk of depression due to an increase in peer sexual harassment (Lindberg et al., 2007; Salk et al., 2017). With research indicating that women are almost twice as likely as men to experience depression, there is the real risk that depression has become a stereotyped disorder. This stereotype may lead to overdiagnosis, and consequently overmedication of women (Salk et al., 2017). Conversely, for men, this may mean that they are being overlooked and underdiagnosed. In some cultures, it is more acceptable for women to show emotion and seek professional help when struggling. Of course, seeking help is what results in a diagnosis. Men who do not seek help when they are struggling with depressive symptoms will not receive a diagnosis. This may further contribute to gender differences in depression.

Diagnosis and Assessment

In order to diagnose MDD, the individual must meet at least five of the following criteria: sad mood, sleep disturbance, diminished interest in activities, weight loss, psychomotor agitation or retardation, loss of energy, feeling worthless or guilty, inability to concentrate, or recurrent thoughts of death (APA, 2013). These symptoms need to last at 2 weeks (1 week in children). It is very important when assessing for MDD to determine whether the individual has a history of manic episodes. A history of manic episodes (even one) would indicate a diagnosis of bipolar disorder and would require a different course of treatment. When diagnosing it is important to note whether the depressive episode is a single episode with no remission or whether it is recurrent. In addition, the severity should be noted.

For a diagnosis of PDD, the individual must meet a least two of the criteria listed for depressive episode that persist over the course of 2 years (1 year for children). The episodes indicated a change from their normal level of functioning. And remember, as is the case with all disorders, it must be causing significant impairment in their functioning.

Alesha

Alesha is a 19-year-old multiracial cisgender female who is a second-year college student majoring in biology. She is currently living on campus in the dorms and has one roommate and five additional "suite mates." She does not have a steady boyfriend but has been dating "on and off" since coming to college. She came to the University Counseling Center at the suggestion from a friend after she had shared that she had been having thoughts of suicide. During the assessment, Alesha reported that she grew up in a medium-size suburb with her two parents and her younger sister. She speaks to her parents at least once a week, and reports that she has always had a strong relationship with her parents. She is close with her younger sister and texts with her throughout the day. She says there is no history of abuse; however, she did admit that she has a history of self-injurious behavior (SIB) that began at the age of 13. She states that over the past few years when "things get really stressful" she would scrape her skin with a push pin or paperclip but did not draw blood. As a teenager, she described herself as a loner, not fitting in, and somewhat shy. She shared she had just a very small group of friends she connected with. She shared that more recently it has been getting harder for her to get out of bed and move through her day. She reported that she "feels down" every day, stating, "I just feel empty … like I'm never going to be happy or good at anything." She spends most of her day watching television. She reports that she began having intermittent feelings of self-harm approximately 4 to 5 weeks ago and recently shared this with her friend. Alesha has admitted to having thoughts of suicide but denies having a plan on any follow through. Alesha stated that she feels the urge to cut herself with sharper objects to release the "inner pain." She further shared that lately she has not been able to concentrate as well, has been feeling distracted, and has not been sleeping much at night. She has a difficult time falling asleep, and she is up numerous times during the night when she cannot "shut up" her mind. She reported that she has gained about 10 pounds in the past 2 months and has been feeling "cranky" toward friends and family. Additionally, she shared, "I have a hard time concentrating and feeling motivated with my schoolwork because I just don't have any energy at all." She reported that her grades have been falling and she is in danger of being placed on academic probation.

Diagnostic Impression

Alesha presents with several signs and symptoms of MDD, including depressed mood, loss of energy, difficulty concentrating, insomnia, weight gain, and recurrent thoughts of death. A diagnosis of MDD can be made if the symptoms are severe enough to interfere with a person's ability to sleep, study, eat, and enjoy life (National Institute of Mental Health [NIMH], 2015). Alesha shared that she has had difficulty with school, and that her sleep, energy, and motivation have all been impacted. As such, these symptoms support a MDD diagnosis.

Diagnosis Conclusion

Major depressive disorder, single episode, severe

DIFFERENTIAL DIAGNOSIS I: BIPOLAR DISORDER

Rationale: Alesha presents with symptoms commonly associated with the depressed phase of bipolar disorder, such as a depressed mood and suicidal ideation. People experiencing a depressive episode of bipolar disorder have a very similar clinical presentation to a person with MDD. A key aspect of bipolar disorder that differentiates it from MDD is that people with bipolar disorder also experience manic episodes. In order to diagnose a person like Alesha with bipolar disorder, the clinician would have to assess for a past history of manic episodes. Because Alesha did not describe a history of manic episodes, the clinician would likely not make a diagnosis of bipolar disorder at this encounter.

It is important to note that antidepressants show little to no efficacy for depressive episodes associated with bipolar disorder (Hirschfield, 2014). Consequently, correct identification of bipolar disorder among people exhibiting signs of depression is critical for effective treatment and improved outcomes (Hirschfield, 2014).

DIFFERENTIAL DIAGNOSIS II: ATTENTION DEFICIT HYPERACTIVITY DISORDER (ADHD)

Rationale: Alesha presents with symptoms of distractibility, irritability, and low frustration tolerance. These symptoms can be present in both ADHD and MDD. When the criteria are met for both, ADHD can be diagnosed in addition to this mood disorder.

Note that clinicians must be careful not to overdiagnosis major depressive episodes in children with ADHD whose disturbance in mood is characterized by irritability rather than by sadness or loss of interest (DSM-5). Additionally, as with all disorders, a full comprehensive assessment should be conducted ADHD.

DIFFERENTIAL DIAGNOSIS III: ADJUSTMENT DISORDER WITH DEPRESSED MOOD

Rationale: There are some key differences between situational (adjustment) and clinical (MDD) depression. An adjustment disorder with depressed mood is a short-term form of depression that occurs as the result of a traumatic event or change in a person's life. Triggers can include divorce; loss of a job; the death of a close friend; a serious accident; or a major life change, such as retirement. Situational depression stems from a struggle to come to terms with dramatic life changes. Clinical depression is more severe than situational depression. In this case, Alesha has a history of depressive features that occur most days than not and there does not appear to have been a recent trigger that would warrant a situational (adjustment) depression. Therefore, MDD is the appropriate diagnosis.

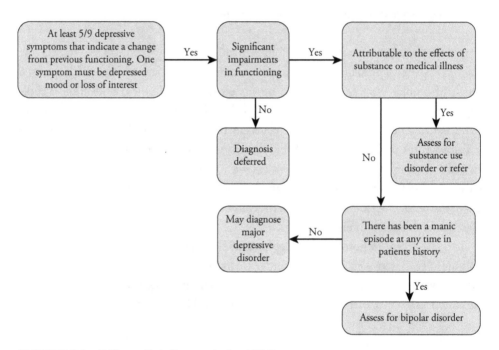

FIGURE 5.1 Differential diagnosis for MDD

Biopsychosocial

BIOLOGICAL

Alesha reports an increase of self-injurious ideation and recently "feeling down," sleeping more, and having difficulty concentrating. She would benefit from a visit to her primary care physician for a physical examination and bloodwork to rule out any medical conditions that may be causing her symptoms.

PSYCHOLOGICAL

Alesha admitted to a history of self-injurious behavior and a recent increase in suicidal ideation. It is important to determine how often and when these thoughts occur. Alesha can gain coping skills in session with her social worker to later generalize outside of session and reduce and prevent the self-injurious behavior. Her grades seem to be impacted by her recent depressive symptoms, and she is now at risk of academic probation. Further assessment needed to assess Alesha's self-esteem and the correlation between her academic success and identity as a student.

SOCIAL

Alesha has an established social support network that includes her parents and younger sister. She states that she was a loner and didn't fit in with her peers during her teenage years. Further assessment should be done on how Alesha has adapted to her new life at the university and her ability to form friendships within her dorm and in her classes.

Michael

Michael is a 65-year-old healthy Black/African American male who currently resides in a 55 and over community in Florida. His wife of 40 years passed away 2 years ago. Two months ago, he moved to the community after becoming "fed up" with the Buffalo winters, after having lived in Buffalo his whole life. He has two grown daughters (Karen and Nancy). When Michael lived in Buffalo he lived on the same street as Karen and was able to see her and two of his grandkids almost daily. Nancy lives in Florida, appropriately 50 miles from Michael's community. Michael stated that Nancy comes to visit every few weeks with her two boys, but she is busy with her job and the boys are heavily involved in sports He requested a visit with the community social worker because he is just feeling "out of sorts." Michael says he has a group of friends in the community with whom he plays golf and cards. He says they are very nice people and have made him feel welcome. He has also been on a few dates with some "nice ladies." He said despite his active social life and the sunshine almost every day, he still feels out of place. He says he feels "down in the dumps" a lot and often tears up for seemingly no reason. He feels himself starting to isolate from his friends, and that makes him worried. He stated that other than when his wife passed, he has not had these issues before.

Diagnostic Impression

Michael has recently moved to a new state after living in Buffalo his entire life. He has a friend group in Florida, but is beginning to isolate from them because he is feeling down and tearful.

Diagnostic Conclusion

Adjustment disorder with depressed mood

DIFFERENTIAL DIAGNOSIS I: MAJOR DEPRESSIVE DISORDER

Rationale: Although Michael as a few symptoms of depressive mood (down in the dumps, tearful, isolation), he does not meet full criteria. Most important, Michael has experienced a significant event (the move from Buffalo) and is likely having a difficult time adjusting to his new home and separation from his daughter. It is likely that with some intervention and support these depressive symptoms will dissipate.

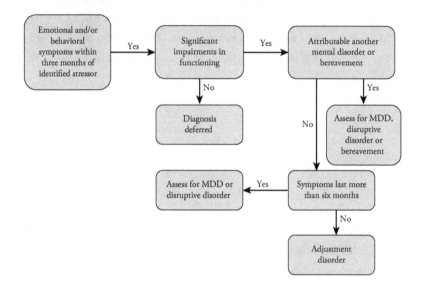

FIGURE 5.2   Differential diagnosis for adjustment disorder with depressed mood

Biopsychosocial

BIOPSYCHOSOCIAL

Although Michael reported that he is in good health, is it important that he be evaluated by a healthcare professional to determine if there are any physiological reasons for his symptoms (such as thyroid or cardiac issues).

PSYCHOLOGICAL

You may be thinking that adjustment disorder is in the "Trauma" chapter in the DSM-5, and so it is out of place here. We wanted to illustrate that sometimes depressive symptoms are the result of a major life event and, although causing significant impairment for the individual, do not warrant a diagnosis of MDD. If Michael's symptoms persist, increase in intensity, or new symptoms appear, then a new assessment would be needed to determine if a diagnosis of MDD would be appropriate.

SOCIAL

Michael has a group of new friends in Florida with whom he socializes. However, given that he has only been in Florida for 2 months, it is not likely that has formed tight bonds with the new friends. His daughter who lives 50 miles away can serve as a source of support, if needed. It may be beneficial to involve his daughter in a session if she is willing. This may help to alleviate some of the isolation Michael is feeling.

TERMINOLOGY

biopsychosocial model   A model that considers an individual's biological, psychological, and social systems.

endogenous depression   Depression caused by a biological condition.

psychomotor agitation   Anxious restlessness that causes a person to make movements without meaning to.

psychomotor retardation   Slowed thoughts, emotional reactions, and physical movements.

reactive depression   Depression caused as a result of psychosocial stressors.

rumination   Repetitively going over a thought or a problem.

REFLECTION QUESTIONS

1. What are the primary differences between MDD and PDD?

2. Why do some by clinicians and researchers consider DMDD be a controversial disorder?

3. If a client presents with depressive symptoms, who should the social worker refer them to?

4. How does depression present in children?

5. Which type of depression is less likely to respond to antidepressant medications, but more likely to respond to psychotherapy?

Anxiety Disorders

Characteristics of the Disorders

The DSM-5 (APA, 2013) identifies six anxiety disorders: separation anxiety disorder, specific phobia, social anxiety disorder, panic disorder, agoraphobia, and generalized anxiety disorder. This chapter examines five of these disorders, omitting separation anxiety disorder.

Specific phobia is an intense fear of specific object or situation. Most individuals fear certain items or situations. However, for a diagnosis of specific phobia the fear must be out of proportion to the situation or object and the fear needs to last at least 6 months (APA, 2013). The individual must have an intense fear almost to or to the point of panic of the object upon exposure or even the thought of the object. It is perfectly normal for an individual to have a fear of a spider; however, if the individual has a panic attack or refuses to leave the house for fear of encountering a spider, this rises to the level of being out of proportion. The DSM-5 lists five phobic situations: animal, natural environment (weather situations, water, etc.), blood, injection, injury (needles, going to doctor, etc.), situational (flying, elevators, etc.), and other (vomiting, life size plush characters, clowns, etc.). Animal and heights have been found to be the most prevalent fears among those with a diagnosis of specific phobia, at 4.7% and 4.5%, respectively (APA, 2013).

Social anxiety disorder is an intense fear about one or more social situations in which an individual fears the possibility of scrutiny by others. These situations include, but are not limited to, parties, performing, giving a presentation, or having a conversation. The individual fears that they will do or say something that will cause them to be embarrassed, humiliated, or rejected. As with specific phobia, feeling nervous or scared when making a presentation or performing in front of others is normal. In the case of social anxiety disorder the fear is out of proportion to the situation and the individual fears being judged by others. To warrant a diagnosis of social anxiety disorder the individual must almost always express fear in the situation and the fear must be out of proportion with the situation. For example, many individuals have symptoms of anxiety or fear (sweating, fast heart rate, shaking) before a presentation in front of a class; however, most individuals can get through the presentation without significant issues. An individual with social anxiety disorder may have a panic attack or other severe symptoms (vomiting, fainting, etc.) at the thought of presenting. The symptoms must persist for at least 6 months (APA, 2013).

Panic disorder is characterized by recurrent unexpected panic attacks. A panic attack is an intense fear that manifests with physiological and psychological symptoms, including, but not limited to, heart palpitations, sweating, shaking, shortness of breath, chest pain, nausea, and/or fear of dying (APA, 2013). Individuals who experience panic attacks, particularly the first time, often feel that they are having a heart attack and will be diagnosed by a medical professional in an emergency room. It is important that clients who are experiencing the physiological symptoms such as chest pain, heart palpitations, and nausea be referred to a medical professional to rule out physiological disorders.

Agoraphobia is characterized by fear or anxiety about being in situations in which escape would be difficult (APA, 2013). The individual will avoid these situations. Agoraphobia is often thought of (and portrayed by the media) as an individual who is a "shut in" and will not leave their homes. Although this is a more severe form of agoraphobia, most cases are related to being in crowds, enclosed spaces, or open spaces. To warrant a diagnosis, the individual must display a fear in two or more situations, such as public transportation, open or enclosed spaces, being in a crowd, or being outside the house (APA, 2013). The situation must almost always elicit fear and must persist for at least 6 months. Individuals with this diagnosis may avoid the situations completely or insist that someone accompany them at all times. As mentioned earlier, severely impacted individuals may refuse to leave the house.

Generalized anxiety disorder (GAD) is an intense, excessive worry about events of activities more days than not over the course of 6 months. The worry is not targeted to one object or situation, and the individual finds it extremely difficult to control (APA, 2013). Many students and some clinicians have historically seen this diagnosis as one to use for an individual who is experiencing "normal" anxiety but does not meet criteria for other disorders. This disorder is characterized by intense worry or fear. It is important to note that in GAD the worry is *excessive* and causes significant impairment. Because of the comorbid physiological symptoms that have no medical basis, those diagnosed with GAD may become annoying to their general physicians, which then, in turn, can result in increased anxiety in the patient. Because of the very high comorbidity with depression, it is important for mental health clinicians to assess for GAD in clients who have depressive symptoms with or without somatic complaints because it is often underdiagnosed.

History

The DSM-I (APA, 1952) defined anxiety as the primary characteristic of the psycho-neurotic disorders. It was said to be produced by a threat from within the personality, such as from repressed emotions such hostility and resentment. These repressed impulses gave rise to anxious reactions such as dissociation, conversion (anxiety converted into physical symptoms), phobic reactions, obsessive compulsive reactions, or depressive reactions. The DSM-II (APA, 1968) had an overarching category for anxiety symptoms called neuroses. It stated that anxiety was the chief characteristic of neuroses and that the anxiety might be felt directly or unconsciously through physical symptoms such as fatigue or exhaustion or other emotional symptoms such as depressive neuroses, phobic responses, or obsessive compulsive neuroses. The DSM-III (APA, 1980) created a chapter for anxiety disorders with three categories. The first category, phobic disorders, was subdivided into agoraphobia (with or without panic attacks), social phobia, and simple phobia. The second category was anxiety states and was subdivided into panic disorder, GAD, and obsessive compulsive disorder (OCD). The third category was posttraumatic stress disorder (PTSD). Note that the DSM-III, DMS-III-R (APA, 1987), and DSM-IV (APA, 1994) had a separate chapter for childhood and adolescent disorders that contained separation anxiety, avoidant disorder of childhood, and overanxious disorder. The DSM-III-R and DSM-IV made some changes with regard to mixed anxiety and depressive symptoms. Acute stress disorder was added to the DSM-IV.

The DSM-5 introduced major changes to the anxiety disorders. First, the DSM-5 does not include a chapter for childhood disorders. Second, anxiety disorders, OCD, and trauma- and stressor-related disorder are now in three separate chapters. This change was made based on increasing knowledge about the brain circuitry underlying stress, panic, and obsession. The anxiety disorder chapter is composed of separation anxiety, selective mutism, specific phobia, social anxiety disorder, panic disorder, agoraphobia, and GAD.

Etiology

As is the case with most mental health disorders, there is no one cause of anxiety disorders. What is agreed upon by researchers is that anxiety is likely caused by a combination of genetic, neurobiological, and psychosocial factors.

Genetics and Neurobiological

All of the anxiety disorders have been shown to have a genetic component. Family studies have indicated heritability to be between 30% and 50% (Shimada-Sugimoto et al., 2015). Panic disorder has the highest genetic component, with 50% of those with panic disorder having at least one affected relative. Twin studies of anxiety disorders have estimated that the heritability in twins is between 65% and 74% (Shimada-Sugimoto et al., 2015).

NEUROTRANSMITTERS

Three neurotransmitters have been implicated in anxiety disorders: norepinephrine, serotonin, and Y-aminobutyric acid (Gamma-Aminobutric Acid). The chronic symptoms experienced by people with anxiety disorders such as panic attacks, insomnia, and autonomic hyperarousal (extreme physical symptoms of anxiety in absence of stressor) are associated with an increase in epinephrine, referred to as an increased noradrenergic function. It is thought that affected people may have poorly regulated noradrenergic systems that result in seemingly random bursts of activity (Sadock et al., 2015).

Serotonin was discovered to play a role in anxiety through the observation that antidepressants that increase serotonin also have therapeutic effects in terms of reducing the symptoms of anxiety (Sadock et al., 2015). However, elevated levels of serotonin can actually lead to anxiety. Illicit drugs such as LSD and MDMA have been linked to the release of high levels of serotonin and increases in anxiety in the short term. However, long-term use or high doses will inhibit serotonin production (Yubero-Lahoz et al., 2015).

The role of GABA in anxiety disorders was discovered similarly to that of serotonin, that is, through the use of medications. In this case the medications are the benzodiazepines. It is thought that benzodiazepines enhance GABA activity. Studies have also indicated that administering drugs that decrease GABA leads to more frequent panic attacks in patients with panic disorder. This led researchers to hypothesize that people who have anxiety disorder may have abnormal functioning in their GABA receptors (Hodges et al., 2014).

Psychological Factors

Freud described the presence of anxiety as a signal that anxiety was present in the unconscious. It was viewed as a conflict between unconscious aggressive or sexual desires and threats from external reality. The defense by the ego resulted in anxiety responses to prevent these thoughts from coming into awareness (Sadock et al., 2015). Although Freud's theories are not widely used by psychologists today, his theories shed light on the fact that although it is important that the symptoms of anxiety be treated, it is also important to determine the root cause of the anxiety.

According to cognitive theory, dysfunctional thoughts lead to extreme emotions, which, in turn, then lead to maladaptive behaviors. From a cognitive perspective, anxiety results from a person's overestimation of harm or danger or an underestimation of their coping ability. Our behavior is not determined by what is happening in the environment, but rather by the perception or thoughts about what is happening. The perception of danger, lack or loss of control, and/or inability to cope leads to anxious response or behaviors (Meichenbaum, 1976). These behaviors are often caused by cognitive distortions such as all-or-nothing thinking (things are thought of in extremes), catastrophizing (assuming the worst possible outcome), emotional reasoning (using feeling as fact), or "should statements" (evaluating oneself based on what they should have done or should be doing).

Some mental health disorders are predictive of the development of an anxiety disorder. For example, six disorders predict the onset of GAD: agoraphobia, panic disorder, specific phobia, dysthymia, major depressive disorder, and mania (Stein et al., 2017).

Prevalence and Comorbidities

The National Comorbidity Study (Harvard Medical School, 2007) reported that 31% of individuals in the United States will have a diagnosis of at least one anxiety disorder in their lifetime. Women are more likely to have a diagnosis of anxiety disorder than men, with 23.4% of women having a diagnosis of an anxiety disorder, as compared to 14.3% of men.

The lifetime prevalence of specific phobia is approximately 11%; it is more common in women (12%) than in men (5.5%) (McLean et al., 2011). Having more than one fear is not uncommon. Research has indicated that 21.2% of those with specific phobia have two fears, 15.9% have three fears, and 11.4% have four fears. Those individuals with two or more fears have significantly higher levels of social impairment and dysfunction than those with only one fear. The mean age of onset is 5 to 9 years, based on the type of phobia. Specific phobia is comorbid with a number of disorders, the most common being alcohol use disorder, agoraphobia, and bipolar II (Stinson et al., 2007).

The lifetime prevalence of social anxiety disorder is approximately 7% of the population, with rates being similar in women and men (10.3% and 8.7%, respectively) (McLean et al., 2011). The average age of onset is 13 years. An international study conducted in 2017 found that the prevalence rates of social anxiety disorder are lower in the low- and lower-middle income countries and African and Eastern Mediterranean regions and highest in higher-income countries, the Americas, and the Western Pacific regions (Stein et al., 2017). Comorbid diagnoses are common with social anxiety disorder. Approximately 60% will meet the criteria for other anxiety disorders and 47% will have a comorbid depression or bipolar disorder. The rate of comorbid substance use disorder is approximately 27% (Stein et al., 2017). A diagnosis of social phobia in adolescence (ages 14 to 24 years) significantly predicts the onset of alcohol use disorder at the 4-year follow-up (Zimmerman et al., 2003).

The lifetime prevalence of panic disorder is approximately 2% to 3% in both children and adults (APA, 2013). The lifetime prevalence is significantly higher in women with women being 1.3 to 5.8 times more likely to have a diagnosis (Barzega et al., 2008) Native Americans tend to have significantly higher rates (4.1% in women and 2.6% in men) (Sawchuk et al., 2017), whereas lower rates are seen among Black/African Americans and Asian Americans (Breslau et al., 2006). The median age of onset is approximately 22 years. Comorbidities are extremely common in panic disorder, with 91% having at least one other disorder (Sadock et al., 2015). Approximately one-third of individuals with panic disorder are diagnosed with major depressive disorder prior to onset and two-thirds are diagnosed with panic disorder after the onset of depression (Kessler et al., 2015). As is the case with social phobia, a diagnosis of panic disorder in adolescents and young adults significantly predicts alcohol use disorder (Zimmerman et al., 2003).

The total lifetime prevalence of agoraphobia is approximately 1.4% (0.3% with panic disorder and 1.0% without panic disorder) (Roest et al., 2019). The disorder is comorbid with a number of other disorders, including mood disorders (55%), disruptive disorders (26%) and substance use disorders (31%) (Roest et al., 2019).

The lifetime prevalence of GAD is 3.7% with rates being highest in high-income countries (Meron Ruscio, et al., 2017). Being female and unmarried are risk factors associated with GAD. The onset is typically in adulthood, with 25% of cases occurring by age 25. Although the onset of GAD is typically in adulthood, when diagnosed in children, 75% had a comorbid diagnosis of major depressive disorder (Masi et al., 2004). Mental health comorbidities are common in GAD (81.9%), with other anxiety disorders and major depressive disorders being the most common (51.7% and 52.6%, respectively) (Meron Ruscio et al., 2017). In fact, GAD and depression have substantial genetic overlap (Morneau-Baillancourt et al., 2019).

Course and Prognosis

The Global Burden of Disease study (Yang et al., 2021) found that in 2010 anxiety disorders were the sixth leading cause of disability accounting for 29.68 million disability-age adjusted life years. Women reported significantly higher rates of anxiety.

Social anxiety disorder is generally considered to be a chronic disorder and is associated with substantial impairment. Approximately 21% of patients with social anxiety disorder reported having severe impairment in quality of life (Rapaport et al., 2005), Adults with social anxiety disorder miss an average of 25 workdays per year; however impairment is often more severe at home and in relationships than at work (Stein et al., 2017). Recurrence of social anxiety disorder is more common in women, early age of onset, and being unmarried Stein, et al., 2017).

Specific phobia is associated with long-term impairment. Studies have found the average duration of episodes is 19.7 years (Stinson et al., 2007) to 22.4 years (Goisman et al., 1998). Unlike the other anxiety disorders with symptoms that wax and wane, the level of severity typically remains constant.

Panic disorder is a chronic disorder that typically has an onset in early adolescence and tends to continue into adulthood. Studies regarding long-term follow-up indicate that 50% of patients were in partial or full remission and were able to regain normal functioning (Svanborg et al., 2008). The frequency of panic attacks often fluctuates, ranging from several in one day or less than once a month.

Agoraphobia often results in severe impairment at home, work, and in social situations. One study indicated that 43.3% of respondents with agoraphobia reported having severe impairment and that the mean number of days per month that the individual was out of their role (either at home, work, or socially) was 3.6 (Roest et al., 2018).

GAD is a chronic disorder with half of cases still experiencing symptoms after 2 years (Rodriguez et al., 2006). Factors associated with a full recovery include older age of onset of disorder, being female, married, being in good physical health, having social support, and not having comorbid depression or substance use disorders (Fuller-Thomson, & Ryckman, 2020). Those individuals who had a comorbid diagnosis of depression had a reduced likelihood of recovery. GAD is associated with somatic symptoms such as gastrointestinal pain, headache, and back and joint pain (Bensenor et al., 2003; Grothe et al., 2004) and sleep disorders (Belanger et al., 2004), which result in frequent visits to healthcare professionals.

Cultural and Gender-Related Considerations

Mental health practitioners should consider the cultural and social environment of the individual being assessed for GAD. Things to consider would be whether worries are excessive or beyond that of expected members of the client's culture. Some studies report that symptoms of GAD may be culturally determined (Lewis-Fernandez et al., 2010), such as an anxiety disorder presenting with somatic symptoms such as muscle tension, sleep disturbance, fatigue, and generalized aches and pains; additionally, symptoms can present as difficulty concentrating on tasks or the person feeling that their mind is going blank. The cultural content should be considered during the evaluations as excessive symptoms somatic symptoms. Similar to other mental health diagnoses, although Black/African Americans have lower prevalence of anxiety disorders (Gibbs et al., 2013), their diagnosis is more likely to persist and be much more debilitating.

Women have a higher prevalence of anxiety disorders compared to men, at 30.5% and 19.2%, respectively (Kessler et al., 1994). A more recent study by Pesce et al. (2016) found the female-to-male ratio to be 1.73 to 1. Gender differences were less pronounced in social phobia. Compared to men, women tend to have more severe self-reported symptoms (12.3% higher than men). Women are also more likely to suffer from comorbid major depressive disorder and bulimia nervosa, whereas men are more likely to suffer from substance abuse. The reason for the gender differences in the prevalence rates of anxiety disorders is not well known, but a number of biological, social, and demographic explanations have been offered (McLean & Anderson, 2009). The differences in severity between men and women and treatment seeking may also be responsible for the gender differences. Many patients with mental health disorders do not seek treatment. If men with anxiety disorders do not seek treatment (often due to the stigma that surrounds treatment and the diagnoses of mental health disorders), it would stand to reason that the rates for women would seem higher (Pesce et al., 2016).

Diagnosis and Assessment

Everyone experiences anxiety at some point in their lives. Some more than others, of course. But anxiety is normal and needed for survival. It is what allows us to recognize a potentially dangerous situation. It is what prevents (most) children from jumping off a slide. The adrenal system triggers our flight-or-fight response. When anxiety becomes a problem is when it is present when there is not a stressful event, the stressful event has ended, or it is out of proportion with the stressful event. As with all diagnoses, when the symptoms cause impairment in everyday life, it indicates a problem.

As mentioned earlier, unlike the other anxiety disorders, GAD is characterized by distress rather than a reaction to a specific fear. Consequently, when encountered in primary care practices it often goes undiagnosed or misdiagnosed. It is important to assess for GAD when a patient or client presents with symptoms of depression, because oftentimes the underlying cause of the depression is worry from the GAD.

Prior to the DSM-5, agoraphobia was not defined as an independent disorder, it was coded with or without panic disorder. Agoraphobia can now be diagnosed with or without panic disorder. If criteria are met for both panic disorder and agoraphobia, both disorders are diagnosed. The decision to create an independent diagnosis of agoraphobia was based on research that indicated that a significant number of individuals with agoraphobia did not have panic disorder or panic attacks (Kessler et al., 2006). As a result, individuals with agoraphobia without panic symptoms had significant impairment but had no diagnosis, making treatment difficult.

Eve

Eve is a physically healthy 17-year-old Latina/Hispanic cisgender female who resides with both her parents and two younger siblings (Mark and Elena). She and her parents (Jack and Diane) have come to the outpatient mental health clinic to discuss Eve's recent behaviors. Her parents state that Eve has become a "hermit" since the COVID-19 stay at home orders. She is refusing to go to school and no longer spends time with her friends. She has tried on several occasions to go to school. She will shower and do her hair and makeup but when she goes to walk out the door, she freezes and starts shaking. She says that she has trouble breathing whenever she thinks about going to school and having to see other people. She has stated that she will say something stupid and her peers will make fun of her. She is completing her work and submitting it by email. The school, however, has emailed her mother to tell her that she is being marked absent, and is therefore considered truant unless they provide documentation of illness. Eve's friends have encouraged her to "hang out with them," but again, when she tries to leave the house to meet them, she is overcome with dread and cannot leave the house. Eve reports that, prior to the COVID-19 stay-at-home orders, she was "super anxious" at school and around her friends but "sucked it up." She says there were times she would have to excuse herself and go to the restroom to "get it together." She says that when school was back in session (after being remote for 8 months), and she was able to see her friends again, she was "terrified." As she is speaking of going to school and interacting with her friends, she becomes tearful. She states that nothing happened at school or with her friends that was embarrassing or made her feel stupid, but she is "just afraid it is going to happen." When asked if she would leave the house to go grocery shopping or to the mall with her parents, she says she is fine with that because she doesn't "have to talk to people." Jack and Diane report that as a child, Eve had many friends and was "pretty out going" They reported that when she got into high school she became a bit more reserved and spent less time with friends, but never expressed any concerns.

Diagnostic Impression

Over the past 8 months or longer, Eve has experienced extreme anxiety about both school and being with her friends and avoids both situations. She has reported that she is afraid that she will say something stupid, and she will be made fun of. There was no precipitating event that has led to these fears. She is at risk of being considered truant from school.

Diagnostic Conclusion

Social anxiety disorder (social phobia)

DIFFERENTIAL DIAGNOSIS I: AGORAPHOBIA

Rationale: Although Eve tends to stay in the house, her fear is not about leaving the house; it is directly related to being afraid of doing something embarrassing or stupid in front of her peers. Because this fear is limited to social situations, agoraphobia can be ruled out.

DIFFERENTIAL DIAGNOSIS II: ADJUSTMENT DISORDER WITH ANXIETY

Eve's parents had stated initially that Eve had become a "hermit" since the stay at home orders resulting from the COVID-19 pandemic. However, Eve reports experiencing anxiety around her peers before the pandemic therefore it is apparent that the stay at home orders are not the trigger for her current anxiety. Therefore a diagnosis of Social Anxiety disorder is more appropriate.

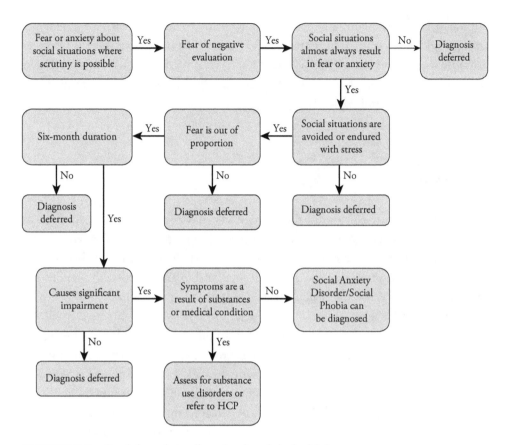

FIGURE 6.1 Social anxiety disorder (social phobia)

Biopsychosocial

BIOLOGICAL

Eve is reported to be physically healthy. She does report having difficulty breathing at times; this seems to be limited to when she is faced with having to go to school or spend time with her friends. It is recommended that Eve have a medical examination by a medical professional.

PSYCHOLOGICAL

Eve is reporting a (seemingly) irrational fear about going to school or spending time with her friends. While she states that she had these fears prior to COVID-19, it is important to explore whether Eve is afraid of COVID-19 transmission. It is important to note if she has had any friends or family who have had COVID-19, because this may contribute to her current fears.

SOCIAL

Although Eve is not willing to spend time with her friends for fear of doing something stupid, her friends seem to be reaching out to her, indicating there is likely no animosity. Eventually involving her friends in her treatment is something that should be explored. Eve seems to have a supportive family; however, more information is needed regarding family dynamics.

Michael

Michael is a 50-year-old White single man who has never been married. He has been dating the same woman (Alexa) for the past 10 years and, until recently, their relationship has been stable. Over the past year or so, however, he has become increasingly worried about the status of their relationship and whether she is cheating on him. He says he has no evidence that she is cheating but cannot stop thinking about it. When he asks her about it, she tries to be reassuring, but he can tell she is getting frustrated with him, and now he is afraid that she will leave. During the 1-hour intake session, Michael is continuously wringing his hands and looking very concerned. He says he is also having problems at work (he is the manager of a local pharmacy). He feels like his work is not good enough, no matter how many hours he puts in, and he is worried that he will be replaced by a younger worker. When asked about his sleep patterns, he said he is having difficulty falling asleep, because he cannot stop thinking about all the things he has to do and recent conversations in which may have said "the wrong thing". Alexa joins the session for the last 10 minutes and reports that their relationship is strained lately (becoming increasingly more so over the past year), because Michael is "super on edge" and "jumps down her throat" for no reason. She says that she loves Micahel and has never cheated on him but he still keeps worrying about it. She says he is like this most days, and nothing she says or does helps. Michael agrees that he has been very irritable lately because "he has a lot on his mind." He has tried to meditate and clear his mind of the worry, but it just will not go away. He has tried going to the gym, but he just does not have the energy lately. They have even tried going on a vacation to the mountains to try to clear his mind. He says he just worried more about work and then also worried about being attacked by a bear. Michael reports that he is not taking any medication or using any drugs. He has a glass of wine with dinner on occasion, but otherwise, he rarely drinks alcohol.

Diagnostic Impression

Michael is experiencing what is often referred to as "free-floating worry." He is worried most of the time, but the worry cannot be linked to any one source. He is on edge (as evidenced by "jumping down Alexa's throat"), irritable, and having trouble sleeping. He also reports fatigue (no energy for the gym). These symptoms have persisted most days for over a year.

Diagnostic Conclusion

Generalized anxiety disorder

DIFFERENTIAL DIAGNOSIS I: SPECIFIC PHOBIA

Rationale: Although Michael does mention being afraid of being attacked by a bear, this does not seem to be an irrational fear. They were in the mountains and a fear of bears is considered normal.

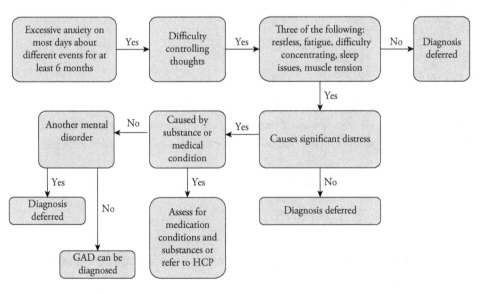

FIGURE 6.2   GAD

Biopsychosocial

BIOLOGICAL

There is no evidence to suggest that Michael is experiencing any physiological reason for his worry, and he does not use alcohol or other drugs. It is, however, always recommended that individuals experiencing mental health symptoms have a physical exam by a healthcare professional in order to rule out physiological causes.

PSYCHOLOGICAL

Other than his anxiety disorder, Michael does not seem to be suffering from any other mental health issues. It is important that Michael receive ongoing mental health treatment and be evaluated for major depressive disorder, because GAD and major depressive disorder are often comorbid.

SOCIAL

Michael has a support system in Alexa. However, at this point, their relationship is suffering. It is important that, in addition to individual treatment, Michael and Alexa receive couples therapy to ensure positive communication. It is unclear as to whether Michael has friends outside of Alexa. It is important to explore the possibility of not only possible therapeutic groups but also social groups, so that Alexa is not the only source of support and entertainment for Michael.

TERMINOLOGY

selective mutism   Severe anxiety disorder in which person is unable to speak in certain situations. Usually begins in childhood but can persist into adulthood if untreated.

REFLECTION QUESTIONS

1. How did Freud's psychodynamic theory of the unconscious contribute to treating symptoms of anxiety?

2. Which anxiety disorder was once coded with panic disorder but became its own independent disorder in the DSM-5, and why?

3. What makes GAD different from other anxiety disorders in the DSM-5?

CHAPTER 7

Obsessive Compulsive and Related Disorders

LEARNING OBJECTIVES

1. Gain a basic understanding of the causes, prevalence, and comorbidities of the obsessive compulsive disorders.

2. Become familiar with the criteria for the obsessive compulsive disorders.

3. Be able to differentially diagnose the obsessive compulsive disorders.

Characteristics of the Disorders

The obsessive compulsive and related disorders chapter of the DSM-5 (APA, 2013) outlines criteria for obsessive compulsive disorder (OCD), hoarding disorder, trichotillomania (hair pulling disorder), excoriation disorder (skin picking disorder), and other related disorders. This chapter is new to the DSM-5, because in past editions of the DSM, OCD and related disorders were located with the anxiety disorders (which also included trauma-related disorders).

Obsessive Compulsive Disorder

Obsessive compulsive disorder (OCD) is characterized by persistent obsessions or compulsions or both. Obsessions are defined as persistent thoughts, images, or urges that cause disturbance and are seen as intrusive and unwanted (APA, 2013). The individual attempts to ignore the thoughts images or urges or to neutralize them by performing an action or ritual (i.e., a compulsion). Intrusive thoughts on their own is not sufficient to diagnose OCD, because up to 90% of community-dwelling adults experience intrusive thoughts, images, or impulses that they find difficult to control (Julien et al., 2007). Compulsions are defined as repetitive behaviors that the individual feels driven to engage in and must be performed to neutralize an obsession (APA, 2013). These acts are either not connected to the obsession in a realistic way or they are excessive. Common types of obsessions include contamination (e.g., germs, dirt, illness), safety or harm (causing harm to a loved one), unacceptable sexual or religious thoughts, or the need for order. The compulsions tend to include excessive cleaning, handwashing, checking, arranging, counting, or repeating activities (e.g., turning a light on and off). Most compulsions are not observable behaviors but mental rituals such as counting, reciting song lyrics, or prayers.

Trichotillomania (Hair Pulling Disorder)

Trichotillomania is characterized by excessive hair pulling that results in significant hair loss (APA, 2013). The individual has had repeated attempts to stop but is unsuccessful. The most common location for hair pulling is the scalp (73%), followed by eyebrows (56%) and pubic regions (51%) (Grant & Chamberlain, 2017). Importantly, as with all mental health disorders, the hair pulling must result in significant distress. It is important to rule out other disorders such as dermatological disorders or schizophrenia or side effects of medication.

Excoriation Disorder (Skin Picking Disorder)

Excoriation disorder is the recurrent picking of skin resulting in skin lesions. The individual has attempted to stop or decrease the skin picking (APA, 2013). The picking can occur on any part of the body, with the face, arms, legs, and hands being the most common. The majority of individuals pick at their skin with their fingernails; however, some will use instruments such as tweezers. The amount of time spent picking can range from minutes to hours several times a day. While some people with the disorder have "focused" skin picking, which helps to regulate negative emotions, others have an automatic type. In the automatic type, the individual does not realize that they are engaging in the behavior. Some individuals have both types.

Hoarding

Hoarding disorder is characterized by difficulty parting with possessions and distress upon discarding with them (APA, 2013). The difficulty with discarding items results in the accumulation of possessions that results in clutter in living areas. The specifier of "with excessive acquisition" refers to a situation in which the difficulty discarding possessions is paired with excessive acquisition of items that are not needed or for which there is no space available to accommodate them (APA, 2013).

Body Dysmorphic Disorder

Body dysmorphic disorder is a preoccupation with perceived defects in personal appearance that are not apparent to others (APA, 2013). The individual will engage in repetitive behaviors (looking in mirror, picking at skin, grooming) in response to these perceived flaws. A specifier of muscle dysmorphia is used if the preoccupation is centered around the idea that they are not muscular enough (APA, 2013). The most common areas of concern are the skin, hair, and nose (Buhlmann et al., 2010).

History

The term *obsessive compulsive disorder* is a relatively modern 20th-century term. Prior to the coining of the term, people with obsessions and compulsions were thought to have a condition called scrupulosity. Many of the descriptions about these obsessions and compulsions refer to religious beliefs and practices (Cefalu, 2010). Individuals with the affliction were considered to be suffering from doubts of sin and expressing their suffering through obsessions. The obsessions and compulsions were treated through bloodletting. At the time, it was thought that emotions and behaviors were controlled by bodily fluids (ocduk.org). By changing the levels of body fluids, it was thought that the individual's mood or behaviors would improve through adjustment of the "humors" (OCD. Throughout the 19th century and into the early part of the 20th century, doctors noticed that individuals obsessive thoughts often were focused on biological contamination and aggressive or distressing sexual thoughts. The view of OCD had begun to shift toward a more psychological explanation (Fornaro et al., 2009).

Previous editions of the DSM placed OCD in the chapter on anxiety and trauma-related disorders. OCD is now located in a chapter on OCD and related disorders in the DSM-5 (APA, 2013). This move came after a wide range of evidence indicated significant differences in genetic risk factors, course of illness, personality correlates, and treatment response between OCD and anxiety disorders.

Trichotillomania has been discussed in the medical literature since the early 1900s, but it was not included in the DSM until the DSM III-R (APA, 1980), where it was classified as an impulse control disorder not elsewhere classified. In the DSM-IV-TR (APA, 2000) one of the diagnostic criteria was that the hair loss must be noticeable to others. This is no longer a criterion in the DSM-5 (APA, 2013). Another change from the DSM-IV-TR to the DSM-5 is the sense of tension followed by relief after hair pulling is no longer required. A new requirement of trying to stop the pulling is now in the DSM-5.

Excoriation disorder is new to the DSM-5 (APA, 2013) as its own disorder. In the DSM-IV-TR (APA, 2000), skin picking could be diagnosed under impulse control disorders not otherwise.

Hoarding, now its own disorder in the DSM-5 (APA, 2013) was originally a criterion of obsessive compulsive personality disorder in the DSM-IV-TR (APA, 2000). Research has found that most individuals who hoard do not meet criteria for OCD (Van Ameringen et al., 2014).

Body dysmorphic disorder was first introduced in the DSM-III (APA, 1980) as an atypical somatoform disorder called dysmorphophobia. In the DSM-IV-TR (APA, 2000), it became its own disorder under somatoform disorders. In the DSM-5 (APA, 2013), body dysmorphic disorder is classified under obsessive compulsive and related disorders. The move to this chapter also included a new criterion of performing repetitive behaviors such as looking in the mirror, excessive grooming, skin picking, seeking reassurance, or mental acts (comparing appearance to others) in response to their concerns about their own appearance (APA, 2013). Two specifiers were also added, one for muscle dysmorphia and one regarding their level of insight.

Etiology

To date, studies have not been able to determine the causes of the obsessive compulsive and related disorders. Family studies have indicated that the disorders do run in families; however, it unknown if this is due to genetics, environmental risk factors, or a combination of both. Some families have at least four successive generations with clear diagnostic cases of OCD (Rector et al., 2009). However, it is possible (even likely) that the family members may have learned these behaviors from relatives; the presence across generations is not sufficient to prove inheritance. Interestingly, although OCD seems to be inherited (at least to some degree), the family members often have different obsessions and compulsions, indicating that the obsessions and compulsions themselves were not learned but rather the OCD response to common life experiences (Fornaro et al., 2009).

Genetics

Twin studies have indicated that the heritability of the obsessive compulsive and related disorders ranges from 27%–47% (Van Grootheest et al., 2005). A study by Monzani et al. (2014) found the heritability of OCD to be 48%; hoarding disorder, 51%; trichotillomania, 32%; and excoriation disorder, 47%. The heritability of body dysmorphic disorder was found to be 43%, consistent with a later study by Enander et al. (2018) that found heritability to be 49% at age 15, and decreasing with age.

Neurobiological

One (often controversial) suggested cause of OCD is pediatric autoimmune neuro-psychiatric disorders associated with streptococcal infections (PANDAS) (Orlovsake et al., 2017). PANDAS is characterized by an acute onset of OCD following a strep-tococcal infection. In a study of 1,067,743 children, Orlovska et al. (2017) found an elevated risk of OCD in children who had streptococcal infections (51%). Children with other infections also had an increased risk of OCD, indicating that other im-mune factors may be at play.

Research based on neuroimaging has indicated that there are subtle structural and functional abnormalities in numerous parts of the brains of people with OCD (Schiepek et al., 2007). It is possible that parts of the brain get overwhelmed with information. For example, caudate nuclei located near the center of the brain are responsible for filtering information. It has been hypothesized that if too many mes-sages regarding how things "should be" get to the caudate nuclei and are not filtered properly, they can spill over and overwhelm the consciousness. Caudate nuclei are involved in repetitive behaviors, and other parts of the brain, such as the anterior caudate putamen and the anterior cingulate cortex, as well as other structures, may play a role in the impulsive or repetitive behaviors of OCD and the related disorders (Fornaro et al., 2009).

Psychosocial

Cognitive models of OCD posit that the level of responsibility the individual feels over their situation contributes to the etiology of OCD symptoms (Rachman, 1998). It is the interpretation of the content and the presence of the intrusive thoughts that will determine whether an individual develops obsessions that result in extreme anxiety and ultimately compulsions (Rachman, 1998). Cognitive models identify six key belief domains that can contribute to OCD: inflated sense of responsibility, estimation of threat, perfectionism, intolerance of uncertainty, overimportance of thoughts, and a need to control thoughts (Obsessive Compulsive Cognitions Working Group, 1997).

Prevalence and Comorbidities

The lifetime prevalence of OCD is approximately 1.3%, with women being 1.6 times more likely to experience OCD symptoms as compared to men (Fawcett et al., 2020). The lifetime prevalence of OCD in women is 1.5% and 1% in men. The reason for the gender difference in prevalence is unknown. However, it could be explained at least in part by hormonal influences during pregnancy, the postpartum period, premenstrual period, or menopause. Younger adults are more likely to experience OCD than older adults (Fawcett et al., 2020). Several comorbidities are associated with OCD, including depression (30%), and anxiety disorders (21%) (Viswanath et al., 2012), bipolar disorder (10.9%) (Ferentinos et al., 2020), lifetime alcohol use disorder (19%) (Osland et al., 2018), and eating disorders (3% to 13%) (Bang et al., 2020).

The prevalence of body dysmorphic disorder in the United States is approximately 1.9% in the adult population, with the rates being slightly higher in women (Veale et al., 2016). The highest rates are found in settings where rhinoplasties are performed (20%). Rates of body dysmorphic disorder outside of the United States are slightly lower. For example, in Italy the prevalence was found to be approximately 1.6% (Cerea et al., 2018). Body dysmorphic disorder is highly comorbid with depression (75%), social anxiety disorder (37%), OCD (32%) (Gunstad & Phillips, 2003), and excoriation disorder (37%) (Grant et al., 2006).

Estimates of the prevalence of hoarding disorder range from 1.5% to 6%. A study by (2019) et al. found a prevalence of 2.5%, with rates being similar in males and females. Rates of hoarding disorder seem to increase with age. A study by Cath et al. (2017) found that the prevalence rate of hoarding in those over the age of 70 years was 6%. Hoarding symptoms are highly comorbid with OCD. 20% of individuals with OCD engage in hoarding behaviors (Mathews et al., 2014). In addition, depression is more common in individuals with OCD and hoarding (42.9%), as compared to those with OCD and no hoarding symptoms (21.9%) (Boerema et al., 2019).

The prevalence of trichotillomania is approximately 0.5 to 2% in adults, and is disproportionately present in women, with a ratio of 4:1 female to male (Duke et al., 2010). However, the female-to-male ratio is equal in children. Studies have found that when people are asked about only one criterion, "hair pulling at least once a week," 16.5% of respondents replied in the affirmative. Comorbid OCD is found in up to 13% of individuals with trichotillomania (Duke et al., 2010).

The prevalence of excoriation disorder is approximately 1.5% in the adult population. Rates are higher among college students worldwide, at 2% to 9% (Calikusu et al., 2012; Odlaug et al., 2013; Siddiqui et al., 2012). However, research indicates that rates of occasional skin picking range from 20% to 92% (Hayes et al., 2009). There are significant gender differences in excoriation disorder, with approximately 75% of those with the disorder being female. This may, however, be attributed to increased treatment-seeking behaviors among women and underreporting by men. Of people with excoriation disorder, 42% will have lifetime comorbid conditions, the most common being anxiety disorders (12.5%), trichotillomania (3.8%), and depressive disorders (26.3%) (Odlaug et al., 2013).

Course and Prognosis

Fifty percent of those with a diagnosis of OCD had onset in early adulthood and 50% in childhood or adolescence. Onset after age 40 is not common (Ruscio et al., 2010). Without treatment, recovery rates in adults are typically low, approximately 20% at 40 years follow up (Skoog & Skoog, 1999), and symptoms will be chronic and tend to wax and wane. Approximately 5% to 10% of those with OCD will have spontaneous remission, and 5% to 10% will have progressive worsening of symptoms (Eisen et al., 2010). Approximately 70% of adults with OCD have reported that their family functioning is significantly impacted by their OCD symptoms, 60% reported issues at work and 63% in social situations (Hollander et al., 1997). Individuals with OCD often avoid situations that they find pleasurable in effort to avoid anxiety. This avoidance often leads to a reduced quality of life.

The average age of onset of trichotillomania is 13 years (Flessner et al., 2010). Fifty percent of those with the disorder will seek treatment, and of those who do, only 15% report experiencing a moderate to significant reduction in symptoms (Woods et al., 2006). If untreated, trichotillomania is a chronic illness that may result in significant psychosocial dysfunction, such as low self-esteem, avoidance of work or social situations, and low quality of life. Approximately 5% to 20% of individuals with trichotillomania engage in the ingestion of the hair, which can lead to serious medical complications (Grant & Chamberlain, 2017).

The onset of excoriation disorder can occur at any age. A high number of cases begin around the start of puberty, often with a dermatological condition such as acne (APA, 2013). Limited data is available regarding the course or prognosis of excoriation disorder; however, it does seem to be a chronic disorder. Excoriation disorder is associated with significant distress. Individuals with the disorder often spend considerable time covering their lesions and often avoid social situations (Odlaug et al., 2013).

The average age of onset of body dysmorphic disorder is approximately 17 years. Those with an early onset (prior to age 17 years) tend to have a more gradual onset and are more likely to have lifetime eating disorder (Bjornsson et al., 2013). Body dysmorphic disorder is associated with severe impairment in psychosocial functioning at home and work and/or social functioning and low quality of life, with the psychosocial impairments enduring over time. Research indicates that only 10% of those with the disorder attain functional remission after 3 years (Phillips et al., 2008). People with body dysmorphic disorder have high rates of suicidality. Bjornsson et al. (2013) conducted one study on two separate samples of adults who were seeking treatment for body dysmorphic disorder. In the first sample, 55% of those with younger onset had suicidal ideation due to body dysmorphic disorder and 11% had attempted suicide. Older onset saw lower rates of ideation (53%) and attempts (10%). The second sample had much higher rates in both younger and older onset. In the younger-onset group, 70% had ideation and 21% had attempted suicide. In the older-onset group, 73% had ideation and 6.4% had attempted suicide (Bjornsson et al. (2013).

The average age for onset of hoarding disorder is approximately 12 years, and it seems to be a chronic, progressive disorder. The majority of individuals (70%) with hoarding disorder report that their symptoms began in childhood and increased in severity throughout their lifetime (Cath et al., 2017). Hoarding can cause significant impairment. In older adults, hoarding is often seen as a form of self-neglect. The extreme clutter interferes with basic hygiene and poses health issues. Dong et al. (2012) found that hoarding was more common among older adults who reported fair or poor health status.

Cultural and Gender-Related Considerations

There are gender differences in presentation and onset of OCD. Males are more likely to be single, have a higher level of education (Torresan et al., 2009; Tripathi et al., 2018), have an earlier onset (Lochner et al., 2004; Torresan et al., 2009), a chronic course of the disorder (Tripathi et al., 2018), and more social impairment (Tripathi et al., 2018). Men are also more likely to have comorbid substance use disorders (Bogetto et al., 1999; Sobin et al., 1999; Tripathi et al., 2018). Women are more likely to report precipitating factors (Tripathi et al., 2018), have cleaning compulsions (Karadag et al., 2006; Tükel et al., 2004), and experience comorbid depression (Karadag et al., 2006; Torresan et al., 2009).

Mental health clinicians should be aware that cultural factors may shape the content of obsessions and compulsions. During the assessment clinicians should also differentiate between diagnosable obsessions and compulsions and those that are motivated by cultural influences. If obsessions and compulsions exceed those of cultural norms as judged by other members of the same culture, and interfere with social role functioning, a diagnosis of OCD may be warranted (APA, 2013). Religious rituals such as repetitive washing, checking and ordering objects, and/or prayer or repeating of phrases silently may be culturally appropriate (Paniagua, 2014). These cultural practices should not be pathologized by a clinician. Racial and ethnic cultural factors to consider include Black/African Americans in comparison to Latinx/Hispanic Americans and White Americans have lower rates of OCD (APA, 2013).

The research surrounding gender differences of body dysmorphic disorder has been inconsistent. Some studies have found no differences between men and women (Pope et al., 2000; Rief et al., 2006), others have found higher rates among women (Koran et al., 2008; Phillips et al., 2005), and still others have found that it is more common in men (see Ishigooka et al., 1998; Taqui et al., 2008). There have been few studies surrounding racial and ethnic differences in body dysmorphic disorder. The studies that have been conducted have suggested that European Americans and Latinx Americans report higher levels of body dissatisfaction as compared to Black/African Americans, Indigenous individuals, or those with Asian backgrounds (Poran, 2002; Ricciardelli et al., 2004; Yang, 2005).

Diagnosis and Assessment

As with most mental health disorders, many of us engage in behaviors that meet one or more of the criteria for a disorder. This is also true of OCD and related disorders. You may check the front door four times to make sure it is locked. You may smell the milk before you drink it, even though you just bought it that morning. Some people need order in their lives and have all their items lined up or a certain number of items in groupings. This does not necessarily warrant a diagnosis. It may just be part of one's personality. Remember that to diagnose a mental health disorder there must be significant impairment in functioning.

Maria

Maria is a 34-year-old Hispanic/Latina woman who has been brought to an inpatient facility by her husband, Jorge. Maria is in great distress. She is sobbing and rocking back and forth. She has refused to let the admitting nurse examine her and has screamed at him not to touch her. Face masks are required by the facility; however, Maria is wearing two masks and two pairs of latex gloves. She has the hood of her sweatshirt pulled close around her face and her pants tucked into her socks. When asked why Jorge brought Maria to the facility, he states that when he got home from work he found Maria kneeling on the floor with a bucket of bleach. He states that the entire apartment smelled like bleach; it made him so lightheaded that he had to open all the windows. When he tried to talk to Maria, she kept repeating, "We must get the virus out of this house." He finally convinced her to get off the floor and into the car so he could drive her to the facility. During the drive to the facility, Maria kept repeating, "The virus is going to kill us; we are going to die." Nothing Jorge said could "get through."

Jorge says that Maria has always been a bit of a "germaphobe." When they first started dating, he noticed that her apartment was always spotless and smelled of cleaning solution. He also noticed that she washed her hands numerous times a day. He said he found these traits endearing, and they did not interfere with their lives at all. He smiles and states that after they were married he never had to worry about cleaning, because it was always done. Three years ago, after the birth of their son Alex, her "germaphobia" got "out of control." Not only was Maria constantly cleaning the house, but she was constantly checking Alex's diaper (about every 10 minutes) and was giving him two to three baths a day, if not more. Jorge had told her that so many baths were not good for Alex, but she could not help herself. Jorge did insist that Maria go to therapy, and she did agree. The therapist recommended inpatient treatment and Maria agreed for the "sake of the baby." She was in treatment for 3 months in the facility of the current intake. When she came home, she was still cleaning often, but not excessively, and she left the bathing of Alex to Jorge. Things seemed to be "getting back to normal when COVID hit." When news of COVID-19 virus was first reported, Jorge started to see a change in Maria. She started to clean more—about 3 to 4 hours a day. Alex, who is now a toddler and, by nature, messy, became a source of stress for Maria. She was constantly wiping his face and hands, even when they were not dirty. She began bathing him two to three times a day. Alex, who typically likes baths, has begun to resist the baths. Maria and Jorge are potty-training Alex, and he is doing well, but being only 3 years old, accidents happen. Maria becomes angry and very stressed when Alex has an accident. Jorge saw that Alex was becoming upset and began bringing him to grandma's house during the day when he was at work. During the stay-at-home orders, Jorge would have to monitor Maria to make sure that she was not excessively cleaning or becoming frustrated with Alex. He began taking Alex to Grandmas during the stay-at-home orders as well. Maria seemed very relieved not to have Alex at home during the day. Maria was spending all day cleaning. When Jorge returned to work when the orders were lifted in his county, Maria would make him strip his clothes off at the front door and put them directly into the wash. He then had to put on paper slippers to walk to the shower. Maria would no longer touch or kiss Jorge or Alex in fear of contracting the virus. Jorge said he understood these pre-cautions but the anger that was becoming directed at Alex for being a normal messy toddler who had accidents was concerning. Maria was also beginning to develop a cough. She was tested for COVID-19 three times and has tested negative. Jorge says that he is worried about the safety of both Maria and Alex. The precipitating event leading to today's intake was particularly concerning for Jorge.

Diagnostic Impression

Maria is exhibiting obsessive thoughts about germs and is attempting to neutralize these thoughts through excessive cleaning. She is spending a great deal of time on these behaviors (3 hours to all day), and her obsessive thoughts and compulsions are causing significant distress in her husband and son.

Diagnostic Conclusion

Obsessive compulsive disorder with absent insight

DIFFERENTIAL DIAGNOSIS I: SCHIZOPHRENIA

Psychotic symptoms can lead to obsessions and compulsions. However in Maria's case she is not exhibiting any of the other characteristics of schizophrenia, such as hallucinations or disorganized speech, thoughts, or behaviors.

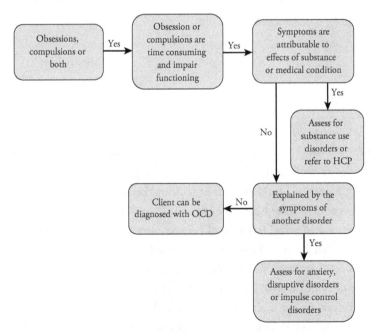

FIGURE 7.1   Differential diagnosis for OCD

Biopsychosocial

BIOLOGICAL

Maria has had negative tests for COVID-19, but she does have a chronic cough. It is important to determine the reason for the cough. Maria has had excessive exposure to cleaning supplies; therefore, it is extremely important that she have a physical examination by a healthcare provider to determine if the cleaning supplies have caused damage to her lungs or other organs.

PSYCHOLOGICAL

Maria has been admitted for inpatient care for OCD in the past. Although she was not "cured," she was able to manage the amount of time she spent engaging in her compulsions. COVID-19 seemed to trigger her illness and have led to the current diagnosis. The fact that she was able to gain control over her behaviors in the past can indicate a more positive prognosis. However, her current absent insight and almost delusional thinking may prove to be more difficult in terms of treatment.

SOCIAL

Maria's behaviors have had a significant impact on her family. Jorge seems genuinely concerned for her health and is a strong source of support. Of course, it will be very important to involve Jorge in Maria's treatment once she is stabilized. It will also be important for Jorge to continue to use his mother as not only a source for childcare but also for emotional support.

Ramon

Ramon is a 17-year-old physically healthy White male. He is currently a senior in high school. He has come to a counseling appointment at the local mental health center. He is very well dressed in pressed khaki pants and a button-down shirt. He is wearing a pair of black shoes that look as though they have never been worn before. His fingernails have been recently manicured, and his hair is perfectly gelled in place. When asked what has brought Ramon to the clinic, he looks down at his hands and says that he is feeling really depressed. He says he feels like he is on the verge of tears all the time. When asked how long he has been feeling this way, he states that he does not know, but it has been many years. The therapist notices that Ramon is not making eye contact and keeps looking out at the door. The door has a tinted window, and every time he looks at the window, he frowns and fixes his hair. When asked what he thinks is making him so sad, he replies, "I am really ugly." This response comes as a bit of a surprise to the therapist, as Ramon is very attractive. When asked why he feels he is ugly, he replies, "my hair is dry and always a mess, my nose is absolutely hideous, my eyes are too close together, and don't even get me started about my skin." When the therapist replies that she thinks he is indeed very attractive, Ramon responds: "You get paid to say that." The therapist responds that yes, she does get paid to talk to her clients; however, she does not have to tell them they are attractive. Ramon just rolls his eyes. When asked about his social life, he says that he had a girlfriend for a few months, but she broke up with him because he spent more time in front of the mirror than she did. When asked to say more about this, Ramon becomes tearful and says that he spends hours getting ready to go out because he feels like he is not as attractive as his friends. When asked to define "hours," he says 4 or 5. When asked about his friend group, he states that he has a group of friends, but they do not ask him to "hang" anymore because he is always late—"and yes, it is because I am still getting ready." When asked about school, Ramon states that he gets up at 4 AM to start getting ready for school, and his mom often must literally push him out the door. His mother has gone so far as to remove all the mirrors in the house (other than the ones in the bathrooms) because he is "driving her insane." Ramon says that he typically earns straight As but has gotten quite a few detentions for leaving class to use the restroom and not returning or for skipping class altogether. He says he gets stuck in front of the mirror. Ramon says he has begged his parents to allow him to have a nose job and Botox injections, but they refuse. They say he is very attractive, and he does not need any procedures. Ramon states that he takes biotin and collagen pills to "help with his skin issues" and uses face and eye creams to prevent more wrinkles. When the therapist asks if he has wrinkles because she cannot see them, he smiles and says, "Well, not really, but I might." When asked about his sleeping habits, Ramon says he goes to bed early because he wakes so early. He always sleeps on his back to avoid wrinkles and will only sleep on silk pillowcases to "protect his hair."

Diagnostic Impression

Ramon reports that he spends hours in front of a mirror grooming himself ("getting ready") and has a preoccupation with perceived defects (his nose, skin, and hair) that others do not see. He reports that he feels "depressed" because he feels ugly. His preoccupation with his perceived flaws and his grooming habits have led to significant impairment at school (as evidenced by his detentions) and in his social life (his friends do not call him anymore; girlfriend broke up with him). He does seem to realize that his preoccupations are unrealistic on some level, as evidenced by his acknowledging that he likely does not have wrinkles.

Diagnostic Conclusion

Body dysmorphic disorder, with fair insight

DIFFERENTIAL DIAGNOSIS I: MAJOR DEPRESSIVE DISORDER

Rationale: Ramon sought out treatment for what he called "depression," and it would likely be tempting to give him a diagnosis of major depressive disorder. However, Ramon does not meet the full criteria for major depressive disorder. Although he is sad and tearful, his sadness is directly related to preoccupation with his appearance. He exhibits no other symptoms of major depressive disorder.

DIFFERENTIAL DIAGNOSIS II: OBSESSIVE COMPULSIVE DISORDER

Rationale: Although Ramon has obsessive thoughts, his only focus is on his appearance; therefore, a diagnosis of body dysmorphic disorder is more appropriate.

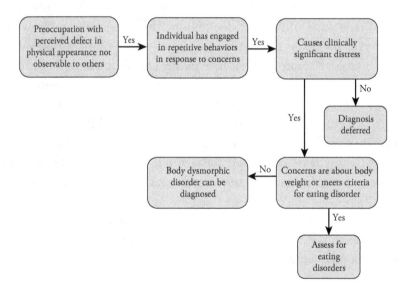

FIGURE 7.2   Differential diagnosis for body dysmorphic disorder

Biopsychosocial

BIOLOGICAL

Ramon is a physically healthy 17-year-old with no known physical health problems.

PSYCHOLOGICAL

Ramon is experiencing sadness and some social anxiety surrounding his perceived defects. People with body dysmorphic disorder have high rates of major depressive disorder, anxiety, and a significant risk of suicide. It is important that Ramon be periodically reevaluated for anxiety disorders and major depressive disorders and continuously monitored for suicide risk.

SOCIAL

Body dysmorphic disorder is highly comorbid with social anxiety disorder. He is not yet exhibiting signs of social phobia; although he has stated that his friends have stopped calling him, he is not avoiding them. It is important to encourage Ramon to reach out to his friends to add another level of support.

TERMINOLOGY

compulsion   Repetitive behaviors that an individual feels driven to engage in and that must be performed to neutralize an obsession.

dysmorphia   A perceived deformity or abnormality in size or shape of a body part.

obsession   Persistent thoughts, images, or urges that cause disturbance and are seen as intrusive and unwanted.

REFLECTION QUESTIONS

1. Why was OCD reclassified from the anxiety disorders to its own chapter in the DSM-5?

2. Which disorder is highly comorbid with OCD and was originally a criterion of obsessive compulsive personality disorder in the DSM-IV-TR?

3. What negative health outcomes are common in individuals who meet the criteria for trichotillomania but do not seek treatment?

4. When diagnosing an individual with trichotillomania, what other disorders should be ruled out before concluding the diagnosis?

5. Individuals with body dysmorphic disorder are most concerned over which areas of their body?

CHAPTER 8

Trauma- and Stressor-Related Disorders

with *Lynell Hodge*

LEARNING OBJECTIVES

---

1. Gain a basic understanding of the causes, prevalence, and comorbidities of the trauma- and stressor-related disorders.

2. Become familiar with the criteria for the trauma- and stressor-related disorders.

3. Be able to differentially diagnose the trauma- and stressor-related disorders.

Trauma- and-stressor-related disorders develop due to exposure to stressful or traumatic events that happen in an individual's life. Disorders characterized under this category are reactive attachment disorder, disinhibited social engagement disorder, posttraumatic stress disorder, acute stress disorder, and adjustment disorders. Psychological distress following exposure to a traumatic or stressful event is the precursor to disorder diagnosis. In many cases, the response to trauma and/or acute stress is exhibited through symptoms such as anxiety, withdrawal, anger, aggression, and dissociation.

Trauma is a negative physiological or emotional reaction to a horrific event (APA, 2013). Trauma occurs when an event or series of events have lasting harmful effects physically or emotionally. These effects have lasting adverse effects on the person's functioning and physical, social, emotional, or spiritual well-being. Traumatic events can include interpersonal violence; community, school, or workplace violence; sexual abuse; physical abuse; health-related trauma; natural disasters; motor vehicle accidents; homicides; suicides; and other traumatic losses.

Characteristics of the Disorder

The DSM-5 (APA, 2013) chapter on the trauma- and stressor-related disorders includes reactive attachment disorder, disinhibited social engagement disorder, acute stress disorder, posttraumatic stress disorder, and adjustment disorder.

Reactive Attachment Disorder

Reactive attachment disorder (RAD) is characterized by a pattern of developmentally inappropriate attachment behaviors, in which the child rarely turns to a caregiver, parent, or other attachment figure for comfort, support, or protection (APA, 2013). The disorder emerges in infancy or early childhood and is linked to conditions of severe social and/or emotional neglect early in the child's life (prior to age 5). The essential feature of RAD is an absence or an underdeveloped attachment between the child and parent or other caregiving adults. Children with RAD are believed to have the ability to form selective attachments; however, due to an absence of healthy attachments formed in early childhood, children fail to show the behavioral manifestation of an attachment. Thus, when in distress, children with RAD show no consistent effort to obtain support, comfort, or protection from caregivers. Additionally, they may only respond minimally to comfort and support when provided by a caregiver. Children with RAD display a diminished or absent expression of positive emotions during routine interactions with caregivers that involve comforting. In addition, their emotion regulation capacity appears to be compromised, and they can display episodes of fear, sadness, or irritability because of a caregiver trying to provide comfort. A diagnosis of RAD should not be given to a child under the age of 9 months, but the symptoms must be present prior to the age of 5 (APA. 2013). This recommendation does not necessarily mean a diagnosis cannot be given after the age of 5, but rather that when conducting a retrospective analysis the symptoms must have been present prior to the age of 5. A child who has been in and out of foster care placements and begins to have behavioral issues, such as anger or becoming socially withdrawn after the age of 5 (with no symptoms prior), is likely reacting to their situation (rightfully so), but this does not meet the criteria for RAD. In this case, a disruptive disorder may be considered, or no disorder, taking into account that this may be a normal reaction to a very unpleasant situation.

Disinhibited Social Engagement Disorder

Disinhibited social engagement disorder (DSED) is a pattern of behavior in which children will actively approach and interact with unfamiliar adults (APA, 2013). Children with this disorder appear to have a reduced or complete lack of understanding of social norms and cultural boundaries as they apply to strangers. This disorder typically manifests in the first months of life as a result of conditions of social and/or emotional neglect. It is different from RAD in that the child is actively seeking attention from any adult instead of rejecting attention and comfort. DSED can be diagnosed from as young as 9 months of age. Unlike RAD, DSED may be diagnosed into adolescence. This disorder is displayed in several ways:

- The child approaches and interacts with strangers in public.

- The child ventures away from caregivers into unfamiliar settings.

- The child lacks fear or display of any discomfort when approached by an adult that they do not know.

DSED is often mistaken for attention-deficit/hyperactivity disorder (ADHD) because of the impulsivity displayed by the child. This disorder is comorbid with an intellectual or developmental disability.

Posttraumatic Stress Disorder

The essential feature of posttraumatic stress disorder (PTSD) is the development of symptoms following exposure to one or more traumatic events. PTSD is a triggering emotional response to perceived fear, helplessness, or horror from a conscious and sometimes subconscious reliving of the emotion of the traumatic event (APA, 2013). It is marked by the presence of one or more recurrent, involuntary, and intrusive symptoms associated with the traumatic event(s). PTSD symptoms can vary in intensity over time; when stressed in general, or when individual comes across reminders of the traumatic event.

Symptoms of PTSD are grouped into four categories: intrusive memories, avoidance, negative changes in thinking and mood, and changes in physical and emotional reactions. Individuals with PTSD are 80% more likely to have comorbid symptoms that meet the diagnostic criteria associated at least one other mental disorder. It is also not uncommon for individuals with PTSD to have a substance use disorder.

Individuals diagnosed with PTSD may have experienced traumatic events ranging from natural disasters (earthquake, hurricane, tornado, etc.) to human-caused events (rape, assault, abuse, terrorism, kidnapping, etc.). The traumatic event produces long-lasting symptoms. Note the PTSD patients may experience the traumatic event indirectly or vicariously; the exposure still provokes reminders or triggers of the event, which could include anniversaries and sensory triggers.

Acute Stress Disorder

Acute stress disorder is the development of characteristic symptoms lasting 3 days to 1 month following exposure to one or more traumatic events. These events include but are not limited to exposure to war, a violent personal assault, being physically attacked, childhood physical or sexual abuse, physical or sexual violence, being involved in a natural or manmade disaster, or being involved in an automobile accident or other type of accident. Individuals may have experienced the traumatic event directly or indirectly (i.e., learning of the death or injury of a loved one). Watching events on television, viewing websites or pictures, or playing video games does not qualify as an indirect traumatic event.

Symptoms of acute stress response include symptoms of intrusion (e.g., distressing memories and dreams), negative mood (e.g., inability to feel happiness), dissociative symptoms (e.g., altered state of reality), avoidance (i.e., efforts to avoid memories and reminders), and arousal (e.g., difficulty sleeping, issues with concentration, exaggerated startle response) (APA, 2013) Many of the symptoms of ASD are very similar to those of PTSD, and many of those who are diagnosed with ASD do not develop PTSD. However, it is thought that having ASD may increase an individual's risk of developing the PTSD.

As mentioned above, the duration for ASD is 3 days to 1 month. What this means is that within the first 72 hours of the traumatic event no diagnosis is given. This is because after a trauma the brain will do whatever it takes to protect itself. Any reaction within this time frame should be considered normal and a direct result of the trauma. This does not, of course, mean that the individual should not receive treatment or support, it simply means that there is no pathology involved. There is nothing wrong with the individual; they are just processing what they have experienced.

It is also important to note that when discussing a trauma impact or diagnosis the literature acknowledges two types of trauma: type 1, or acute, trauma, which results from exposure to a singular overwhelming event (e.g., a natural disaster or terror attack); and type 2, or complex, trauma, which results from continued exposure to traumatizing situations and events (e.g., physical or sexual abuse) (APA, 2013). This distinction helps provide space to accurately discuss and diagnosis a patient.

Adjustment Disorders

An adjustment disorder is the presence of emotional or behavioral symptoms in response to a major stressor or recent traumatic event. Adjustment disorders are stress-related conditions and considered an excessive reaction to an identifiable life stressor. The stressor may be a single event or multiple stressors (APA, 2013). The stressors impact the way individuals view themselves. Symptoms may start within 3 to 6 months of the stressors or they may be continuous with stressors. Examples of major life stressors include the breakup of a relationship, marital problems, having a loved one with a painful illness or disability, living in a community with high crime rates, or living through a natural disaster. The reaction to the stressor is more severe than would normally be expected and can result in significant functional impairment in social, occupational, or academic domains.

Adjustment disorder is associated with increased risk of suicidal behavior and substance abuse, as well as the prolonging of medical disorders or interference with medical treatment (Carta et al., 2009). When the stressor persists, it may progress to a more severe condition such as major depressive disorder. Adjustment disorder often prompts depressed mood, anxiety, norm-violating or inappropriate conduct, or other maladaptive reactions, such as problems at work or school, physical complaints, or social isolation (APA, 2013).

Other Specified Trauma- and Stressor-Related Disorder

This category applies to a diagnosis in which symptoms and characteristics of trauma- and stressor-related disorders cause clinically significant distress or impairment in social, occupational, or other areas of functioning but do not meet the full criteria for other disorders in the trauma- and stressor-related disorder category. The other specified trauma- and stressor-related disorder category is used for situations in which the clinician chooses to communicate the specific reason that the presentation does not meet the criteria for a specific trauma- and stressor-related disorder; this can be done by a diagnosis of other specified trauma and stress related disorder followed by the specific reason.

Examples include:

- Adjustment-like disorder with a delayed onset of symptoms (more than 3 months after the stressor)

- Adjustment-like disorder with prolonged symptoms lasting more than 6 months (without prolonged duration of stressor)

- *Ataque de nervios* ("attack of nerves")

- Other cultural syndromes ("*cultural concepts of distress*")

- Persistent complex bereavement disorder, characterized by severe and persistent grief and mourning

History

PTSD first appeared in the DSM-III (APA, 1980). The addition of the disorder to the DSM-III and its corresponding criteria implied that the cause of the disorder was outside the individual (i.e., a traumatic event), rather than an internal weakness. The authors of the DSM-III had in mind events such as the Holocaust, nuclear bombs, war, natural disasters, car crashes, or fires. The DSM-III made the distinction between traumatic events, such as the ones mentioned earlier, and normal stressors, such as divorce, financial issues, and illness. The DSM-IV (APA, 1994) and the DSM-IV-TR (APA, 2000) included a history of trauma (not just recent trauma) to the diagnosis and added three symptom clusters: intrusive recollections, avoidant/numbing symptoms, and hyperarousal symptoms. It also added a duration of symptoms and a caveat that the symptoms must cause significant distress. The DSM-5 (APA, 2013) made significant changes to the diagnosis. The most notable change was that the diagnosis was no longer categorized as an anxiety disorder but as a disorder in a new category, trauma- and stressor-related disorders. The DSM-5 also included indirect exposure to trauma, such as learning about a trauma perpetrated on a loved one or repeated indirect exposure to the consequences of trauma, such as those experienced by a first responder. Another significant addition to the PTSD diagnosis in the DSM-5 is the addition of dysphoric symptoms, marked by negative cognitions and/or mood states (anger, recklessness).

Attachment disorders were first formally defined in the DSM-III (APA, 1980) and revised in the DSM-III-R (APA, 1987) and the DSM-IV (1994). However, because the disorders are underresearched, the revisions were made with little research to support them. The DSM-5 separated attachment disorder into two separate disorders, RAD and DSED.

Etiology

Although exposure to trauma may lead to PTSD, it remains unclear why some people who experience or are exposed to trauma will develop PTSD and others will not.

Sociodemographic factors associated with a diagnosis of PTSD include lower socio-economic status, less education, and less social support (Berwin et al., 2000). Women are twice as likely to have a diagnosis of PTSD than men (Koenen et al., 2017).

Adverse childhood experiences (ACEs) are traumatic events that occur in childhood (0 to 17 years), specifically abuse, neglect, and household dysfunction. Consequently, ACEs and associated conditions, such as living in underresourced or racially segregated neighborhoods, frequently moving, and experiencing food insecurity, can cause toxic stress (extended or prolonged stress). Toxic stress from ACEs can change brain chemistry and affect such things as attention, decision making, and learning. It is particularly important to consider the impact of ACEs, because children who experience prolonged toxic stress may have difficulty forming healthy and stable relationships. Many also have unstable work histories as adults and struggle with finances, jobs, and life satisfaction. Women, Black/African Americans, Latinx/Hispanic, and American Indian groups are at greater risk for experiencing four or more ACEs (Afifi & Asmundson, 2020). American Indians/Alaskan Natives report the highest rates of PTSD (APA, 2013).

Beginning in the 1940s and continuing to present day, studies have indicated that children raised in institutions often exhibit unusual social behaviors, such as social inhibition, unresponsiveness, social disinhibition, and boundary violations (Dobrova-Krol et al., 2010; Goldfarb, 1947; Tizard & Rees, 1975). These behaviors are now classified as reactive attachment and disinhibited social engagement disorder. These disorders arise when the child's first attachment relationships are compromised by neglect, suggesting that this is a sensitive period for the onset of these disorders.

Prevalence and Comorbidities

RAD is underresearched, and there is limited data on its prevalence. In foster care samples, the prevalence of RAD ranged from 3% to 35% (Jonkman et al., 2014; Zeanah et al., 2004). Longitudinal data on RAD are even more scarce. One study of Romanian children found that the number of children meeting criteria at 30 months was 3.3%; at 42 months, 1.6%; and at 54 months, 4.1% (Gleason et al., 2014). It should be noted that the sample sizes of these studies were small.

The lifetime prevalence rate of PTSD ranges from 6.1% to 9.2% in national samples of adults in the United States and Canada, with 1-year prevalence rates of 3.5% to 4.7% (Goldstein et al., 2016). In a study of more than 5,500 respondents, approximately 83% were exposed to severe or traumatic events, and 8.3% were diagnosed with lifetime PTSD (Koenen et al., 2017).

The majority of individuals with a diagnosis of PTSD will have at least one co-morbid disorder. The most common comorbid disorder is major depressive disorder; Rytwinski et al. (2013) found that 52% of adults have comorbid depression with a diagnosis of PTSD. Anxiety disorders and substance use disorders are also common comorbidities with PTSD (Bangasser & Valentino, 2014).

Course and Prognosis

The symptoms of RAD and DSED can persist into adolescence and early adulthood. Even with intervention, children with either of these disorders are likely to encounter difficulties in every aspect of their lives. The resulting persistent stress created by neglect or maltreatment diminishes their capacity for resilience (Ellis et al., 2021). Many will have difficulties with self-esteem and relationships. Some will have anger management issues, antisocial behaviors, and/or comorbid substance use disorders, depression, or anxiety. Those with DSED may engage is risk-taking sexual behaviors.

There has been little research conducted on the long-term course of PTSD. Data from the World Mental Health surveys (as reported by Rosellini et al., 2018) indicate that 20% of individuals recover within 3 months, and 27% within 6 months. Fifty percent of cases recovered in 2 years and 77% by year 10. Those who had an onset of PTSD after age 60 had the lowest recovery rate, whereas the highest recovery rate was for those with an onset of PTSD between 25 and 44 years.

PTSD is a significant risk factor for suicidal ideation and death by suicide. A study conducted between 1994 and 2006 found that death by suicide was 5.3 times higher in those with a diagnosis of PTSD (Gradus et al., 2010). A more recent study found that the suicide rates of men diagnosed with PTSD were 6.74 times higher than those not diagnosed with PTSD (Fox et al., 2021). Suicide rates for women with a diagnosis of PTSD were 3.96 times higher than those without a diagnosis of PTSD (Fox et al., 2021). Some factors that aid in promoting recovery after trauma include having a support system, having positive coping strategies, and being able to respond to adverse events effectively despite feeling fear (Koenen et al., 2017).

Cultural and Gender-Related Considerations

Cultural concepts of distress refer to the ways that cultural groups experience, understand, and communicate suffering, behavioral problems, or troubling thoughts and emotions. The three main types of cultural concepts of distress may be distinguished as cultural syndromes, cultural idioms of distress, and cultural explanations or perceived causes of distress (APA, 2013; Paniagua, 2014). Black/African Americans, Latinx/ Hispanic Americans, American Indians/Alaskan Natives, and Asian Americans experience higher rates of PTSD as compared to White Americans; this prevalence can be a result of racism, microaggressions, and racial trauma (Comas-Diaz et al., 2019; Nadal, 2018).

Cultural implications may be instrumental in the trauma dynamics, and media influences may shape perceptions about traumatic incidents. Traumatic events associated with gendered violence, racial and ethnic violence, and age-related violence (child or elder abuse) can cause specific types of trauma with particular symptoms.

- *Racial/cultural trauma:* This includes trauma due to race-based stress, which refers to the reactions of individuals of color to dangerous events associated with racial discrimination. These events and be real or perceived and may include threats of harm and injury, humiliating and shaming events, and witnessing racial discrimination and violence toward other people of color (Comas-Diaz et al., 2019).

- *Intergenerational/generational trauma:* Passing on of trauma from one generation to the next; may occur due to phenomenon such as war, the Holocaust, genocide, slavery, etc. (Doctor & Shiromoto, 2010).

- *Racial battle fatigue:* Cumulative result of natural, race-related stress response to distressing mental and emotional conditions. These conditions emerged from constantly facing racially dismissive, demeaning, insensitive comments and/or interfacing in hostile racial environments (Smith, 2004).

- *Posttraumatic slave syndrome:* The adaptive and/or survival behaviors by Black communities deployed throughout the diaspora. The strategies used are a consequence of multigenerational and intergenerational oppression of Black (African) Americans and their descendants, due to centuries of chattel slavery, discrimination, and oppression (Degruy, 2005).

- *Microaggressions:* Subtle verbal and nonverbal insults directed at people of color, often unconscious but layered insults based on one's race, gender, class, sexuality, language, immigration status, or nationality; these covert insults cause unnecessary stress to people of color or marginalized communities (Sue et al., 2007).

- *Insidious trauma:* Refers to the daily incidents of marginalization, objectification, dehumanization, and intimidation experienced by members of marginalized or disenfranchised groups. These groups are targeted through systemic oppressive mechanisms such as racism, heterosexism, ageism, ableism, sexism, and poverty (Root, 1992; Nadal, 2018).

- *Toxic stress:* Occurs when an individual experiences frequent and/or prolonged adversity or stressors—such as physical or emotional abuse, child neglect, caregiver substance abuse or mental illness, exposure to violence, and/or the accumulated burdens of family economic hardship—without adequate support (Shern, Blanch & Steverman, 2016).

Diagnosis and Assessment

Although the criteria of acute stress disorder and PTSD are very similar, the distinct difference is duration. For acute stress disorder, a diagnosis should not be made until 48 hours after the traumatic event. Any reaction an individual has immediately following the traumatic event should be considered a just a reaction or being in a state of crisis (APA, 2013). This does not mean that you do not treat the individual or give them psychological first aid. After 48 hours passes and if the individual meets full criteria for acute stress disorder, it may be diagnosed. If the symptoms persist past one month and the individual meets full criteria, then a diagnosis of PTSD is warranted.

Teresa

Teresa is a 49-year-old Black/African American woman who is meeting with the hospital psychologist. She is a surgeon in a very large hospital in New York City. She states that she has become very overwhelmed lately. At the height of the COVID-19 pandemic, she worked 16-hour days and spent most of her days in the emergency room. She states that she often slept at the hospital because it was easier than going home. Teresa reports that during the height of the pandemic she watched dozens of people die every day. She said that the hospital ran out of ventilators and ICU beds. She reports that she responded to numerous "codes" and had to perform CPR daily. She states that as a surgeon, she has seen a lot of trauma, but that "this was different." She says that it seemed that no matter how hard she and her team worked people "just kept dying, day after day." She recalls a story of a 26-year-old man who came into the ER with shortness of breath and chest pain. The staff determined that he had a blood clot in his lung and needed emergency surgery. He died before they could get him upstairs. She recalls that the waiting room was not large enough and tents had been set up outside for triage. She says that there were a number of people who had died waiting to see a healthcare professional. Teresa says that the hospital ran out of room for bodies in the morgue, and at one point bodies were being stored in refrigerated trucks in the parking lot. She would walk past them on the rare occasion that she returned home. Teresa stated that the hospital had a very limited supply of protective clothing, and the staff said that they were scared to be at work. She says that things have slowed down considerably at work, she is working fewer hours, and there are an "almost normal number of patients." She has returned to performing surgeries. Over the past month, she said she has had difficulty falling asleep, and when she finally does, she often has nightmares about people dying or struggling to breathe. She says that sometimes in her dreams it is her parents who are struggling to breathe. Teresa says it feels like the "world has gone to hell" and is "a very dangerous place." She says that she feels like she could have done better; she could have saved more people. Teresa states that she is glad to be back in the operating room and being back to normal hours, but she still thinks about the past few months "constantly." She said she has a hard time staying focused, and while this has not impacted her surgical skills, she has had difficulty performing small tasks, such as charting. She also reports that when she comes to work in the morning she no longer parks in her normal spot because she can't bear to be in the parking lot, where the refrigerated trucks were. She also states that when there is a surgical consult needed in the ER, she sends a resident whenever possible. She says that she just cannot "deal with being in the ER." During the stay-at-home orders, she could not spend time with her friends and did not even have time to speak with them by phone. Now that she is vaccinated and has continuously tested negative for COVID-19, she still has not met up with friends. She says that she just does not "feel like it" and feels that she would bring everyone down. She has tried returning to the gym now that it is open again, but she just does not find working out enjoyable anymore. When asked what she does find enjoyable, she simply shakes her head. Teresa states that she has tried going for walks in the park and to the local farmers market but "people annoy the hell out of her." She says that she finds herself snapping at her surgical residents, something she had never done before. When asked about life "prepandemic," she states that she had worked long hours but would meet up with friends at least twice a week. She also states that she would run every morning or work out before work. She said that working out was her "happy time." Teresa states that she would sometimes have a glass of wine or two after work but otherwise did not use drugs. She says she does not take any medications, other than those to treat her asthma.

Diagnostic Impression

Teresa has experienced repeated exposure to death and trauma. She has watched dozens of people die every day, despite her efforts to save them. She has witnessed death in numerous ways. She reports intrusion symptoms in the form of nightmares of people struggling to breathe. She now avoids going to the ER or parking near where the refrigerated trucks once were. She has negative alterations in cognition, in the form of feeling that world is going to hell. She is also experiencing guilt for not being able to save more patients. She is no longer interested in spending time with her friends or working out, an activity she once enjoyed. She also is exhibiting alterations in arousal as evidenced by her difficulty falling asleep, her issues with concentrating on small tasks, and her irritability with her surgical residents.

Diagnostic Conclusion
Posttraumatic stress disorder

DIFFERENTIAL DIAGNOSIS I: MAJOR DEPRESSIVE DISORDER
Rationale: Although Teresa is exhibiting some of the symptoms of depression (i.e., difficulty sleeping, decreased concentration, diminished interest in pleasurable activities), she has experienced a trauma. She reported that she did not have these issues prior to the traumatic events; therefore, a diagnosis of PTSD is more appropriate.

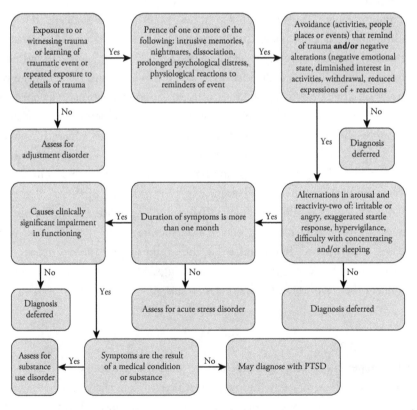

FIGURE 8.1 Differential diagnosis for PTSD

Biopsychosocial

BIOLOGICAL

Teresa reports that she has had repeated negative COVID-19 tests. However, given the fact that she has asthma and is exposed to COVID-19 on a daily basis, it is important for her to follow up with her general practitioner. It is important not to assume that because she, herself, is a physician that she will automatically take the initiative to seek medical treatment; medical professionals who experience trauma often neglect their own health. Physical activity is known to have a positive effect on mood; it is important that Teresa be encouraged to engage in physical activity.

PSYCHOLOGICAL

Teresa will need psychological intervention to help her process and cope with what she experienced during her time at the hospital during the pandemic. At this point, her symptoms are a direct result of the trauma she has experienced. However, it is important that she be assessed for major depressive disorders, should her symptoms become worse. Although Teresa states she has a glass of wine or two after work, it is important to reassess for substance use in the future, because substance use disorders and PTSD are highly comorbid.

SOCIAL

Teresa is socially isolating outside of work. She has not been reaching out to her friends. Although Teresa may not be ready to spend time with friends, because they may have a difficult time understanding what she has experienced, it may be helpful for Teresa to join either a treatment or support group of others who have had similar experiences during the COVID-19 pandemic.

David

David is a 6-year-old White boy who presents as shy and thin. He is wearing a clean T-shirt, clean jeans, and dirty tennis shoes. His hair is dirty. David was brought into the agency by his grandmother. She arrived with David, his older brother (age 9), and his baby sister (approximately 1 year old). The baby was wearing only a diaper, and it was very full. His older brother was wearing dirty jeans and tennis shoes, but his shirt was clean. The grandmother is very friendly but visibly under duress. Her hair is disheveled, and her face is red. David's mother and father have both been in prison for 3 weeks for various drug charges; they are scheduled to stand trial and will likely be serving long sentences. Six weeks ago, DEA agents raided the motel room

David was living in with his mom, dad, and three siblings. His parents were forcibly removed from the room in handcuffs and the children were kept in the back of a police car until their grandmother arrived to pick them up. His parents were cooking methamphetamine in the room. David is currently living with his grandmother and three siblings in a single-family home in a rural area. Grandmother has managed to find beds for all of the children. David and his older brother are still attending the same school and have only missed the three days following the raid. Grandmother is struggling to pay the bills and put food on the table. Her boyfriend of 5 years recently left because "he is way too old to deal with small children." David was referred to the agency because he seems to have retreated into a "shell." He has become very withdrawn and rarely smiles. He no longer wants to play with his friends, whom he used to see every day. He simply sits on the couch and watches TV or does nothing at all. Throughout the course of the sessions, he draws pictures portraying his mother as an enormous bug, spraying him with bug spray trying to kill him. David has a very difficult time falling asleep and often has bad dreams. He reports that, during the day, he can see his parents being arrested over and over in his mind. Whenever grandma drives past the motel where mom and dad were arrested, he begins to sob. When he plays with his toys, he often acts out the scene of his parents' arrest in his head. He says that, sometimes, he can hear his parents' voices in the house, even though he knows they are not there. Oftentimes, when he hears a knock at the door, he becomes very startled. His grades in school are suffering, and his teachers state that he is having trouble focusing on his work. He was also sent to the principal's office 2 days ago for stabbing a child in the hand with a pencil. David has lost more than 10 pounds and often refuses to eat. He walks around aimlessly and when he does eat, he does so very slowly. Grandma confirms that these behaviors began after mom and dad were taken away in handcuffs and seem to be getting worse. During a session with his social worker, he stated that he feels like it might be better for everyone if he were not around anymore. He feels like it is his fault that his parents were taken away by the police.

Diagnostic Impression

David presents with many signs and symptoms of PTSD, including upsetting memories, intrusive thoughts and dreams, flashbacks, distress when exposed to the motel (evidenced by crying while driving past), and psychological distress (evidenced by being startled at door knocks). David has experienced negative emotional states, such as withdrawal and guilt, stating that it is his fault that his parents were arrested.

A diagnosis of PTSD in children 6 years and younger has specific criteria in the DSM-5. The symptoms must cause impairment in the client's functioning in relationships with his parents, siblings, peers, or caregivers, or in school behavior, which is clear in this case. David witnessed, in person, the traumatic event of the DEA's raiding his family's motel room and arresting his parents for cooking methamphetamine.

David presents with several depressive symptoms, such as depressed mood, social withdrawal, loss of interest in playing with friends as he used to, significant weight loss of 10 pounds, trouble concentrating on schoolwork, difficulty sleeping, and psychomotor retardation, evidenced by walking around slowly. David also shares that he is experiencing suicidal ideation, stating "it might be better for everyone if I were not around anymore." These symptoms have caused significant impairment and distress in his social interactions with his friends, at home, and in school. David's grandmother shares that these symptoms began after his parents were arrested 3 weeks ago and continue to worsen.

Diagnostic Conclusion

Diagnosis I: Posttraumatic stress disorder for children 6 years and younger
Diagnosis II: Major depressive disorder, single episode, moderate

DIFFERENTIAL DIAGNOSIS I: ATTENTION DEFICIT HYPERACTIVY DISORDER (ADHD)

Rationale: David presents with some inattentive symptoms commonly seen in ADHD. David's teacher observed that he is experiencing difficulty concentrating on his schoolwork, and his grades in school are suffering. In order to diagnose David with ADHD, the clinician would have to further assess if the inattentive symptoms are present in another location in addition to school. Because David did not describe a history of difficulty concentrating at home, the clinician would likely not diagnose him with ADHD.

DIFFERENTIAL DIAGNOSIS II: ADJUSTMENT DISORDER WITH DEPRESSED MOOD

Rationale: David meets full criteria for major depressive disorder; therefore, a diagnosis of adjustment disorder with depressed mood can be ruled out.

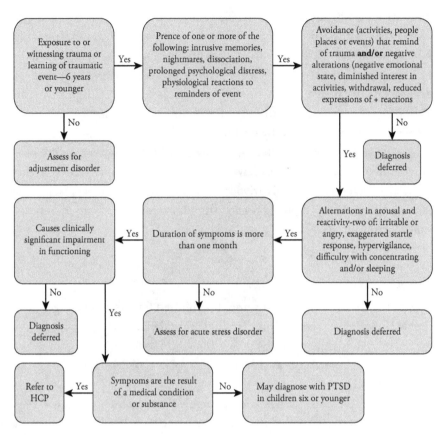

FIGURE 8.2 Differential diagnosis for PTSD in children 6 or younger

Biopsychosocial

BIOLOGICAL

David and his siblings were exposed to the methamphetamine that his parents were cooking in their motel room. David should have a physical examination by his pediatrician. The social worker notices that David and his family appear to live in filthy, unhygienic conditions. It is apparent that the grandmother is distressed. The social worker should consider the health conditions of the entire family, including David's nutritional health, considering his significant weight loss. There is also a history of parental drug use. Although it is unclear if David was exposed to drugs in utero, exposure could have significant biological consequences.

PSYCHOLOGICAL

David is experiencing withdrawal, bad dreams, and auditory delusions. David's social skills in his school setting are being impacted, evidenced by his stabbing of a student with a pencil. Also of concern is the history of parental drug use. Again, exposure is unclear; however, if exposed, he could be at risk for a variety of mental health disorders, including, but not limited to, depression, anxiety, and ADHD.

SOCIAL

David's home life has recently been disrupted by his parents' recent incarceration, and he is now living with his grandmother and siblings. According to the case study, David's traumatic experience is causing disruption in his functioning at school, which led to his stabbing one of his peers. It appears that these new behavior problems are caused by the lack of structure in his new home life, which is creating chaos in school. A needs assessment should be completed on the family to assess the dirty appearance of the children. The social worker can connect the family to local agencies to assist with food, day care, clothing needs and mental health support for grandmother.

REFLECTION QUESTIONS

1. DSED is often mistaken for which neurodevelopment disorder due to the child's impulsive behavior?

2. In the latest revision of the DSM, which diagnosis was once considered an anxiety disorder but is now its own disorder in a new category?

3. Why should therapists wait 72 hours to diagnose an individual after a traumatic event?

CHAPTER 9

Feeding and Eating Disorders

<hr/>

LEARNING OBJECTIVES

1. Gain a basic understanding of the causes, prevalence, and comorbidities of the eating disorders.

2. Become familiar with the criteria for the eating disorders.

3. Be able to differentially diagnose the eating disorders.

Overview of Disorders

Eating disorders are characterized by significant disturbances in both eating behaviors and body weight. Six specific eating disorders are included in the "Feeding and Eating Disorders" chapter of the DSM-5 (APA, 2013). These disorders include pica, rumination disorder, avoidant/restrictive food intake disorder, anorexia nervosa, bulimia nervosa, and binge eating disorder. For the purposes of this chapter, we will focus on the three primary eating disorders: anorexia nervosa, bulimia nervosa, and binge eating disorders. Pica, rumination disorder, and avoidant/restrictive disorders are diagnosed by medical professionals and are rarely if ever diagnosed by social workers and other mental health professionals.

Characteristics of the Disorders

Eating disorders are serious mental health disorders that can lead to several medical, cognitive, social, and emotional issues that often lead to significant impairment in quality of life and even death.

Bulimia Nervosa

Bulimia nervosa is characterized by recurrent episodes of uncontrollable binge eating that are coupled with a purge-type behavior such as vomiting, fasting, enemas, laxatives, or excessive exercise to prevent weight gain (APA, 2013). A *binge* is defined as eating an excessive amount (a much larger amount of food that most people would eat in the same time period) of food within a discrete period of time, such as a couple of hours. The individual has a sense that they lack control over their food consumption. To be classified as bulimia nervosa the binge–purge behaviors must occur, on average, once a week for 3 months. The individual's perception of self is excessively influenced by body weight and shape. The disorder has four severity specifiers that are based on the number of binge–purge episodes per week and the individual's current level of impairment.

Anorexia Nervosa

Anorexia nervosa is characterized by restricted eating behaviors and a significantly low body weight, taking into context age, sex, development, and physical health (APA, 2013). The individual has an intense fear of gaining weight despite already being at a low body weight. The individual often has a distorted view of their own body weight and does not recognize the seriousness of their low body weight (APA, 2013). People with anorexia nervosa perceive body parts such as the head, thighs, and abdomen as larger than they appear in reality (Smeets et al., 2009). There are two types of anorexia nervosa: restricting type, wherein the past 3 months, the individual has not engaged in any binge eating or purging behaviors, weight loss is achieved by food restriction and/or excessive exercise, and binge/purge type where The individual has engaged in recurrent episodes for binge eating an purge behaviors. Anorexia Nervosa has four severity specifiers based on current body mass index (BMI) and the individual's current level of impairment (APA, 2013).

Binge Eating Disorder

Binge eating disorder is characterized uncontrollable eating episodes without a compensatory behavior. It is associated with a feeling of being out of control and marked distress related to food intake (APA, 2013). The binge eating behaviors occur at least once a week for at least 3 months. Research has indicated that in addition to the binge eating episodes, individuals with binge eating disorder also tend to overeat during regular meals (Heaner & Walsh, 2013). They are also reported to engage in more snacking. People with binge eating disorder have reported greater propensity toward cravings, emotional eating, and eating as a coping mechanism (Leslie et al., 2018) and report a greater hedonic hunger, meaning that they have a greater motivation to eat for pleasure than for caloric need (Espel-Huynh et al., 2018).

History

Starvation and/or the symptoms of anorexia are certainly not a modern-day phenomenon. Eating disordered symptoms have been reported since before the Middle Ages and have long been associated with a drive for thinness and perfectionism (Dell'Osso et al., 2016). The term *anorexia nervosa* was first coined by Gull (1874, as cited in Dell'Osso et al., 2016), distinguishing the disorder from the other "hysterical" disorders. Bulimia nervosa was first described by Gerald Russell, a British psychiatrist, who stated that it was a "phase" of anorexia nervosa where patients overeat and then use a compensatory behavior such as vomiting or prolonged starvation (Castillo & Weiselberg, 2017). The term *bulimia* is from the Greek word for "ox hunger," which was used to describe the defining feature of "gross overeating." Russell differentiated patients with bulimia nervosa from anorexia as being of normal weight.

Anorexia nervosa was accepted as a psychogenic disorder in the late 19th century and was included in the DSM-I (APA, 1952) as a neurotic disorder. The DSM-II (1968) categorized anorexia nervosa as a feeding disturbance, along with pica and rumination. The DSM-III (1987) required that a diagnosis of anorexia nervosa required a weight of at least 15% below normal for age and height. In addition, the DSM-III was the first version to include bulimia as a distinct disorder, classifying it as an eating disorder under disorders of childhood or adolescence. The disorder was simply defined as the presence of binge eating behaviors. The DSM-III-R used the term *bulimia nervosa* and added a requirement that a compensatory behavior (vomiting, laxatives, fasting, exercise) must be present to warrant a diagnosis (in the DSM-III it was optional). In addition, the DSM-III-R required a minimum number of episodes (at least two per week). The DSM-IV (1994) moved eating disorders into its own chapter. The diagnosis required binge eating and compensatory behaviors that occurred twice per week for at least 3 months. It added two subtypes: purge type, which referred to those who engaged in vomiting, laxative use, diuretics, and/

or enemas, and the nonpurge type, which referred to those who used compensatory measures such as excessive exercise or fasting. The DSM-IV (APA, 1994) had the category eating disorders not otherwise specified (EDNOS), which encompassed those individuals who did not meet the full criteria for anorexia nervosa or bulimia nervosa. There are many patients who purge or have purge like behaviors but do not binge; these individuals would be diagnosed under EDNOS.

The DSM-5 (APA, 2013) has a chapter entitled "Feeding and Eating Disorders" and features a number of changes from the DSM-IV-TR (2000). One momentous change is that three disorders that were previously categorized under "Disorders Usually First Diagnosed in Infancy, Childhood, or Adolescence" were added to the chapter. These disorders include rumination, pica, and avoidant/restrictive eating disorder. As mentioned earlier, these disorders are typically diagnosed by medical professionals. Another significant addition to this chapter was the new diagnosis of binge eating disorder. In addition, some changes made to the actual criteria for bulimia nervosa and anorexia nervosa. For bulimia nervosa, the number of binge episodes and the compensatory behaviors was reduced from twice per week to once per week for 3 months and the two subtypes of purge and nonpurge were removed. A severity specifier was also added. In anorexia nervosa, the criterion of amenorrhea was removed. The DSM-5 also added a category called "Other Specified Feeding or Eating Disorders." A new diagnosis in this category is purging disorder, which describes individuals who purge but do not binge. This is a particularly important diagnosis for teens and adolescents who are more likely to fit into this category than adults.

Etiology

Eating disorders are complex conditions that arise from a complex combination of factors. Research has indicated that both genetic and environmental influences contribute to eating disorders.

Genetic

Twin studies of anorexia nervosa indicate that anorexia is highly familial, with 28% to 74% of the variance being attributed to genetic factors (Yilmaz et al., 2015). Family studies indicate that female relatives of those with anorexia nervosa are 10 times more likely to develop anorexia than those without the disorder (Schaumberg et al., 2018). Genome studies suggest that there are both metabolic and psychiatric risk factors for anorexia nervosa, and research also suggests that anorexia nervosa may be influenced by epigenetics (Algería-Torres et al., 2011). Epigenetics refers to the regulation of gene expression without a change in sequencing. In other words, epigenetic markers can be influenced by environmental factors beginning at conception. These environmental factors include, but are not limited to, hormones, nutrition, lifestyle, and intestinal microbiota.

Twin studies of bulimia nervosa have estimated the heritability of bulimia nervosa to be 28% to 83% (Munn-Chernoff et al., 2015). Studies of the symptom of binge eating (not the disorder, which will be discussed later) estimate its heritability to be 4% to 82% (Bulik et al., 2007; Reichborn-Kjennerud et al., 2003; Sullivan et al., 1998). The operationalization of the terms *large amount*, *short period of time*, and *loss of control* make estimates of both genetic and environmental influences difficult (Mazzao et al., 2010). A study of individuals who engage in self-induced vomiting found that the heritability was approximately 51%, and it is thought to be the most heritable symptom of bulimia nervosa (Peterson et al., 2016). These data are consistent with earlier studies (Mazzeo et al., 2010; Sullivan et al., 1998).

There are few genetic studies of binge eating disorder; however, twin-based studies have indicated a heritability of between 41% and 57% (Mayhew et al., 2018; Yilmaz et al., 2015). In addition, research has found significant genetic correlations between binge eating and bulimia symptoms and binge eating and alcohol dependence (Munn-Chernoff et al., 2016). Molecular genetic studies have found involvement of both dopamine and μ-opioid receptor genes. This indicates that the risk for binge eating may be through a hypersensitivity to reward, which is likely to foster binge eating, particularly in an environment where calorie-dense, processed foods are highly available (Hilbert, 2019)

Neurobiological

Brain imaging studies indicate a reduction of grey and white matter in acutely underweight patients with anorexia. However, both normalize fairly rapidly after recovery (Seidel et al., 2020). Magnetic resonance imaging (MRI) imaging indicates alterations in the parts of the brain that influence reward processing, food-cue reactivity, emotion recognition, and visual processing. Functional MRI (fMRI) studies of those with binge eating disorder have found hypoactivity in the prefrontal networks and hyperactivity in the medial orbital frontal cortex as compared to those without binge eating disorder (Culburt et al., 2015).

Neurocognitive similarities have been found with binge eating disorder and substance use disorders, which has led to the common (and controversial) food addiction hypothesis. This hypothesis asserts that certain foods, particularly those high in sugar and fat, may elicit addictive type responses in individuals with high impulsivity and reward sensitivity (Gearhart, 2011). Although there are shared characteristics between the two disorders, there are also distinct differences. More specifically, substance use disorders are defined by specific symptoms of withdrawal or tolerance.

Psychobehavioral

There have been a number of hypotheses as to the reason that people develop eating disorders. Some early hypotheses focused on the association of reward (weight loss) with food restriction, resulting in "starvation dependence", essentially an addiction (Bergh & Sodersten 1996). More recently it is hypothesized that eating disorders are part of a model of uncontrolled behavior centered around a reward system (Zink & Weinberger, 2010). The dietary restriction may be rewarding due to a sense of self-mastery over hunger or weight and or/the social reinforcement from the weight loss.

Body image is a conscious representation of the perception and feelings of one's body size shape or weight. Studies have shown that the perceptions and feelings about appearance are dysfunctional in anorexia nervosa (Risso et al., 2020). These studies have shown that although the individual's self-perception is distorted (i.e., they see themselves as being fat or their shape is distorted), their perception of the shape of others is not. Although these studies demonstrate a disturbance in body image perception, they do not explain why the distortions exist. A number of theories of have been offered as to what causes the disturbances, including negative mood (Gadsby, 2017), tactile perception of distance (Spitoni et al., 2015), and multisensory integration issues (Gaudio et al., 2014).

Environmental

The ideal body shape for women has changed over time along with cultural and social norms. Thirty years ago, women were expected to have a curvaceous and ample figure. Over the past 30 years, the ideal body type has become increasingly thinner. There is now a popular misconception that thinness and health are synonymous. In the Western world, there is a conflict between the excessive availability of inexpensive, high-calorie (yet highly palatable) food and the value placed on slimness, and dietary restraint has made weight and shape concerns and dieting the norm among young women (Dell'Osso et al., 2016). Anorexia nervosa has been identified across time and globally; however, the cultural idealization of thinness has been associated with higher rates or anorexia nervosa. Interestingly, no cases of bulimia nervosa have been found in absence of Western influences, and rates in non-Western cultures have increased after exposure to Western influences (Keel & Klump, 2003). Media exposure, the perceived pressure to be thin, thin-idea internalization, and thinness expectations have all been shown to predict increased levels of eating disordered behaviors. Whether individually these factors lead to diagnoses of eating disorders is still unknown (Culbert et al., 2015).

As mentioned earlier, there are overlaps in the symptoms of anorexia nervosa and bulimia nervosa. Etiological overlaps have been seen as well. Relatives of individuals with anorexia have over a four times higher risk of bulimia nervosa as compared to the relatives of individuals without anorexia nervosa. The same is true in the other direction. Relatives of individual with bulimia nervosa have a higher risk of anorexia nervosa as compared to relatives without bulimia nervosa (Strober et al., 2000). Further research has found that the shred overlap is explained by a combination of both genetic and environmental factors (Yao et al., 2019).

Prevalence and Comorbidities

The lifetime prevalence of eating disorders is approximately 8.4% for women and 2.2% for men (Galmiche et al., 2019). Specifically, for anorexia nervosa the lifetime prevalence is approximately 1.4% for women and 0.2% for men, and for bulimia nervosa it is 1.9% and 0.6% for women and men, respectively. The lifetime prevalence for binge eating disorder is 2.8% for women and 1% for men. In a review of past studies, Galmiche et al. (2019) found that 5.7% of women and 2.2% of men meet the criteria for an eating disorder at some point in their lives. Anorexia nervosa and bulimia nervosa are more common in women (approximately 10% are men), and men account for approximately 36% of those with binge eating disorder. Seventy-five percent of individuals with anorexia and 83% of those with bulimia nervosa have an onset before the age of 22 (Volpe et al., 2016). The rates of eating disorders tend to be highest in the United States, followed by Asia and Europe.

Anorexia nervosa is highly comorbid with several disorders, with the prevalence rate of comorbidities with anorexia nervosa reaching as high as 97% in adults and 57% in adolescents (Brand-Gothelf et al., 2014). The most common comorbidities including anxiety disorders, major depressive disorder (50% to 75%) (Godart, 2015; Iwaskaki et al., 2000), obsessive compulsive disorder (35% to 44%) (Levinson et al., 2018), and substance use disorders (22%) (Baker et al., 2012). Bulimia nervosa is highly comorbid with major depressive disorder (60%) (Godart et al., 2015), ADHD (30%), oppositional defiant disorder (11%), anxiety disorders (53%), and alcohol or stimulant use disorder (30%) (Castillo & Weiselberg, 2017). A recent study by Udo and Grilo (2018) found binge eating disorder is highly comorbid with major depressive disorder

(65.5%), anxiety disorders (59%), substance use disorders (67.7%), and posttraumatic stress disorder (PTSD) (31.6%). Evidence actually suggests that major depressive disorder and bulimia nervosa share genetic risk factors (Slane et al., 2011).

Course and Prognosis

The course and the prognosis vary by disorder. Multiple biopsychosocial factors influence how the disorders will develop and progress and the response to various treatments.

Anorexia Nervosa

Anorexia nervosa has a wide range of long-term physical health complications, including, but not limited to, metabolic issues, cardiac issues (e.g., bradycardia, mitral valve prolapse), endocrine issues (e.g., low bone density, amenorrhea), gastrointestinal issues, and anemia (Cass et al., 2020). Anorexia nervosa comorbid with obsessive compulsive disorder is associated with a younger age of onset as well as a poorer prognosis (Crane et al., 2007; Simpson et al., 2013). Similarly, research has indicated that premorbid depressive symptoms are associated with a poorer outcome of anorexia nervosa (Eskild-Jensen et al., 2020). A study by Levinson et al. (2018) found that concerns over making mistakes is associated with a higher severity in both anorexia nervosa and OCD.

Weight gain is a key outcome in the treatment of anorexia nervosa. The long-term prognosis for anorexia is often poor, with a relapse frequency of approximately 31% (Berends et al., 2018). Approximately 33.5% of those with the disorder will improve (Jagielska & Kacperska, 2017). Many will go on to have chronic anorexia nervosa. Only one in three individuals diagnosed with anorexia nervosa will receive specialist care. Of those in treatment, 20% to 51% are inpatients; however, 23% to 73% of those receiving outpatient care dropped out of their inpatient care. Interestingly, studies have indicated that hospitalization can actually worsen outcomes for individuals with anorexia nervosa (Jagielska & Kacperska, 2017).

Anorexia has the highest mortality rate of all the mental health disorders (approximately 5%) (Cass et al., 2020). The high mortality rate is due primarily to medical complications and suicide. Suicide is a significant cause of the high mortality rate (Arcelus et al., 2011), with up to 26% of patients attempting suicide (Forcano et al., 2011). A diagnosis of major depressive disorder has been associated with higher rates of suicide attempts (Bulik et al., 2008) and suicide-related mortality (Crow et al.,

2009). It is estimated that only about 50% of cases of anorexia are being diagnosed (Jagielska & Kacperska, 2017). This is due to several factors, including denial of having the disorder, effectively hiding symptoms, and avoiding treatment.

Bulimia Nervosa

A number of medical complications are associated with bulimia nervosa, with the most serious being an electrolyte imbalance that can lead to cardiac arrhythmia, seizures, and in extreme cases, death. The self-induced vomiting associated with bulimia nervosa can lead to hyperchloremic alkalosis (significant decline of chloride) and ultimately severely low potassium, which is called hypokalemia. Potassium is an electrolyte that is responsible for nerve and muscle functioning, including the heart. Other complications that are largely due to the vomiting include subconjunctival hemorrhages (burst blood vessels), dental erosion (from stomach acid washing over teeth), other dental issues, and an inflamed larynx and vocal cords, which can lead to sore throat, hoarseness, and cough. Excessive laxative use can lead to diarrhea and hemorrhoids. A serious concern with excessive laxative use is the development of severe constipation. This is a result of damage to the nerves in the colon, which can render the colon unable to move fecal material (Castillo & Weiselberg, 2017).

Bulimia nervosa has a lower mortality rate (approximately 3.9%) than anorexia nervosa (Crow et al., 2009). Mortalities from bulimia nervosa are often a result of suicide. Approximately 7% of adolescents with bulimia nervosa will attempt suicide and approximately 6% will have multiple suicide attempts (Crow et al., 2014).

Adolescents tend to have better outcomes than adults (Castillo & Weiselberg, 2017). A review of 27 studies by Steinhausen & Weber (2009) found that 45% of patients had a full recovery, 27% had partial remission and 23% had a chronic course of bulimia nervosa. A better prognosis is also associated with an earlier age of onset, absence of laxative use, shorter duration of symptoms, and a strong familial support system. Those who have a continuous overemphasis on body shape and weight, a history of physical abuse, unstable family relationships, a history of self-injury, and comorbid personality disorders tend to have a poorer prognosis (Castillo & Weiselberg, 2017). Research also indicates that depressive symptoms have been found to predict a poor treatment and outcome and relapse (Puccio et al., 2016).

Binge Eating Disorder

Although binge eating disorder was initially thought to be an "adult disorder," recent research suggests that it begins in childhood or adolescence (Amianto et al., 2015). The average age of onset ranges from late teens to mid-20s and has a mean duration of symptoms of 15.9 years (Udo & Grilo, 2018). An earlier onset is predictive of poorer outcomes and likely requires more intense intervention (Kessler et al., 2013). As with anorexia nervosa and bulimia nervosa, a number of medical conditions are associated with binge eating disorder. These conditions are those that are associated with obesity, including type 2 diabetes, hypertension, asthma, gastrointestinal issues, neurological problems, sleep and pain disorders, and gynecological conditions (Mitchell, 2016; Olguin et al., 2017). Limited data are available regarding the long-term outcomes of binge eating disorder; however, research does indicate that binge eating disorder has a chronic course with tendencies toward recovery and relapse. Unlike bulimia nervosa and anorexia nervosa, binge eating disorder is not likely to migrate to another eating disorder (Hilbert, 2019).

Cultural and Gender-Related Considerations

Anorexia nervosa, bulimia nervosa, and binge eating disorder are generally more common in industrialized countries where attractiveness is associated with being thin, which may explain high prevalence rates of this disorder (Castillo, 1997, as cited in Paniagua, 2014). The DSM-5 (2013) points out that the prevalence for anorexia nervosa appears to be low among Latinx/Hispanic, Black/African Americans, and Asian Americans. However, the low prevalence of anorexia nervosa among racial and ethnically diverse groups may be a result of significantly lower mental health utilization by these groups compared to White Americans (APA, 2013). Further research indicates that the risk for anorexia nervosa for Asian Americans may actually be higher than for White Americans (Wildes & Emery, 2001). Additionally, Latinx/ Hispanic and Black/African American women are underdiagnosed and undertreated for anorexia nervosa (Keel & Brown, 2010; Goeree et al., 2011).

There is a stereotype that eating disorders are "female disorders." Although eating disorders are more prevalent in women, about 25% of cases are reported by men (Hudson et al., 2007). Research is consistent in reporting that girls are more likely to perceive themselves as being fat, despite being of normal weight, and they are more likely to engage in weight control behaviors (Fayet et al., 2012; Hautala et al., 2008; Robinson et al., 2014). Men appear to have lower awareness of the clinical symptoms of anorexia nervosa (Shingleton et al., 2015), are less likely to see anorexia as a real disorder, are more likely to trivialize the illness, and believe that individuals are personally responsible (Griffiths et al., 2014). Men are also more likely to perceive men with anorexia to be less masculine (Griffiths et al., 2015). Gay men are at greater risks for eating disorders then lesbian women and heterosexual men (Muise et al., 2003).

Diagnosis and Assessment

Anorexia nervosa and bulimia nervosa are two distinct disorders; however, they do have common symptoms. In both disorders there is an overemphasis on body weight and shape and the individual engages in behaviors to control their weight. Students (and some clinicians) often ask: What is the difference between bulimia nervosa and anorexia nervosa binge–purge type? The primary difference is that individuals with bulimia nervosa maintain their weight, whereas those with anorexia have a significantly low body weight. Another difference is that in anorexia nervosa binge–purge type the individual may binge *or* purge. Meaning that they may eat a small amount of food that they will then purge. However, crossover between the two disorders is not uncommon. Approximately 10% to 54% of individuals with anorexia nervosa will develop bulimia nervosa, and 2% to 27% of those with bulimia nervosa will develop anorexia during the course of the illness (Eddy et al., 2008; Tozzi et al., 2005).

The defining difference between binge eating disorder and bulimia nervosa is the presence of compensatory behaviors. In both disorders there are discreet periods of excessive food consumption and feelings of disgust and/or guilt. However, in bulimia nervosa the individual engages in a compensatory behavior such as vomiting, excessive exercise, fasting, and/or laxatives.

Lisa

Lisa is a 28-year-old White woman who lives with her husband, David. Lisa has been brought to the emergency room by David after she fainted during their morning run. After a physical examination, it is determined that Lisa is severely dehydrated and her kidney function is low. When asked when she ate last, Lisa reports that she had a "green juice" for breakfast. When asked when last she had any solid food, she has a difficult time remembering. The nurse asks Lisa to step on the scale, but Lisa refuses. David asks her why she will not get on the scale, and she states that she has gained weight over the past few weeks. David tells her she looks great, and after much convincing, Lisa finally gets on the scale. Her current weight is 85 pounds (Lisa is 5 feet 5 inches). David is shocked that she weighs so little. He says he knows she has lost some weight but had no idea how much. The nurse informs Lisa that she will need to insert an IV for fluids. Lisa becomes very upset and asks what is in the IV and if it will make her gain weight. She finally tearfully agrees to the IV but looks very frightened. The nurse is concerned and asks Lisa if she can send in a social worker to speak with her. After first refusing, Lisa finally agrees.

The social worker arrives in Lisa's room and begins chatting with her. When she asks if Lisa understands why the social worker was called, she replies, "Because the doctor thinks I do not weigh enough." The social worker asks if she agrees with the doctor, and she states that she does not and feels that she still needs to lose a few pounds, as she is still "pretty chunky." During the interview, Lisa tells the social worker that she and David have been married for just over 2 years. She states that, before her wedding she began dieting and running to fit into her wedding dress. She says her goal weight for the wedding was 120, and she was very proud to get down to 110. Lisa has continued to diet, and she is running 4 to 10 miles per day. David reports that they often run together, and he has noticed that she has become thin, but "didn't think much of it." He also states that Lisa often tells him that she is not hungry, and her dinner is often left untouched. When asks her about it, she often says she had had a big lunch or a late lunch. The couple reports that they have been trying to start a family for about a year, but Lisa has been unable to get pregnant. She and David have both been tested extensively, and there does not seem to be anything wrong with either of them, reproductively. At her last visit to the gynecologist, her nurse noted that she had lost 10 pounds since her previous visit and was underweight for her height. At the time, Lisa weighed 100 pounds. Her gynecologist told her that being underweight can sometimes lead to difficulty conceiving and inquired about her diet. Lisa reports that she told the doctor that she often "did not have time to eat" and that she "does not have much of an appetite." Concerned that Lisa may be suffering from an eating disorder, the gynecologist referred Lisa to a therapist. Lisa admits that she never called the therapist. Lisa has denied eating large amounts of food at one sitting or ever throwing up after eating.

Diagnostic Impression

Anorexia nervosa, restricting type, severe

Diagnostic Conclusion

Lisa is suffering from cognitive distortions surrounding her weight. She is 5 feet 5 inches and weighs 85 pounds, which gives her a BMI of 15. A healthy BMI is between 18.5 and 24.9. She feels that she has gained weight, when, in fact, she has lost weight. She has an intense fear of gaining weight, as evidenced by her aversion to the IV fluids. She has been restricting her food intake by skipping meals or drinking only juices. She has a difficult time remembering when she last had solid food. She denies any bingeing.

DIFFERENTIAL DIAGNOSIS I: A MEDICAL CONDITION

Lisa has been seeing a doctor, so it is likely that physical reasons for her weight loss have been ruled out.

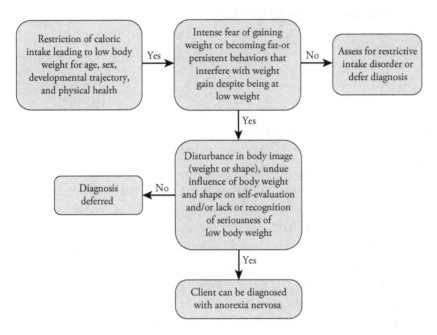

FIGURE 9.1   Differential diagnosis for anorexia nervosa

Biopsychosocial

BIOLOGICAL

Lisa is significantly underweight for her height. She is having acute issues related to her weight/eating habits. She fainted during her run, she is severely dehydrated, and her kidneys are not functioning properly. People with anorexia nervosa are at risk of several health issues including cardiac problems, gastrointestinal issues, and metabolic issues. Given Lisa's extremely low body weight and lack of insight, inpatient treatment for further medical assessment and stabilization is likely warranted.

PSYCHOLOGICAL

People with anorexia nervosa are at an elevated risk of suicide. Therefore, it is extremely important that Lisa be periodically assessed for suicidal ideation. At this point, there is no mention of depressive symptoms; however, the two disorders are highly comorbid. Further assessment for depressive symptoms is indicated.

SOCIAL

Given societal pressure for thinness, it is important for Lisa to associate with those who have a healthy lifestyle and positive body image. Therapeutic groups are often helpful for individuals who suffer with body image issues.

Miranda

Miranda is a 25-year-old White woman who lives in the Pacific Northwest. A social worker is meeting with her to do a psychosocial assessment. Miranda is very reluctant to talk to the social worker, but her mom has convinced her to "at least" talk to someone about her current situation. Miranda has been "very unhappy" over the past 4 months. She states that, while she has never really been a "joyful" person, lately she has been "really cranky" and feels like she does not have the ability to be happy. She has been avoiding all social contact. When asked if anything has happened to change her mood, she becomes visibly uncomfortable. When asked what has been happening, Miranda states that, about a year ago, she went on a date with a man she met on a dating app. She says she had chatted with him by text message and had spoken with him on the phone a few times and that he had seemed "normal." They met at a bar and had "way too many drinks." Miranda becomes tearful and says that she knows it was "stupid," but she went home with him. She recalls being at his house, having another beer, and kissing him while on the couch. She does not remember anything until the next morning, when she woke up in his bed. She snuck out while he was sleeping. She reports that she was "very sore" and could barely walk home; her wrists hurt, and she had a bruise on her abdomen, which she found strange. She felt ashamed that she had "let that happen," but decided to put it behind her. She says, however, that as the days passed, she began having memories of that night. She states that she remembered telling him she wanted to go home and his saying that he was not going to let her. She says she can remember him "practically dragging" her to the bedroom. She says she remembers telling him repeatedly that she did not want to be there anymore. He laughed and said, "Sure you do." Her last memory is of him pinning her arms above her head. Miranda says that she has nightmares about the incident every night. Miranda states that it is her fault this happened; she should never have gone home with him. She cannot sleep at night, because she keeps playing the incident in her mind over and over. Miranda reports that, over the past 6 months, she has gained more than 50 pounds. She says that she just cannot seem to stop eating. She says that food is the only thing that makes her "even a little happy." She reports that she will often feel that she cannot get food into her mouth fast enough, even when she is not hungry. When asked for an example, she states that, the night before, she had ordered a large pizza, a large order of garlic knots, a 2-liter bottle of soda and "ate it all." Then, she ate four doughnuts that she had bought earlier in the day (she had eaten the other eight of the dozen prior to dinner). She says she felt "disgusting" afterward and like she was going to "explode." When asked how often she does this, she states that it happens three to four times a week. She states that no one in her family knows about her eating behaviors and that she only eats alone; she would be "mortified" if anyone saw her eating. Miranda denies any compensatory behaviors (i.e., throwing up or taking laxatives to purge) after her "eating episodes." Her doctor has informed her, however, that she is at risk of diabetes.

Diagnostic Impression

Miranda has clearly suffered a traumatic event, the details of which she has only just begun to remember. Over the past 4 months, she has been experiencing nightmares, difficulty sleeping, irritability, and distorted cognitions about the event (she feels that it was her fault and has also isolated herself from her family and friends). Although Miranda had trouble remembering the events of the evening until recently, it is unclear as to whether this is a result of the alcohol or suppression of the memories. These symptoms and the duration of 4 months indicate a diagnosis of PTSD. Because she began experiencing the symptoms a year after the event, the specifier of *with delayed expression* is required.

Miranda also reports that she is eating excessive amounts of food at one sitting, three to four times a week. She has stated that she feels out of control (she cannot get the food in mouth fast enough and feels as though she cannot stop), she hides her eating because she would be mortified if anyone saw, and she reports that she feels uncomfortably full afterward (like she is going to "blow up"). She has also stated that she eats like this even when she is not hungry. Given these symptoms and the fact that she does not engage in any compensatory behaviors, Miranda meets the criteria for binge eating disorder. She reports these behaviors three to four times per week, and she has stated that she is at risk of health issues; therefore, a specifier of *moderate* was given.

Diagnostic Conclusion

Diagnosis I: PTSD with delayed expression
Diagnosis II: Binge eating disorder moderate

DIFFERENTIAL DIAGNOSIS I: MAJOR DEPRESSIVE DISORDER

Rationale: Although Miranda is experiencing symptoms consistent with major depressive disorder (sleep issues, avoiding social contact, weight gain), she experienced a traumatic event prior to the onset of her symptoms; therefore, a diagnosis of PTSD is most appropriate.

DIFFERENTIAL DIAGNOSIS II: BULIMIA NERVOSA

Rationale: Although Miranda is engaging in binge eating behaviors, she has denied any compensatory behaviors; therefore, a diagnosis of binge eating disorder is warranted.

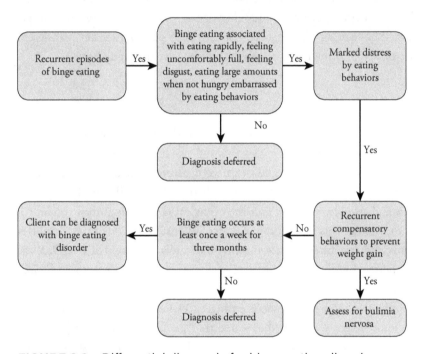

FIGURE 9.2   Differential diagnosis for binge eating disorder

Biopsychosocial

BIOLOGICAL

Miranda has revealed that her doctor has told her that she is at risk of developing diabetes; therefore, it is very important that her eating behaviors are addressed by both a mental health professional and by a medical professional. Regular appointments with her primary care physical are recommended to monitor her weight and her blood sugar. It is also recommended that Miranda work with a nutritionist to ensure that she is eating a balanced diet.

PSYCHOLOGICAL

Miranda has experienced a traumatic event. It is important that her feelings surrounding this event are explored. It is also important to determine if her eating behaviors are a result of the traumatic experience. Both her binge eating disorder and her PTSD will likely need to be treated simultaneously. Under the guidance of a physician, Miranda should implement a physical activity regimen.

SOCIAL

Miranda seems to have a support system in her mother. It would also be helpful for Miranda to join a support group for women who have been sexually assaulted.

TERMINOLOGY

arrhythmia A condition in which the heart beats irregularly.

pica An eating disorder in which people eat nonfood items (e.g., clay, dirt, paper).

rumination eating disorder The regular regurgitating of food that occurs for 1 month.

REFLECTION QUESTIONS

1. What are the some of the suspected causes of eating disorders?

2. What is the difference between anorexia nervosa binge–purge type and bulimia nervosa?

3. What is the difference between bulimia nervosa and binge eating disorder?

Gender Dysphoria

The World Health Organization (WHO) no longer recognizes transgender or gender dysphoria as a "disorder." The most recent version of the International Classification of Diseases (ICD), ICD-11, defines *gender incongruence* as "a marked and persistent incongruence between a person's experienced gender and assigned sex" (WHO, 2019). It was removed from the section on mental health disorders based on research that indicated that the incongruence was not a mental health issue but rather a physical disorder. Gender incongruence is now placed in the chapter on sexual health. It is hoped that the reclassification will not only improve access to care but also reduce stigma and discrimination. However, the DSM-5 (APA, 2013) still recognizes gender dysphoria as a disorder. A diagnosis of gender dysphoria is required for those experiencing gender incongruence to receive treatment; therefore, we are including the diagnosis in this text. Note that the authors fully agree with the WHO in the classification of gender incongruence as a sexual health disorder as opposed to a mental health disorder.

Characteristics of Gender Dysphoria

Gender identity refers to the extent to which an individual sees themselves as being like one gender. Gender identity is usually expressed by gender role behaviors. *Gender roles* are concerns, behaviors, attitudes, and personality traits that within a given society are typically attributed, expected by, or preferred by individuals of one gender (Beek et al., 2016). In most cases, gender identity and physical sex characteristics are congruent; a baby with male genitalia is assigned as being male gendered, and a baby with female genitalia is assigned as being female gendered. If an individual experiences distress resulting from an incongruence between their gender identity and their assigned gender, the individual is considered to be gender dysphoric (APA, 2013).

Gender dysphoria in children is characterized by a marked incongruence between one's experienced or expressed gender and their birth-assigned gender. The duration must be for at least 6 months and include at least six of eight additional criteria, including a strong desire or insistence that one is a gender other than the one assigned, a strong preference for wearing the clothing typical of the opposite gender, a strong preference for cross-gender roles in play, a strong preference for toys typically used by other gender, a rejection of toys that are typical of assigned gender, a strong preference for playmates of other gender, a strong desire for the sex characteristics of the preferred gender, and dislike of one's own sexual anatomy.

Gender dysphoria in adolescents is characterized by a marked incongruence between one's experienced or expressed gender and their birth-assigned gender and at least two of the following six criteria: a strong desire to be rid of one's primary and secondary sex characteristics, a strong desire for the primary and secondary sex characteristics of the other gender, a marked incongruences between one's experienced or expressed gender and their primary and secondary sex characteristics, a strong desire to be of gender other than that assigned a birth, and a strong conviction of having feelings or reactions of gender other than the one assigned at birth. As with the childhood criteria, the duration must be for at least 6 months. And as with all disorders, there needs to be a significant impact in functioning.

History

The psychiatrist Richard Freiherr von Krafft-Ebing (1886) (as cited in Beek et al., 2016) was among the first to recognize that there were some individuals who wanted to live or were living as a member of the opposite sex. Another psychiatrist, Magnus Hirschfeld (1923) (as cited in Beek et al., 2016), was the first to refer individuals with gender dysphoria for surgery (hormone treatment was not yet available). Many practitioners (both health and mental health) were against the use of hormones and surgery as a treatment for gender identity problems because it was considered to be a severe neurotic or delusional condition that should be treated with psychotherapy and reality testing (Beek et al., 2016). As public awareness was raised by media attention paid to individuals who shared their stories of gender reassignment surgery, interest in studying gender incongruence increased. It was then acknowledged that sexual orientation and transvestism had to be distinguished from transsexualism. In 1975 and 1980 transsexualism (now referred to as gender dysphoria) was added to the ICD-9 and the DSM-III, respectively.

The diagnosis of transsexualism appeared in the DSM-III (APA, 1980) under the class of psychosexual disorders. The psychosexual disorders included transsexualism, gender identity disorder of childhood, and atypical gender identity disorder. The primary features of these disorders were an incongruence between anatomical sex and gender identity. For transsexualism, the individual had to have the presence of two criteria: "a persistent discomfort and inappropriateness about one's anatomic sex and a persistent wish to be rid of one's genitals and to live as a member of the opposite sex" (APA, 1980, pp. 261–262). The disturbance had to be present for at least 2 years and not be associated with intersex (APA, 1980). Gender identity disorder of childhood was a strong persistent desire to be the opposite gender, a boy wished to be a girl and a girl wished to be a boy. The child also had to display significant discomfort or hatred for or refusal to accept their genitalia or have a preoccupation with the opposite gender's stereotypic activities (APA, 1980). According to this criterion, boys were focused on dissatisfaction and hatred for having a male body and girls were more focused on the denial that they had a female body. Atypical gender identity was a "residual" category for those who did not fall under transsexualism or gender identity disorder of childhood.

The DSM-III-R (APA, 1987) had three diagnoses for postpubertal individuals: transsexualism, gender identity disorder of adolescence and adulthood, non-transsexual type (new to the DSM-III-R), and gender identity disorder not otherwise specified. For children, there was a diagnosis for gender identity disorder in children. Other changes in the DSM-III-R included the elimination of the category of psychosexual disorders, which was replaced with sexual disorders. Gender identity disorder was placed under "disorders usually evident in infancy, childhood, or adolescence." The differences between the criteria for gender identity disorder in children became more prominent. Girls had to exhibit extreme distress about being a girl and also state that they desired to be a boy; boys needed to exhibit extreme distress about being a boy and intense desire to be a girl (but it did not have to be explicitly stated) (APA 1987).

The DSM-IV (APA, 1994) eliminated the diagnosis of gender identity disorder of adolescence and adulthood, non-transexual type and transsexualism and combined them into one diagnosis for gender identity disorder. There were different criteria for adults and children. The criterion of stated desire to become the opposite sex was no longer required for a diagnosis, though it was included as one of many symptoms. The criterion of "causes clinically significant distress or impairment" was also added to the diagnosis. The DSM-IV-TR (2000) had no changes to the diagnosis.

The DSM-5 (APA, 2013) introduced many changes to the diagnosis. Most notably was the change in the name of the diagnosis to *gender dysphoria*. The diagnosis was also placed in its own chapter separate from sexual dysfunctions and paraphilias. The criteria of cross-gender identification and not being comfortable in one's assigned gender were combined. In addition, the concepts of gender identity and gender role were no longer considered to be dichotomous (male or female), but rather fluid and occurring on a spectrum. The term *sex* was replaced with the term *gender*. A criterion for duration of 6 months was also included. It is now mandatory that the individual express a strong desire to be the opposite gender or insist that they are the opposite gender (or a gender alternative different to the one assigned at birth). This allows for the identification of children who are without a doubt struggling with their gender identity (Zucker, 2010). The terminology was also changed from a "verbalized desire" to a "strong desire."

Prevalence and Comorbidities

It is difficult to determine the prevalence of gender dysphoria due to a number of factors. Estimates of prevalence have typically relied on number of adults seeking care at specialized clinics in a particular country or the number of clients who have been approved for hormone treatment (Zucker et al., 2016). Population-based estimates in 2009 from European countries indicated the prevalence of transsexualism (defined by those who had undergone sex reassignment surgery) was approximately 1 in every 12,900 for adult males and 1 in every 33,800 for adult females (Zucker & Lawrence, 2009). The DSM-5 (APA, 2013) estimates the prevalence of gender dysphoria to be between 0.0005% and 0.14% for males and 0.002% to .0003% for females.

Some studies indicate that despite the distress that accompanies gender dysphoria the majority of adolescents do not have co-occurring mental health problems. For example, a study by Hoshiai et al. (2010) of adults with a diagnosis of gender dysphoria (at the time it was called gender identity disorder) found mental health comorbidities in 19.1% of male-to-female patients and 12% in female-to-male patients. The most common comorbid diagnoses were adjustment disorder at 6.7%, anxiety disorder at 3.6%, and mood disorders at 1.4%. de Vries et al. (2011) found that 67.6% of their sample of adolescents had no comorbid diagnosis. Anxiety disorders were found in 21% (10% were social phobic), mood disorders in 12.4%, and disruptive disorders in 11.4%. Natal males were found to be more likely to have two or more comorbid diagnoses (22.6%). Autism spectrum disorder is reported to occur at higher rates in adolescents with gender dysphoria compared to the general population. In 2010, de Vries et al. found an autism spectrum disorder rate of 7.8% in children referred to a gender identity clinic. The ratio of boys to girls was 3:1. Pasterski et al. (2014) found symptoms of autism spectrum disorder in 5.5% of their adult sample, with no difference by gender. A more recent study by van der Miesen (2018) found that 14.5% of children and adolescents with gender dysphoria also exhibited symptom of autism spectrum disorder.

It is important to note, however, that though comorbidities appear to be low, this may be because many with gender dysphoria do not seek treatment. Also note that suicidality and self-harm are common among those with gender dysphoria. Hoshaiai et al. (2010) found that of 579 adult patients diagnosed with gender dysphoria, 76.1% of male-to-female patients and 71.9% of female-to-male patients had attempted suicide. A more recent systematic review of the literature found that 28% of gender nonconforming youths expressed suicidal ideation, and 14.8% attempted suicide (Surace et al., 2020). With the prevalence of suicide being significantly higher than in the general population, it is critical to implement interventions and strategies to support youth who may be suffering from the stigmatization and/or bullying related to gender nonconformation (Surace et al., 2020).

Course and Prognosis

Gender nonconformity can manifest at any age group. In children, cross-gender behaviors may start as early as 2 to 4 years of age, which is the same time that children begin showing gendered behaviors. Some children will not begin to express cross-gender behaviors until puberty or well into adulthood. In some children and adolescents, gender atypical behavior, such as wearing the opposite gender's (stereotypical) clothing and engaging in play and activities that are typically associated with the opposite gender, may be a normal part of development. Not all children who display gender incongruence continue to report distress or seek treatment for gender reassignment later in life (Steensma et al., 2013).

Cultural and Gender-Related Considerations

Early studies (1999–2005) indicate that sex ratio of male to female was significantly higher (approximately 1.4–2:1) (Aitken et al., 2015). The opposite was found between the years of 2006–2013 the ratio of male to female was approximately 1:176) (Aitken et al., 2015). Many transgender individuals have gender identities that are not exclusively male or female and are considered to be nonbinary. A study conducted in Australia found that 14% of the sample had a nonbinary gender, with 29% of these individuals being in the 21- to 30-year age group. The authors also found that those who identified as nonbinary had higher prevalence of depression, anxiety, and substance use (Cheung et al., 2020).

The DSM-5 notes that this gender dysphoria has been documented in different countries and cultures, and that clinicians may have problems applying diagnostic criteria with clients "living in cultures with institutionalized gender categories other than male or female" (APA, 2013, p. 487). People who are transgender face heightened risk of stigmatization and harassment compared to nontransgender individuals. Individuals who are stigmatized or isolated are at an increased risk of depression, anxiety, substance use disorders (White Hughto et al., 2015). A study exploring whether transgender people of color are more likely than White transgender individuals to experience poor health outcomes found that transgender people of color had significantly greater odds of having asthma or certain autoimmune disorders. In addition, those with a lower income had worse overall health and indicators of poor physical and mental health, including depression, anxiety, and suicidal ideation (Seelman et al., 2017).

TERMINOLOGY

binary gender   The faulty concept that there are only two genders (male and female).

birth sex   The physical, biological, chromosomal, genetic, and anatomical makeup of the body at birth.

cisgender   A person whose birth sex and gender identity align.

gender expression/presentation   External appearance of one's gender identity, usually expressed through behavior, clothing, haircut, and/or voice.

gender identity   One's innermost concept of being male, female, a blend of both, or neither.

genderqueer/gender nonbinary   A broad descriptor many people use to indicate that a person does not identify as either male or female.

gender role   Dominant mainstream ideas of how one should act according to their gender.

identified pronouns   The way in which individuals prefer to be identified. May be nonbinary (they/them).

intersex   An umbrella term for those who are born with a combination of sex characteristics (genital, genes, hormones).

paraphilias   A pattern of recurring sexually arousing mental imagery or behavior that involves atypical and socially unacceptable sexual practices.

transgender (trans)   Those whose gender identity and birth sex do not align.

transvestism   The practice of dressing in a manner stereotypically identified with the opposite sex. It is often not sexual in nature.

REFLECTION QUESTIONS

1. What were the significant changes in the diagnosis of gender dysphoria between the DSM-IV-TR and the DSM-5?

2. What are the primary features of gender dysphoria?

3. What is the difference between sex and gender?

4. What are the most common comorbidities with gender dysphoria?

CHAPTER 11

Disruptive, Impulse-Control, and Conduct Disorders

LEARNING OBJECTIVES

1. Gain a basic understanding of the causes, prevalence and comorbidities of the disruptive, impulse-control, and conduct disorders.

2. Become familiar with the criteria for the disruptive, impulse-control, and conduct disorders.

3. Be able to differentially diagnose the disruptive, impulse-control, and conduct disorders.

Characteristics of the Disorders

The chapter on disruptive, impulse-control, and conduct disorders is new to the DSM-5 (APA, 2013). The disorders in this chapter were previously part of other chapters in the DSM-IV-TR (APA, 2000), including disorders usually first diagnosed in infancy, childhood, or adolescence (eliminated from DSM-5) and impulse control disorders not elsewhere classified. The DSM-5 disorders in this category include oppositional defiant disorder, conduct disorder, intermittent explosive disorder, pyromania, and kleptomania.

Pyromania and kleptomania are typically first identified by law enforcement officials and thus will not be addressed in this chapter.

Oppositional defiant disorder (ODD) is a disruptive behavior disorder that is characterized by angry and/or irritable mood, argumentative or defiant behavior, or vindictiveness that lasts for at least 6 months. Individuals with ODD often have trouble controlling their tempers and are often seen as disobedient (APA, 2013).

Conduct disorder (CD) is characterized by behaviors that violate the rights of others, social norms, or rules (APA, 2013). Individuals with conduct disorder tend to have a long history of violation of rules and antisocial behaviors. They typically do not have regard for the welfare of others. People with CD often do not see their behaviors as causing a problem and tend to blame others for their mood and behaviors. While at times they may verbalize remorse for their behaviors, they often do not experience feelings of guilt. In addition, people with CD may view others as threatening without evidence of such feelings. Consequently, these individuals may exhibit seemingly unprovoked aggression.

Intermittent explosive disorder (IED) is characterized by impulsive aggressive episodes that are quick and usually triggered by a situation of threat (APA, 2013). The reaction is out of proportion to the stressor or threat. The behaviors include verbal or physical aggression toward people, animal, or property (that does not result in damage). There is typically a very rapid onset with little to no warning.

History

The concept of disruptive behavioral disorders was conceived over 50 years ago, though there have been changes to our biopsychosocial understanding of them. Disruptive behavior disorders were first discussed in the DSM-II (APA, 1972). They were based on reactive behaviors of delinquent boys: runaway unsocialized aggressive and group delinquent. The diagnosis was unreliable because there were no diagnostic criteria. The DSM-III (APA, 1980) introduced oppositional defiant disorder (ODD) and conduct disorder (CD) as diagnoses. The criteria for ODD included violation of rules, rights of others, and/or societal norms; temper tantrums; provocative behaviors; and stubbornness. The DSM-III had specific criteria for ODD, with two of five symptoms being required for a diagnosis. However, the validity of the diagnosis faced criticism (and for some still does), with some saying that it was pathologizing normal child behavior (Loeber et al., 2000). CD was defined as a more severe behavioral disorder that involved the violation of the rights of others and societal norms. The two disorders (CD and ODD) could not be diagnosed comorbidly, because it was believed that a diagnosis of CD would encompass the behaviors of ODD. To address the issue of potentially pathologizing normal childhood behavior, the DSM-III-R (APA, 1987) added two additional criteria: spitefulness/vindictiveness and angry/resentful attitude to the diagnosis of ODD. They also added language stating that the occurrence must be out of proportion to the developmental age of the child and required four of eight symptoms that were present for 6 months or more. A diagnosis of CD required 3 of 15 symptoms within the past year, with at least one present for the past 6 months. Both diagnoses had an addition of a severity specifier (mild, moderate, severe). Other than changes to the number of criteria, there were few changes to the diagnosis of ODD in the DSM-IV (APA, 1994). The DSM-IV conduct disorder diagnosis included two subtypes: childhood onset or adolescent onset. The DSM-5 (APA, 2013) divides the criteria for ODD into three categories: angry/irritable mood, argumentative/defiant behavior, and vindictiveness. In addition, the criterion that criteria for conduct disorder or antisocial personality disorder are not met was dropped. Conduct disorder now includes specifiers of "with limited prosocial emotions," "lack of remorse or guilt," "callous lack of empathy," "unconcerned about performance," and "shallow or deficient affect."

Intermitted explosive disorder (IED), as it is called today, was first introduced in the DSM-III (APA, 1980); however, variations of the disorder have been in the DSM since the first edition in 1952. The DSM-I (APA, 1952) called the disorder *passive-aggressive personality, aggressive type*. It was characterized by persistent reactions to frustration, temper tantrums, and destructive behaviors. The disorder was renamed *explosive personality* in the DSM-II (APA, 1972) and was characterized by intermittent violent behavior, aggressiveness, overresponse to pressures, and generalized excitability. The DSM-III (1980) included IED, but the criteria were not without issue. Individuals who were diagnosed with the disorder could not exhibit aggression in between episodes, which essentially ruled out the majority of people who would now meet the criteria (Cocarro, 2012). The DSM-IV (APA, 2000) had three criteria for IED: discreet episodes of aggressive impulses that result in assaultive acts or destruction of property, the aggressiveness is out of proportion of the stressor, and not accounted for by another disorder. The DSM-5 (APA, 2013) has two separate criteria for aggressive outbursts. The first criterion is episodes of verbal aggression toward people, animals, or property that does not cause physical damage and that occurs on average twice per week for 3 months. The second criterion is physical aggression that results in damage of property or physical harm to people or animals that occurs three times within 12 months.

Etiology

The cause of the disruptive, impulse-control, and conduct disorders is likely a combination of genetics, neurobiology, and environment. Twin studies have found that approximately 50% of the variance in conduct disorder is attributed to genetics and approximately 61% in ODD (Polderman et al., 2015). Research has also indicated that low levels of neurotransmitters such as monoamine oxidase and serotonin and dopamine have been associated with CD (Conner & Lochman, 2010) and ODD (Salvatore & Dick, 2018). Males are two to three times more likely to have a diagnosis of conduct disorders (Patel et al., 2018).

A number of environmental factors can lead to the development of CD and ODD. Prenatal exposure to toxins such as tobacco and alcohol have been linked to both CD and ODD (Baer et al., 2003). Parental substance abuse (Su et al., 2018), psychiatric illness of a parent, marital conflict, child abuse, and exposure to parental antisocial behavior all increase the risk of both disorders (Kazdin, 1997). Absent parenting and inconsistent discipline have also been shown to be a risk factor (Dishion & Kavanagh, 2003) largely due to the fact that the child does not experience consistency between behaviors and consequences. Although conduct disorder is found in all socioeconomic levels, it seems to be more prevalent in lower socioeconomic groups (Patel et al., 2018). The external environment such as congested or violent neighborhoods, deviant peer groups, and peer rejection are also risk factors for both CD and ODD (Frick, 2006).

Family and twin studies indicate approximately a 34% familial rate of IED (Coccaro, 2012). IED has been linked to a history of childhood trauma such as trauma to a family member or friend (Fincham et al., 2009) or childhood maltreatment (Dodge et al., 1990). Recent research has indicated that individuals with IED have reduced emotional intelligence. People with IED have been shown to have altered serotonin functioning and increased activation of the amygdala and reduced activation of the orbitofrontal cortex (Coccaro et al., 2015).

Prevalence and Comorbidities

The prevalence of ODD is approximately 3.3%, though some reports state that the prevalence is as high as 16% (Canino et al., 2010; Loeber et al., 2000). ODD is more common among children from lower socioeconomic status and is more common in boys in childhood, with the gender difference resolving in adolescence (Loeber et al.,

2000). A recent study has indicated that ODD is less common in rural areas and less prevalent among those whose mothers had a master's degree (Mohammadi et al., 2020). Research indicates that 71.4% (Mohammadi et al., 2020) to 92.4% (Nock et al., 2007) of people diagnosed with ODD have another mental health disorder, such as separation anxiety disorder (20.3%), generalized anxiety disorder (14.9%), depressive disorders (13.9%), and CD (11.5%) (Mohammadi et al., 2020). Approximately 14% to 40% of children with ODD will also have a diagnosis of attention deficit hyperactivity disorder (ADHD), with the ADHD likely preceding the ODD (Loeber, et al., 2000).

The lifetime prevalence of CD is approximately 12% in males and 7% in females (Nock et al., 2006). The median age of onset is approximately 11.6 years of age. CD can occur in childhood, with rates of 2% to 5% in children between 5 and 12 years of age and 5% to 9% in adolescents between the ages of 13 and 18 years. Although CD is more common in boys, the gender difference is small in children younger than 5 years of age. CD is comorbid with a number of mental health disorder, including ADHD (up to 41%), depression (up to 46%), anxiety disorders (up to 41%) (Patel et al., 2018), and substance use disorders (38%) (Castel et al., 2006).

The lifetime prevalence of IED is approximately 6.9% in the United States (Ortega, et al., 2008). There is a lower prevalence in some regions, such as Asia and the Middle East. This is likely because questions about aggressive behaviors are not asked about on questionnaires or that aggressive behaviors are less likely to be present due to cultural factors (Coccaro, 2012). IED is more common in males by a ratio of about 2:1 (Kessler et al., 2006). Approximately 66% of those with IED will have a comorbid disorder. The most common lifetime comorbid disorders are personality disorders (91%). The most commonly comorbid personality disorder with IED is antisocial personality disorder (32%), followed by borderline personality disorder (20%), paranoid personality disorder (17%), obsessive-compulsive personality disorder (17%), and narcissistic personality disorder (14%). In terms of the nonpersonality disorders, IED is highly comorbid with anxiety disorders (59%) substance use disorders (41%), depressive disorders (39%), bipolar disorder (17%) and posttraumatic stress disorder (12%) (Coccaro, 2019).

With many disorders, such as depressive and anxiety, the individual's emotions are internalized; however, in the disruptive, impulse-control, and conduct disorders, the individuals are externalizing their emotions, directing them toward other individuals, objects, or animals. ADHD, which is classified as a neurodevelopment disorder, is often categorized as a disruptive behavioral disorder. The comorbidity of IED with disruptive disorders (including ADHD) is approximately 10% to 19% in adolescents and 5% to 14% in adults. ADHD typically has an earlier onset then IED, which suggests that ADHD may actually increase the likelihood of developing IED later in life. However, only about 25% of those with ADHD will have lifetime comorbid IED, which indicates that the majority of those with ADHD will not go on to develop IED (Radwan & Coccaro, 2020).

Course and Prognosis

ODD does not have a "typical course"; however, evidence suggests that approximately 70% of those with ODD will have symptom resolution by age 18 (Nock et al., 2007). The diagnosis can persist into adulthood with earlier onset and males being at higher risk of severe symptoms. Antisocial personality disorder is considered to be a more severe, adult version of conduct disorder. Children with both ODD and CD are at an increased risk of developing antisocial personality disorder (Steiner & Remsing, 2007).

CD is associated with a poor prognosis, particularly if the onset is before age 10. CD diagnosed in childhood may be a predictor of significant issues in adolescence and adulthood, including mental health issues or substance abuse issues; legal, academic and occupation problems; and school dropout (Odgers et al., 2007; 2008). Children younger than 11 years of age have a five times greater rate of psychiatric readmission than adolescents (Patel et al., 2018). Children from low-income families are 1.5 times more likely to have a psychiatric admission as compared to children from high-income families. In addition, these children have 11 times higher odds of having comorbid psychosis (Patel et al., 2018). Persistence of the disorder is high; 50% to 80% of boys with a diagnosis will retain the diagnosis 3 to 4 years later (Lahey et al., 2002). A New Zealand study found that boys who had CD prior to adolescence were 3 times more likely to have an anxiety or depressive disorder, 8 times more likely to be homeless, and 25 times more likely to attempt suicide by the age of 32 as compared to boys without CD (Odgers et al., 2007).

IED is a chronic disorder with an average age of onset of about 13 to 21 years. The duration of the disorder ranges from about 12 to 16 years or, if untreated, an entire lifetime (Coccaro et al., 2004; Kessler et al., 2006; McElroy et al., 1998). What is interesting about IED is that there is typically no prodromal period. This means that there is no aggression or agitation leading up to the explosive episode. The individual seems fine one minute and is throwing a temper tantrum the next. The aggressive outbursts are typically directed toward someone who is close to the individuals and is typically provoked by a minor provocation.

Cultural and Gender-Related Considerations

Research has indicated ethnic minorities, particularly Latinx individuals, have lower rates of ODD and CD (Wiesner et al., 2015). One possible reason for the lower rates may be cultural values. The values such as *respeto* and *simpatia* may result in the acceptability of behaviors in the Latinx culture that would not be accepted in others.

Historically the behavioral disorders have been considered to be a problem that primarily impacted males. The research surrounding the gender differences of behavioral disorders is inconsistent. Some population-based studies have indicated that ODD is indeed more common among preadolescent males (Munkvold et al., 2009); however, the rates become fairly equal after puberty. A study of CD in Dutch children aged 4 to 18 years found the rates to be twice as high for boys than for girls (van Lier et al., 2007). A study in Finland found no gender differences in ODD or CD symptoms, but girls had higher rates of comorbid disorders (Munkvold et al., 2011). Interestingly, although the rates for ODD and CD are lower for girls, research has indicated that when girls are diagnosed their symptoms tend to be more severe (Munkvold et al., 2011). One explanation for inconsistent findings surrounding gender and the disruptive disorders may be due to informant discrepancies. Assessment of symptoms of the disorders relies on parents and teachers. There is often inconsistency between the two sources, particularly if the child has comorbid disorders such as ADHD or anxiety.

Diagnosis and Assessment

For a diagnosis of ODD, at least four symptoms of angry/irritable mood (loss of temper, easily annoyed, resentful), argumentative/defiant behavior (such as, arguing with adults, refusing to follow rules, deliberately annoying others, blaming others for their mistakes) and/or vindictiveness (APA, 2013). The diagnosis contains specifiers of mild, moderate, or severe. Note that many of these behaviors are a normal part of childhood and adolescence: the "terrible twos," puberty, and transitioning to middle or high school are often times when children will act out. Most children go through phases where they do not like one or both of their parents or any authority figure. Again, this is a normal developmental process. For a diagnosis of ODD, the symptoms must be present for 6 months and, most important, not be within the realm of normal behavior. This does not, of course, mean that the symptoms or behaviors should be ignored; parenting skills and behavior management are effective strategies for intervening with these behaviors. However, this can present a problem when working with parents. Raising children is difficult, and many parents want a quick fix. However, it is very important that parents are made aware that these disorders are behavioral and will not be cured with a pill. It takes work from both the parents and the child (with the assistance of a mental health professional).

For a diagnosis of CD, the individual must meet three criteria in 12 months and at least one within the past 6 months. The criteria are broken down into aggression toward people or animals (fighting, intimidating, stealing, being cruel), destruction of property, deceitfulness, theft, and/or serious violation of rules. There are a number of specifiers for this disorder, including age of onset (childhood or adolescent), severity (mild, moderate, or severe), and whether the individual has limited prosocial emotions (lack of remorse or guilt, callousness, lack of concern about performance, or shallow affect) (APA, 2013). As with ODD, is it important to be able to distinguish between normal adolescent behaviors and disordered ones. Children without CD will not usually harm individuals or destroy property, and if they do, the behaviors are isolated and usually a reaction to a stressor, such as bullying or family situations.

For a diagnosis of IED, the aggressive outbursts must occur at least twice weekly for 3 months *or* there must be three outbursts that involve harm to people, animals, or property occurring over a 12-month period (APA, 2013).

It is important to remember that impulsive and/or aggressive behavior can occur in the context of a number of disorders, including, but not limited to, bipolar disorder, ADHD, and, of course, CD. Therefore, clinicians may be reluctant to diagnose IED in absence of other diagnoses (Cocarro et al., 2015). If the aggression or violence occurs as a result of a depressive disorder or psychotic disorder or as part of an adjustment disorder, IED would not be diagnosed. Aggression or violence in absence of a diagnosis of IED may be warranted.

Adam

Adam is a 12-year-old White cisgender male in seventh grade who has been called to the principal's office for a meeting with the school social worker, his parents (Bonnie and Michael), and the principal. Adam's parents have been divorced for 3 years and have a cordial relationship. They have joint custody of Adam. His parents live within a mile of each other so that he can easily ride his bike between the two houses. His mother is remarried to a Black woman named Angela. His dad has been dating a White woman for the past year, and she has recently moved in. Adam is at risk of being expelled from school as a result of his behaviors over the past year. At the beginning of his sixth-grade year, Adam stopped hanging out with his friends from elementary school and began hanging out with kids in seventh and eighth grade who have a history of truancy, suspected alcohol and drug use, and school detentions and suspensions. The teacher has reported that, over the past two semesters, Adam has been talking back to him in class, calling him by his first name, telling other students to "shut up," and making fun of a developmentally disabled classmate. The teacher has spoken to Adam about his behaviors and, reportedly, Adam laughed in his face. Adam has not been turning in his homework, and his grades have gone from As to Ds. He has been given suspension four times over the past school year. Adam has reportedly said being suspended is better than going to school. While home on one of his suspensions, his mother stated that he snuck out of the house to meet his friends down the street. That evening, two of the neighbors reported that their mailboxes had been blown up with M-80 fireworks, and Adam was recorded on a doorbell camera, leaving the scene. The neighbors did not press charges. Bonnie has reported that she just "does not know what to do with him." He ignores his curfew and refuses to do his chores; he pesters the dog by poking at him, taking his food, and waking him up when he is napping. His father reports that Adam does not have a curfew at his house but "rarely stays out all night." His parents confirm that Adam is physically healthy, receives regular checkups, and that there is no history of mental illness in the family. The precipitating event that led to the current meeting was Adam's threatening to punch a classmate for "looking at him funny" and being truant from school three times over the past month.

Diagnostic Impression

As reported by Adam's teacher and his parents Adam has demonstrated a year of behaviors that demonstrates aggression to others (telling a classmate to shut up, threatening to punch a classmate, bullying a classmate with a developmental disability), destruction of property (blowing up mailboxes), and violation of rules (breaking curfew and truancy from school). These behaviors have been present for over a year and have caused significant impairment both at home and school. Because these behaviors began in adolescence, and he does not have a history of ODD in childhood, he has a better prognosis.

Diagnostic Conclusion

Conduct disorder, adolescent onset, moderate

DIFFERENTIAL DIAGNOSIS I: OPPOSITIONAL DEFIANT DISORDER

Rationale: Although Adam is clearly demonstrating behaviors that indicate conflict with others, including adults and authority figures, he does not exhibit any angry or irritable mood, which is typical (though not required) in ODD. In addition, Adam has been aggressive to others and destroyed property, both indicative of CD.

DIFFERENTIAL DIAGNOSIS II: ADJUSTMENT DISORDER WITH DISTURBANCE OF CONDUCT

Rationale: Adam has certainly experienced some significant life events over the past few years (advancing to middle school, parents divorcing, mother remarrying a woman, dad's girlfriend moving in). However, his symptoms have persisted for over a year and began after 3 months of the onset of events, and most important, he meets full criteria for CD, ruling out adjustment disorder.

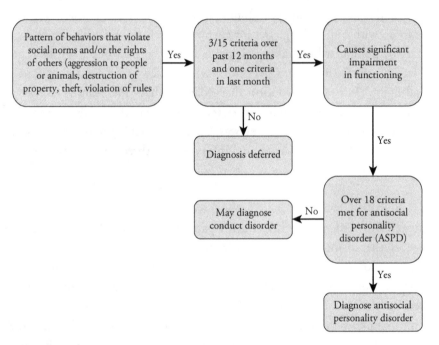

FIGURE 11.1 Differential Diagnosis for CD

Biopsychosocial
BIOLOGICAL

Adam is 12 years old and therefore likely going through puberty. The change in hormones may be partially responsible for his behaviors and should be considered during treatment.

PSYCHOLOGICAL

Although Adam is exhibiting significant behavioral issues, there is no evidence of any disturbances with affect such as depressive episodes. It is still important to explore Adam's feelings surrounding his parents' divorce and subsequent new partners.

SOCIAL

There have been significant changes in Adam's support system. Although his parents are cordial to each other since the divorce, they both have new significant others and Adam splits his time between two houses. He also has a new peer group who engage in negative behaviors. Treatment will need to not only need to involve Adam's parents but also his parents' significant others. It will also be important for Adam to attend group events such as sports teams, clubs, or support groups in order to form positive peer groups.

Andy

Andy is an 8-year-old Latinx/Hispanic cisgender girl who was brought to the community mental health center by her mother, Rosa. Rosa reports that Andy lives with her mother, Rosa, her father, Hector her sister Nancy, and their dog Winston. Andy is currently in third grade. Rosa reports that she is at her "wits end" with Andy. For the past year Andy has been "defiant." When asked to do her chores, Andy will either flat out refuse or lie and say that she did her chores but did not. If asked to get up off the couch she will start yelling, saying to leave her alone. Andy sits in front of the television all day and seems to just "zone out." At dinner time Andy will purposely chew very loudly to annoy her older sister (age 10). She will poke at her sister to the point of a verbal altercation which then in turn leads to yelling on the part of Rosa and Hector. Andy feeds the dog from the table despite the fact that she knows this is not allowed. Rosa reports that Andy "used to be such a good girl" and that she earned good grades and had many friends. Andy's grades have slipped to Ds, and she no longer spends time with her friends. Andy can be heard watching television late into the night. She refused to turn it off when requested. Rosa states that she has not had any reports of negative behaviors from the school; however, the entire family tiptoes around Andy in fear of "setting her off." Rosa also reports that she and Hector have been arguing, typically over how to discipline Andy. Rosa reports that there is "so much tension in the house". She stated that it seems as though everyone is angry or unhappy all the time. She feels that this is mostly due to Andy. During the intake Andy had her arms crossed across her chest and was answering questions when asked but typically in just a few words. When asked about her friends, Andy said that her friends would not want to hang out with her, she is "useless," and they do not like her anyway. Andy reported that she is no longer doing her homework because she cannot concentrate on anything.

Diagnostic Impression

Andy is exhibiting an irritable angry mood as evidenced by her yelling and being "set off." She is deliberately annoying her sister and refusing to follow the rules of the house (doing her chores and feeding the dog from the table). Her behaviors are not only impacting her family but also her grades and her social life.

In addition, Andy is having difficulty concentrating and sleeping. She no longer spends time with her friends and feels useless. She is also spending all of her time in front of the television "zoning out." These symptoms combined with her irritability indicate that she may be suffering from depression.

Diagnostic Conclusion

Diagnosis I: Oppositional defiant disorder, mild (Because Andy is impaired in only one setting, at home, the specifier of mild is most appropriate.)

Diagnosis II: Major depressive disorder, single episode, mild

DIFFERENTIAL DIAGNOSIS I: CONDUCT DISORDER

Andy does exhibit defiant behaviors, but there is no indication that she violates the rights of others or any destruction of property.

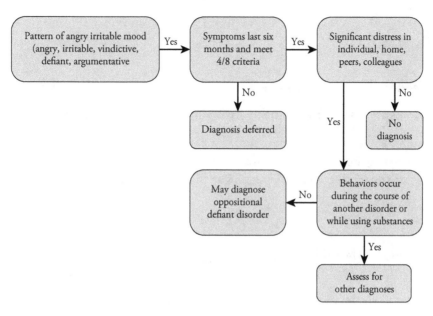

FIGURE 11.2 Differential diagnosis for ODD

Biopsychosocial

BIOLOGICAL

Although there is no mention of any biological issues, it is important to consider that Andy is 8 years old and may be approaching puberty, which may account at least, in part, to her symptoms of ODD or major depressive disorder (MDD). A physical exam and bloodwork are also recommended to rule out and physiological causes for her symptoms.

PSYCHOLOGICAL

Andy is suffering from depression, which may be, in part, due to the unrest within the family. In addition to behavioral interventions, it is important to address the possible reasons for the depressive symptoms.

SOCIAL

Andy seems to have a supportive family who should be involved in her treatment for both disorders. Andy had friends in the past, indicating that she has the social skill necessary to form the bonds of friendship.

TERMINOLOGY

cisgender   Sense of personal identity and gender correspond with birth sex.

kleptomania   A recurrent urge to steal without regard for need or for profit.

pyromania   An impulse control disorder in which the individual is unable to resist starting fires. Setting the fires releases tension and anxiety. The fires are *not* set for financial gain (i.e., insurance money) or revenge.

REFLECTION QUESTIONS

1. Parental substance abuse, psychiatric illness, marital conflict, child abuse, inconsistent parenting, and exposure to parental antisocial behavior are risk factors for which diagnosis?

2. In order to diagnose ODD or CD in childhood or adolescence, the social worker must assess what aspect of the behavior?

3. Which diagnosis would the social worker need to assess for emotional intelligence?

4. Children diagnosed with both ODD and CD are at increased risk for developing which diagnosis in adulthood?

CHAPTER 12

Substance-Related and Addictive Disorders

Characteristics of the Disorders

The substance-related and addictive disorders chapter in the DSM-5 (APA, 2013) outlines the criteria for substance-related disorders for 10 different substances. This chapter also includes gambling addiction, which is new to the DSM-5. For each substance, the criteria for use disorder, intoxication, withdrawal, other substance-induced disorders, and unspecified substance-related disorder are addressed. The criteria for the use disorders include (but are not limited to) using larger amounts or for longer than expected, unsuccessful attempts to cut back, cravings, use despite being harmful or causing psychosocial problems, tolerance, and withdrawal. Use disorder has two specifiers regarding remission: "in early remission" and "in sustained remission."

Remission is based on the Alcoholics Anonymous (AA) model, where 12 months is sustained remission and fewer than 12 months is early remission. There is a third specifier of "in a controlled environment." The assumption is that those who are in a controlled environment (prison, jail, inpatient facility) will not have access to drugs. The final specifier is severity (mild, moderate, severe), which is determined by the number of total criteria they meet (of the 11). The intoxication criteria and withdrawal symptoms differ for each drug (APA, 2013).

History

The DSM-I (APA, 1952) conceptualized substance use disorder as most commonly arising from a personality disorder. It did, however, permit some exceptions. For those with alcohol use issues, it was stated "there is a well-established addiction to alcohol without recognizable underlying disorder" (APA, 1952). It also allowed for a dual diagnosis of personality disorder and addiction. In 1951, the World Health Organization (WHO) and the American Medical Association (AMA) declared alcoholism a medical disorder in 1959 (Robinson & Adinoff, 2016). The DSM-II (APA, 1968) did not include criteria for alcoholism, but it did recognize addiction as a distinct disorder even if it was triggered by another underlying mental health condition. The DSM-III had three categories of alcoholism: episodic (intoxication 4 times a year), habitual (under the influence 12 times a year), and addiction (defined as being dependent) (APA, 1980). The DSM-III also eliminated the term *alcoholic* and set the substance use disorders apart from the other mental health conditions. The terms *abuse* (pathological use) and *dependence* (tolerance or withdrawal) were adopted. The DSM-III-R (APA, 1987) moved some of the criteria that were formerly in the abuse category into the dependence category. It also distinguished physiological dependence from a diagnosis of dependence. The DSM-IV (APA, 1994) further clarified the difference between physiological dependence and substance dependence by specifying that tolerance and/or withdrawal were not necessary for a diagnosis of substance dependence. In addition, specifiers of "with physiological dependence" and "without physiological dependence" were added. The DSM-IV-TR (APA, 2000) added minor revisions further clarifying the differences between abuse and dependence.

Some significant changes were made from the DSM-IV-TR (APA, 2000) to the DSM-5 (APA, 2013). The DSM-5 (APA, 2013) removed the separate categories of abuse and dependence and created one overarching category of substance use. The DSM-5 also added the severity specifiers, with severity being determined by the number of criteria (of a total possible 11) the individual meets: 2 to 3 symptoms indicate mild severity, 4 to 5 moderate severity, and 6 or more severe. Another significant change was the title of the chapter, which is now "Substance-Related and Addictive Disorders." Although the term *addiction* is not part of the diagnostic criteria due to the stigma surrounding the word, it is used to refer to behavioral addiction—in the case of this chapter—gambling addiction, which is a new to the DSM-5.

Etiology

The substance use disorders are caused by a combination of genetics and environmental factors. The genetic risk of substance use disorders is approximately 40% to 70%; however, the environment modifies this risk significantly. Epigenetics refers to the study of how genes are read and acted on by the cells in the body. Chronic stress, trauma, and/or drug exposure can alter the functioning of genes that control neural circuits and influence behavior (Peña et al., 2014).

Neurobiological research indicates that alcohol and other drugs have a potent effect on adolescent brains. The brain does not fully develop until around 21 to 25 years, with the prefrontal cortex being the last part to develop. This area of the brain is responsible for reward, reasoning, and inhibition. Substance abuse in adolescent years can lead to increased vulnerability to substance use disorders (Winters et al., 2014) and other mental illnesses (Barkus et al., 2010). It could also be true that children and adolescents diagnosed with mental health disorders have an increased risk of development of substance use disorders, particularly the internalizing disorders such as depression and anxiety (O'Neil et al., 2011).

A number of neurotransmitters have been implicated in the development of substance use disorders, including dopamine, serotonin, glutamate, GABA, and norepinephrine. For example, dopamine has been implicated in the way in which stress leads to the vulnerability to substance use disorders. Stress is mediated through the hypothalamic-pituitary-adrenal (HPA) axis, which influences the parts of the brain that influence control motivation. Hyperactivity of the HPA axis caused by stress alters dopamine signaling, which may reinforce the effect of drugs (National Institute on Drug Abuse [NIDA], 2020).

Prevalence and Comorbidities

Approximately 17% of individuals (44 million people) in the United States over the age of 12 reported the use of a drug or heavy alcohol use in the past year, and 8% of these individuals (21.4 million) met the criteria for a substance use disorder

(McClellan, 2017). Of those who met the criteria for substance use disorder, 6.4% was for heavy drinking, 1.6% for marijuana use, and 1.1% for opioid use. Although these percentages may seem small, the actual numbers of individuals are 17 million, 4.2 million, and 2.5 million, respectively.

According to a study conducted in 2017, marijuana was the most frequently used drug over the past year (35 million past users), and marijuana use has increased significantly in recent years, most likely due to legalization, either medicinally or recreationally (McClellan, 2017). At the time of this publication, 15 states and the District of Columbia (1 state is still pending) have legalized recreational marijuana, and an additional 19 have legalized medical marijuana. Research suggests that the potency levels of cannabis have increased. For example, the average THC potency in 2017 was 17.1% (Chandra et al., 2019), as compared to 4% in 1990s (Stuyt, 2018)). The higher potency raises concerns about potential adverse effects, such as accidents and medical and mental health issues.

In 2017, in the United States, benzodiazepines were found to be the third most common misused illicit substance (2.2% of the population) with marijuana (15%) and prescription opioids (4.1%) being the first and second. Interestingly, although misuse is common, diagnosis of sedative-hypnotic or anxiolytic-related disorder is relatively low at 0.3% of the population. One explanation for this is that those who were misusing quit by 3-year follow-up (Votaw et al., 2019).

The United States is in the midst of an opioid crisis, with prescription rates quadrupling over the past 15 years (Hedegaard et al., 2015). In 2019 it was estimated that approximately 10.5 million people in the United States had misused opioids (Substance Abuse and Mental Health Services Administration [SAMHSA], 2020). Overdose of both prescription and illicit opioids is the leading cause of deaths in Americans under the age of 50 (Hedegaard et al., 2015). Nearly 50,000 people in the United States have died from opioid-involved overdoses (National Institutes of Health [NIH], 2021).

Researchers from the WHO's World Mental Health Survey (Degenhardt et al., 2019) investigated the lifetime and past-year prevalence of drug use disorders (DUDs) using the criteria from the DSM-IV-TR and found that the average lifetime prevalence of illicit drug use for all countries combined was 24.8% (ranging from Iraq at 1.3% and Italy at 66.8%). In terms of DSM-IV diagnoses, the average combined rate is 3.5%. It was also reported that there was a higher lifetime prevalence of DUDs in higher-income countries (Degenhardt et al., 2019).

Substance use disorders are comorbid with several other mental health disorders. Approximately 50% of those with mental illness during their lives will also experience a substance use disorder. It is thought that individuals with mental health disorders may use drugs as a form of self-medication. Although in the short term the drugs may provide relief from the symptoms of the mental health illness, they can also make the symptoms worse. Individuals tend to use mood congruent drugs, which means they will use drugs that match their moods. For example, an individual who is suffering from depression will likely consume alcohol (a depressant) or take a benzodiazepine. Individuals who are manic are more likely to use cocaine, which, after a period of time, may exacerbate the symptoms (Post & Kalivas, 2013).

Course and Prognosis

Onset of substance use is typically before the age of 17 (74%), and research indicates that 10.2% of respondents reported using at 11 years of age or younger (Poudel & Gautam, 2017). Early onset of drug use is predictive of long-term impairments, including substance use disorder (Chen et al., 2005), conduct disorder, risky sexual behavior, and problems at school with family and friends. A recent study found significant differences in demographic and use-related characteristics of individuals who had early onset substance use. A higher percentage of early onset users were male, unemployed, were currently using both illegal and prescription drugs, and used substances multiple times a day (Poudel & Gautam, 2017). In addition, respondents who reported using substances prior to age 18 were more likely to have physical health, psychosocial, and behavioral issues and more problems within the family, work/ school, and social systems. Note that although there is a high prevalence of those who use substances at a young age, only about 10% of the population will go on to develop a disorder. It is also important to remember that substance use does not necessarily translate into a disorder. Substance use disorder is a clinical mental health disorder, and as with all disorders, there needs to be impairment in functioning in order to be diagnosed, *regardless of substance being used.*

Research indicates that in 2018 more than 21 million people over the age of 12 years needed substance abuse treatment yet only 1.4% (3.7 million people) received treatment. Of those who did not receive treatment, only 5.7% felt that they actually needed it (SAMHSA, 2018). The definition of recovery from substance use disorder is not as straightforward as with other mental health diagnoses. An individual with other mental health diagnoses is seen as being recovered when symptoms remit or diminish and the level of functioning increases. Abstinence is the most traditional treatment for individuals with substance use disorders, with the goal being that the individual remains free of any substances (Corrigan et al., 2019). Relapse is a common component of the abstinence recovery process. Approximately 70% to 80% of clients will return to substance use (Giordano et al., 2013). More recently, harm reduction has emerged as an accepted treatment for substance use disorders. The harm reduction approach focuses on recovery as a process, as is the case with mental illness, rather than an outcome. The goal is decreasing the negative impact of substance use as opposed to eliminating the behaviors (Hawk et al., 2017). Some feel that harm reduction is helpful to those who are overwhelmed by their disorder and cannot fully commit to abstinence. As with all mental health disorders, treatment must be individualized—there is no "one size fits all" treatment.

Cultural and Gender-Related Considerations

Research had indicated that lifetime rates among Native Americans adults is typically lower when compared with other Americans (Spicer et al., 2003; Beals et al., 2003; Mitchell et al., 2003). However people who are Native American who do drink often do some more often with heavy episodic episodes. Other drug use patterns are similar between Native American and other Americans. Epidemiological evidence indicates higher rates and earlier onset of alcohol use among American Indian/American Native adolescents compared with other adolescents (Beauvais et al., 2008; Kunitz, 2008). Those youth who have droppedd out of school and are living on a reservation have the highest rate of use (Beauvais et al., 2008). The rates of substance use among Black/ African Americans and White Americans are similar, (approximately 10%) but lower for Latinx/Hispanics (Breslau et al., 2005). The exception being Latino/Hispanics who believe in "Machismo" (Comas-Diaz, 2019). Asian groups have the lowest rates of substance use (4.2%); this may in part due to a negative physiological response called flushing (characterized as a reddening of the skin) that occurs when several Asian groups (Japanese, Chinese, and Koreans) drink alcohol (Mirin et al., 2002). Cultural traditions in the family often dictate whether the use of alcohol is acceptable and to what degree. For example, if cultural traditions dictate that alcohol should not be consumed, the individual who drinks is more likely to experience impairment in family functioning than those in cultures that accept the consumption of alcohol.

Studies have indicated that lesbian and bisexual women and gay and bisexual men have used alcohol and drugs at greater rates than heterosexual women and men (Drabble et al., 2005; Cochran et al., 2004; McCabe et al., 2009). Research suggests that LGBTQIA+ individuals use substances as a way to cope with societal oppression and self-hatred as a result of discrimination (Green & Feinstein, 2012; Matthews & Selvidge, 2005). There is a lack of substance use treatment facilities that offer special programs for LGBTQIA+ individuals, in fact only 10% of treatment facilities offer programs for sexual minority clients (Senreich, 2012). LGBTQIA+ youth are at risk for substance use disorders as well. A study in 2000 (Hicks, 2000) found that LGBT youth are more likely than their heterosexual peers to engage in alcohol use (Almeida et al., 2009). A study in 2010 found that approximately 85% of self-identifying lesbian, gay or bisexual students reported using alcohol in the past month, 81% reported heavy episodic drinking at least weekly (Reed et al., 2010).

Diagnosis and Assessment

What is most important to remember when assessing for substance use disorders is that (as with all disorders) the individual must experience impairment to be diagnosed. A client may be seeking treatment for another disorder and disclose that they are using an illicit substance on occasion and it is not causing any impairment. Without impairment there is no diagnosis. This can be an ethical dilemma for new clinicians: knowing that an individual is using an illegal substance that has the *potential* for harm but being unable to diagnose. Not diagnosing the substance use disorder does not mean, however, that it should not be addressed and that follow-up assessments cannot be made.

As mentioned earlier, substance use disorder includes specifiers regarding severity. The severity level is chosen by the number of criteria the individual meets for the disorder. There are also specifiers for remission. "Early remission" refers to an individual who once met full criteria for a use disorder but for the last 3 to 12 months has not. "Sustained remission" refers to an individual who has not met any criteria for substance use disorder for the past 12 months. If an individual still experiences cravings (but does not use), they are still considered to be in remission (APA, 2013).

Christopher

Christopher is a 53-year-old Latino/Hispanic male who has been unemployed for 3 years and is living with his elderly parents. He has never married and has one daughter, whom he had with his high school girlfriend. He and his ex-girlfriend coparent their daughter and have a cordial relationship but do not speak very often. Christopher completed high school, and he has held several different jobs as a meat cutter. Christopher grew up in a small rural town in Tennessee, where he lived with his parents and older brother. He describes himself as the "wallflower" of the family and never had many friends in school. He says that he spent most of his time with his dogs and cats. He states that he often felt more comfortable around animals than around people. Christopher does not have medical insurance and has not been to a primary care physician for 7 years. He is financially dependent on his parents, who are both in their 70s and are living on a fixed income. He reports that he has a few friends that he "hangs out with." He states that he used to go to the movies, bowling, and to the pub with them often. However, over the past few months he has not wanted to spend time with his friends. He shares that he feels lonely, sad, and useless. Christopher reports that he spends most of his days alone in his bedroom, watching TV. He says he can barely follow what is happening on TV because his "mind is all weird." He comes out only to eat and to check the mail. His parents keep asking him what is wrong with him; he appears to lack motivation or energy. He often thinks about the past and feels guilty about things he did and said many years ago. Christopher has a history of heavy drinking and self-medication with benzodiazepines (that he typically takes from his parents) that began when he was his 20s. He admits to occasions where he will have more than 20 beers in one evening, because it "takes more to get [him] drunk nowadays." He will then go home and take a "few benzos" to help him sleep. He has attempted to stop drinking and using the medications, but they help him "deal with the loneliness." He has admitted that he often wakes up with a "hangover." He has also stated that he feels guilty for drinking so much, because he lives with his parents, and money is tight for the family. He has attended AA meetings sporadically for the last 10 years but stopped attending due to feeling out of place at gatherings and anxious around new members. He says he is now motivated to be sober, due to his recent health complications, including heart disease and hypertension, as well as his fear of losing his life to drug use. Christopher has told his social worker that he is hesitant to return to work and integrate back into his community, for fear of relapsing, stating, "Things always go wrong when I go back out into the world." He was fired from his last job because he was drunk or hungover and missed too much work. Christopher has used drugs and alcohol to cope with his feelings and does not how to deal with his feelings without the alcohol and drugs. He reports that he sometimes gets aggressive when he drinks and has gotten into fights at bars.

Diagnostic Impression

Christopher exhibits a pattern of excessive alcohol use that has led to significant impairment, occupationally and socially. Christopher has stated that he has tried to stop drinking but has been unsuccessful. He has been fired from his job for his drinking; he has continued to drink, despite the issues it has caused in his life (health and social). He is reluctant to return to work, for fear of relapse. He is also experiencing withdrawal (hangovers) and tolerance (it takes him more to get drunk). Christopher meets six criteria; therefore, a diagnosis of *severe* is appropriate.

Christopher further reports feeling sad and no longer wanting to spend time with his friends. He has neither motivation nor energy and has excessive guilt. He also has difficulty concentrating (his mind is "all weird"). These feelings are impacting his relationships with his family and friends. He is reluctant to "go back into the world," because thing seem to go wrong when he does. Christopher meets the full criteria for major depressive disorder. He has reported that he has had periods when he would engage with his friends and he had a job; therefore, *recurrent* is most appropriate. *Moderate* is the most appropriate severity specifier, given the level of impairment.

Christopher reports that he has been taking benzodiazepines that were not prescribed to him. He reports that he has attempted to stop using benzodiazepines but has been unsuccessful. He has continued to use the drug, despite having health issues. Christopher meets two criteria; therefore, the severity specifier of *mild* is most appropriate.

Diagnostic Conclusion

Diagnosis: Alcohol use disorder, severe
Diagnosis: Major depressive disorder, recurrent episode, moderate
Diagnosis: Sedative-hypnotic or **anxiolytic**-related disorder, mild

DIFFERENTIAL DIAGNOSIS I: BIPOLAR DISORDER

Rationale: Christopher does not report any history of manic or hypomanic episodes; therefore, a diagnosis of bipolar disorder is not appropriate.

DIFFERENTIAL DIAGNOSIS II: DYSTHYMIA

Rationale: Although Christopher has been having depressive episodes for many years (likely since childhood), we are not seeing that the symptoms have a duration of more days than not of 2 years. In addition, his current symptoms indicate full criteria for major depressive disorder.

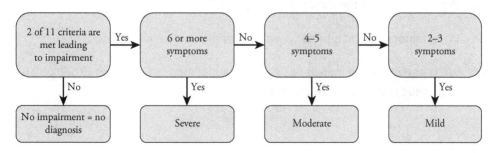

FIGURE 12.1   Differential diagnosis for substance use disorder

Biopsychosocial

BIOLOGICAL

Because of his level of drinking, his current health issues (cardiac), and mental health issues, it is important for Christopher to be evaluated by a health professional to determine if his physical health is contributing to his mental health, or vice versa. It is also important to determine if he is taking medication for his hypertension, if he is compliant with his medication, and if his medication can have adverse interactions with the alcohol and benzodiazepines.

PSYCHOLOGICAL

Christopher is suffering from a number of mental health issues. Christopher relies on alcohol and benzodiazepines to manage his mental health. It is important to support him in exploring healthy coping skills.

SOCIAL

Although Christopher lives with his parents, and they are concerned about him, he has limited interactions with his parents because he spends most of his day in his room. He is also stealing their medication. He has several friends, but due to his drinking and other mental health issues, he has not been in contact with them. As a child, he felt like he did not belong in his family and often felt more comfortable around animals. Further assessment is needed into his relationship with his daughter and his ex-girlfriend to determine if they could be a potential source of support during his recovery process.

REFLECTION QUESTIONS

1. What is meant by the term *mood congruent*?

2. What factors predict a better prognosis with substance use disorders?

3. What percentage of individuals who use substances prior to age 18 will go on to develop a substance use disorder?

CHAPTER 13

Borderline Personality Disorder

Characteristics of the Disorder

A personality disorder is an enduring pattern of inner experiences and behaviors that deviates significantly from social and cultural norms (APA, 2013). Personality disorders are pervasive and inflexible and are stable over time. As with all disorders, they must cause significant impact in functioning. The concept that an individual's personality can be disordered is controversial. This is because, unlike other disorders that are focused on specific aspects of an individual, such as behavior or mood, the focus of a personality disorder is on the whole person. The DSM-5 (APA, 2013) has general criteria for all personality disorders that include deviations from the norm in cognition, affect, interpersonal functioning, and/or impulse control. The DSM-5 has three clusters of personality disorder. Cluster A personality disorders involve thinking and behavior that appear eccentric or unusual to others. These disorders include paranoid personality disorder, schizoid personality disorder. and schizotypal personality disorder. Cluster B personality disorders are characterized by dramatic, overly emotional, or unpredictable thinking or behavior. Cluster B personality disorders include antisocial personality disorder, histrionic personality disorder, narcissistic personality disorder, and borderline personality disorders. Cluster C personality disorders are characterized by anxious, fearful thinking or behavior and include avoidant personality disorder, dependent personality disorder, and obsessive compulsive personality disorder. People with symptoms or diagnoses of borderline personality disorder often present in clinical settings. Borderline personality disorder is the most commonly treated personality disorder by mental health professionals, and therefore will be the focus of this chapter.

Borderline personality disorder is characterized by symptoms that span several domains. It is one of the most common, complex, and debilitating of the personality disorders. Symptoms include instability of affect; impulse control issues, often with intense anger; unstable self-image; and difficulties in interpersonal relationships. Individuals with borderline personality disorder experience rapid changes in mood and may engage is destructive and/or self-harming behaviors (Gunderson & Lyons-Ruth, 2008).

History

The term *borderline personality disorder* was coined in 1938 by Adolph Stern at New York's Mt. Sinai Hospital. The term was developed to categorize individuals who did not meet the criteria for neuroses or psychoses; they were on the borderline of both. In 1967, Otto Kernberg (1967) described borderline personality organization (BPO) as featuring the following behaviors:

- Split-thinking: Viewing things as being black and white, good or bad.

- Primitive idealization: Creating unrealistic figures who are seen as almighty or put on a pedestal.

- Projective identification: Having unconscious fantasies about their therapist or others.

- Denial: Reinforcing the splitting and causing the individual to be unable to see opposing views about a situation.

- Omnipotence of self: May be expressed by grandiosity.

The definition of borderline personality disorder was developed in the late 1970s. The criteria were developed to help distinguish patients with borderline personality disorder from those with major depressive disorder or schizophrenia (Gunderson, 2010). Initially, there were seven criteria for the disorder. Borderline personality disorder was added to the DSM-III (APA, 1980) with an "either" criterion for identity disturbance. The criteria in the DSM-IV (1994) remained the same, with an additional criterion added, "psychotic-like experiences." The criteria for borderline personality disorder have not changed in the DSM-5 (APA, 2013).

Etiology

The etiology of borderline personality disorder is complex and involves biological, social, and psychological factors. Like most mental health disorders, borderline personality disorder is thought to have a multifactorial cause resulting from the interplay of genetics and the environment.

Family studies have indicated that those with relatives diagnosed with borderline personality disorder are approximately four times more likely to have a diagnosis of borderline personality disorder (Gunderson et al., 2011). Twin studies have found the heritability rate to be between 35% (Torgersen et al., 2008) to nearly 67% (Torgersen et al., 2012).

Neuropeptides are small proteinlike molecules that enable neurons to communicate with each other. Oxytocin plays a key role in partnering and other prosocial behaviors. Research has indicated that a dysfunctional oxytocin system is related to borderline personality disorder (Herpertz & Bertsch, 2015). In the study, women with borderline personality disorder had lower levels of oxytocin, as compared to the control group. Oxytocin levels were also negatively correlated with a history of childhood trauma (Bertsch et al., 2013).

Serotonin is a neurotransmitter that has been associated with a number of neurobehavioral processes, including cognition, affect, and impulsivity. Serotonin synthesis issues have been associated with impaired decision making (Maurex et al., 2009) and suicidal ideation in people with borderline personality disorder (Zaboli et al., 2006). The serotonin transporter gene has also been implicated in suicide, impulsivity, and emotional lability, all features of borderline personality disorder (Amad et al., 2014). A study of inpatients found that up to 55% of patients diagnosed with borderline personality disorder had a history of suicide attempts, with an actual suicide rate of between 5% and 10%. Further, up to 80% had committed acts of self-mutilation (cutting), a way to express anger, punish oneself, or grounding oneself during feelings of depersonalization or painful emotions (Brown et al., 2002).

Functional neuroimaging has indicated that the affective instability in borderline personality disorder has been associated with reduced activity in the prefrontal cortex and enhanced activity in the amygdala (Dell'Osso et al., 2010; Minzenberg et al., 2008). Further studies have indicated that the amygdala in those with borderline personality disorder is unable to decrease neural response when a negative stimulus is repeatedly presented. In people without borderline personality disorder, the amygdala activation decreased neural response (Koenigsberg et al., 2014).

Research suggests a correlation between borderline personality disorder and negative events during childhood, such as neglect, sexual abuse, or physical abuse (Zanarini et al., 2002); parental discord or parental physical illness (Bandelow et al., 2005; Winsper et al., 2012); or parental mental illness (Trull, 2001). However, it is important to note that, although there may be a correlation, the belief that borderline personality disorder is a direct result of trauma is a misconception. Research has indicated that the majority (80%) of people with a history of sexual abuse do not meet the criteria for any personality disorder (Paris, 1998).

Prevalence and Comorbidities

The prevalence of borderline personality disorder ranges from 0.5% (Samuels et al., 2002) to 1.4% (Arens et al., 2013), 2.7% (Tomko et al., 2014), or 5.9% (Grant et al., 2008) of the general population and approximately 40% of the psychiatric inpatient population (Marinangeli et al., 2000). The vast majority of those diagnosed with borderline personality disorder are women (75%), a 3:1 ratio (APA, 2013). As a general rule, personality disorders are not typically diagnosed in children younger than 18 years. However, the symptoms and behaviors of borderline personality disorder are typically seen in adolescence, impacting approximately 3% of adolescents (Chanen et al., 2004). A diagnosis of borderline personality disorder is permitted if the symptoms persist for more than 1 year.

Borderline personality disorder has a high comorbidity rate with depression, anxiety disorders, and substance use disorders; in fact, borderline personality disorder is diagnosed as the sole mental health disorder in only 5% of cases. Approximately 80% of individuals with borderline personality disorder experience one or more depressive episodes and half experience ongoing major depressive disorder (Gunderson et al.,

2004). Note that even when a person with borderline personality disorder may not meet the full criteria for major depressive disorder, a number of individuals will have reactive depressions that are triggered by a specific event. Given the nature of borderline personality disorder, these episodes tend to be very intense and out of proportion to the stressor (Rao & Broadbear, 2019). Over time, the mood disorders tend to stay stable.

Approximately 38% of those with borderline personality disorder also have an anxiety disorder. In terms of specific anxiety disorders, approximately 22% of those with borderline personality disorder have panic disorder; 7% social phobia; 10% obsessive compulsive disorder (OCD), and 4% generalized anxiety disorder (GAD) (Silverman et al., 2012). Research has indicated that rates of comorbid anxiety disorders in patients with borderline personality disorder decrease significantly at 6- and 10-year follow-up (Zanarini et al., 2011). Interestingly, it is not common for individuals to have an onset of anxiety disorder after the diagnosis of borderline personality disorder. Silverman et al. (2012) found that the rates of new onsets of anxiety were 17% for OCD, 23% for GAD, and 24% for social phobia. A new onset of panic disorder was higher, at 47%.

Substance use is common in individuals with borderline personality disorder. Studies on the prevalence of comorbid substance use indicate rates of 23% to 84% (Grant et al., 2008). The comorbid use of alcohol ranges from 12% to 66% and other drug use from 3.4% to 87% (Grant et al., 2008). When borderline personality disorder is comorbid with anxiety disorders, substance use disorders tend to decrease over time. A study at 6-year follow-up found that alcohol use disorder was 11.4% and other drug use disorder was 12.9%. At 10-year follow-up, rates of alcohol use disorder and other drug use disorder were 8.8% and 7.2%, respectively (Zanarini et al., 2004; 2011).

Course and Prognosis

Although borderline personality disorder has long been considered a chronic disorder, long-term outcome studies have indicated high levels of remission at 10-year follow-up. For example, one study found that 88% of people with borderline personality disorder achieved remission over 10 years (Zanarini, 2006). Younger age, absence of abuse, lack of family history of substance use disorders, and certain temperamental characteristics (low neuroticism and high agreeableness) are predictive of earlier remission. Recurrence rates are not consistent between studies, however; for example, one study found that 11% of patients had a recurrence within 10 years (Gunderson et al., 2011). Another study found that recurrence rates were approximately 36% if the remission lasted only 2 years, though this rate decreased to 10% at 8 years. A longer remission seems to predict a lower risk of relapse. A 2016 study by Kjaer et al., found that of nearly 11,000 individuals with a diagnosis of borderline personality disorder reported diagnostic stability after 18 years was 37% for women and 25% for men, significantly higher than earlier studies. Although remission from borderline personality disorder is clearly the norm, there are still a significant number of individuals who relapse or have continuous symptoms (Kjaer et al., 2021).

Suicide is a significant risk for individuals with borderline personality disorder; they experience intense emotional pain and extreme fear of abandonment, which often leads to interpersonal instability. This instability, as well as worries about impending loss, can lead to self-harm or suicide attempts in an effort to avoid abandonment. Approximately 60% to 70% of individuals with borderline personality disorder will attempt suicide (Oldham, 2006), and 10% will die by suicide (Paris et al., 2011). A comorbid diagnosis of major depressive disorder and substance use disorders are associated with suicide attempts (Soloff, 2005). A feeling of hopelessness can lead to more severe attempts (Stanley, 2011).

Cultural and Gender-Related Considerations

When comparing prevalence rates of borderline personality disorder between races and ethnicities, the data are mixed. For example, in a systematic review McGilloway et al. (2010) found that in five studies borderline personality disorder was less prevalent in people who were Black/African American. However, in seven studies of raw data, it was found that Black/African Americans were more likely to be diagnosed with borderline personality disorder. A study by Chavira et al. (2003) found that Latinx individuals were diagnosed disproportionaley more than those who were Black/African American or Causcasian. A study of 83 women with borderline personality disorder found that White women reported more severe internalizing symptoms and Black/African American women reported more externalizing symptoms, such as anger, and fewer suicidal behaviors (De Genna & Feske, 2013). Bender et al. (2007) found that people who are Black/African American or Latinx/Hispanic are less likely to have received treatment for borderline personality disorder than people who are white.

Women are diagnosed with borderline personality disorder at a much higher rate than men in clinical populations; however research has indicated the rates of men and women are comparable in community settings (Lenzenweger et al., 2007). In prison settings studies have found a high prevalence of borderline personality disorder in men. For example, Wetterborg et al. (2015) found a prevalence rate of 20% in men on probation or parole, and Black et al. (2007) found a prevalence rate of 27% in prisons.

Men with borderline personality disorder are more likely to present with comorbid substance use disorders (Tadić et al., 2009) and intermittent explosive disorder (Zlotnick et al., 2002), whereas women are likely to present with mood disorders (Tadić et al., 2009), anxiety disorders (McCormick et al., 2007; Tadić et al., 2009), PTSD, and eating disorders (Skodol, 2005).

Diagnosis and Assessment

Individuals with borderline personality disorder have a pervasive history of at least five of nine criteria, as listed in the DSM-5 (APA, 2013). These criteria include unstable and intense relationships alternating between idealization and devaluation; frantic efforts to avoid abandonment; suicidal behavior or self-harm; unstable sense of self; impulsivity; affective instability; chronic feelings of emptiness; uncontrollable anger; and transient, stress-related paranoia or dissociation (APA, 2013).

It is important to remember that borderline personality disorder is a chronic disorder that begins in adolescence and continues into adulthood. This does not mean that children or adolescents should be diagnosed; many teens and young adults who are attempting to find their own identity and navigating through friendships and dating experience at least some of the criteria of borderline. The National Institute for Health and Care Excellence (2009) does acknowledge that borderline personality disorder can occur in younger age groups but states that caution should be exercised due to the stigmatization of the disorder.

Abby

Abby is a 28-year-old single White woman who has presented for treatment because of what she describes as "relationship issues." She is an elementary school teacher at a local school. Abby states that she has been with her current boyfriend (Scott) for 6 months and she says that she is at risk of losing him and "cannot let that happen." She says that lately she feels like he is "pulling away" and does not love her anymore. Abby says that she truly believes he is cheating on her. When asked why she feels this way, she says that he is spending more time at work, he seems to be spending more time on his phone, and he does not answer all her texts. When asked how often she texts him when he is at work or away from her, she says that she will keep texting him until he texts back, which can be 10 or 12 texts over the course of an hour. She says when this happens, he gets angry and then she "feels bad." She admits that she will send him "a bunch of texts" apologizing and telling him how much she loves him. When questioned about any other indications that he is cheating, she says that there are not, but she still believes that he is. She says, at times, she really hates him because he is cheating on her. Abby says that sometimes she becomes so angry and anxious about his cheating that she will drive by his house or his friend's house to "catch him in the act." She never has.

When asked about her relationship up until this point, she says that "it seemed perfect." She says they do "lots of stuff together," such as going to plays, concerts, and hanging out with his friends. When asked if they ever hang out with her friends, Abby states that "his friends are my friends now." She does report that she has one "bestie" that she has been friends with for 10 years. Abby says that she and Scott will often go running together after work or go to yoga classes on Sundays. When asked how long she has been running, Abby replies that she started when she met Scott; the same is true for yoga. When asked if they engage in activities that she likes, she replies that she likes whatever he likes.

Abby reports that she and Scott drank too much over the weekend and got into a "huge fight." She says that she got angry with him for talking to his ex-girlfriend at the bar. When they got home from the bar, she confronted him (she admits aggressively), and he became angry. She says the fight escalated to the point that she said she could not be with him anymore. She left his house and went home. When she woke up the next morning, she was "terrified that she messed everything up" and immediately called him to make sure everything was ok, begging him not to leave her. He said he was not going to leave her, but they needed to discuss what had happened. She says that she got really worried, so she sent him flowers to say that she was sorry. When asked if they fight when they are not drinking, she states that they have gotten into a few fights that usually end up with her throwing things, slamming doors, and then leaving the house. She says she always apologizes the next day.

When asked how her days are when she is not with Scott, she says that she feels all alone and "kinda dead inside." She says that sometimes she feels like she is going to "jump out of her skin" and will pace the house for hours. Then, at other times, she feels "super sad" and just wants to lie in her bed. When asked how often these episodes have been happening, she says, "On and off as long as I can remember." When asked if she ever becomes so sad or anxious that she tries to harm herself, she states that when she and Scott fight she thinks about hurting herself and has told him on a few occasions that she is going to kill herself, but she has never attempted. She admits that she has had thoughts of harming herself for many years. She denies any current suicidal thoughts. Abby reports that drinking wine makes her feel better. She reports having two to three glasses a night. She denies driving while intoxicated or before work.

Abby reports that she has never been married. She says she has been engaged three times but "none of them stuck." She states that she was with her last fiancé for 3 months before they got engaged. Three months later, she met Scott and broke up with her fiancé. She says that Scott "swept her off her feet." She then blurts out, "Yes, I cheated on him; don't judge me!" After being assured that she is not being judged, Abby reveals that her other two engagements ended because she was cheating on her fiancés. She states that sometimes she feels so lonely and needs to feel loved. She also states that her relationships usually start out as a whirlwind and she is "totally in love," but after a few months or so she gets "really sick of them."

Diagnostic Impression

Abby is exhibiting a number of symptoms related to her affect, her relationships, and her identity. She has made frantic efforts to avoid abandonment, evidenced by her compulsive texting, apologizing, begging not be left, and sending flowers. She has a pattern of unstable relationships that start out with Abby being "in love" and ending with her being "sick of them." She is exhibiting signs of identity disturbance, evidenced by essentially losing herself in the relationship: she likes the activities he likes; his friends become her friends; and she seems to need constant reassurance from Scott. Abby has recurrent suicidal thoughts and threats and affective instability. She has periods where she is anxious and pacing and others where she is despondent. Abby has feelings of chronic emptiness, evidenced by her statement of feeling "dead inside." Finally, Abby seems to have a difficult time controlling her anger, evidenced by her starting fights with Scott, throwing things, and slamming doors.

Diagnostic Conclusion

Borderline personality disorder

DIFFERENTIAL DIAGNOSIS I: MAJOR DEPRESSIVE DISORDER

Rationale: Depressive symptoms are present in the majority of individuals with borderline personality disorder. It is often difficult to distinguish between the two. The depressive symptoms in borderline personality disorder are often reactive that may last only for a few days at time (Rao & Broadbear, 2019). If the symptoms last weeks and meet full criteria for MDD then a diagnosis would be warranted Although Abby exhibits some symptoms of major depressive disorder, such as "feeling dead inside" and feeling "super sad" and wanting to stay in bed, she does not meet full criteria; therefore, at this time, a diagnosis of borderline personality disorder is most appropriate.

DIFFERENTIAL DIAGNOSIS II: DEPENDENT PERSONALITY DISORDER

Rationale: Although dependent personality disorder is characterized by a fear of abandonment, in borderline personality disorder the reaction to the fear is rage and anger, whereas someone with dependent personality disorder would react with submission. In addition, people with borderline personality disorder have patterns of intense relationships, but do not typically engage in submissive behaviors.

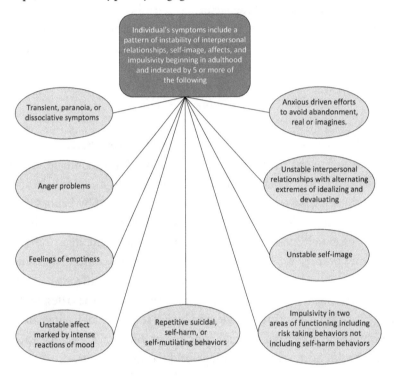

FIGURE 13.1   Diagnosing borderline personality disorder

Biopsychosocial

BIOLOGICAL

Given that the symptoms Abby is reporting are pervasive, long-term, and directly related to her relationships, it is unlikely that they are a result of any physiological cause. However, as with any suspected mental health disorder, a physical exam is always prudent.

PSYCHOLOGICAL

Borderline personality disorder is highly comorbid with major depressive disorder. Given the current information, Abby does not meet the criteria for major depressive disorder, but she should be reassessed later. Oftentimes, assessment of borderline personality disorder and its associated features will take more than one session. Abby has had suicidal thoughts and threats in the past, which is common for those with borderline personality disorder. Although she does not have any current thoughts of suicide, she should be assessed regularly. Suicidal thoughts tend to become more severe under times of extreme stress, particularly when the individual feels betrayed by a loved one. Remember, people with borderline personality disorder often have symptoms of depression (and vise versa). It is important to remember that even in absence of a full diagnosis of MDD, the symptoms must be addressed, particilulary due to the high risk of suicidal ideation in both disorders.

SOCIAL

Given the features of borderline personality disorder and the disorder itself, relationships are a source of stress for someone with borderline personality disorder as well as their partners. Although Abby's symptoms surround her relationship with her boyfriend, it is not unusual for these symptoms to be applied to nonromantic individuals in their lives. Therefore, it is likely that Abby has not been able to maintain friendships due to her behaviors.

TERMINOLOGY

devaluation Reduction or underestimation of the worth or importance of something.

idealization Regarding or representing something as perfect or better than in reality.

transient Lasting only a short time.

REFLECTION QUESTIONS

1. What are the core features of borderline personality disorder?

2. What are the most common comorbid disorders associated with borderline personality disorder?

3. What are the features of borderline personality organization?

References

Achenbach, T.M. (2019). International findings with the Achenbach System of Empirically Based Assessment (ASEBA): applications to clinical services, research, and training. *Child and Adolescent Psychiatry Mental Health 13*, 30. https://doi.org/10.1186/s13034-019-0291-2

Afifi, T. O., & Asmundson, G. J. (2020). Current knowledge and future directions for the ACEs field. In *Adverse Childhood Experiences* (pp. 349–355). Academic Press.

Aitken, M., Steensma, T. D., Blanchard, R., VanderLaan, D. P., Wood, H., Fuentes, A., Spegg, C., Wasserman, L., Ames, M., Fitzsimmons, C. L., Leef, J. H., Lishak, V., Reim, E., Takagi, M. A., Vinik, J., Wreford, J., Cohen-Kettenis, P. T., de Vries, A. L. C., Kreukels, B. P. C., & Zucker, K. J. (2015). Evidence for an altered sex ratio in clinic-referred adolescents with gender dysphoria. *Journal of Sexual Medicine, 12*, 756–763. https://doi.org/10.1111/jsm.12817

Akbaraly, T., Brunner, E., Ferrie, J., Marmot, M., Kivimaki, M., & Singh-Manoux, A. (2009). Dietary pattern and depressive symptoms in middle age. *British Journal of Psychiatry, 195*(5), 408–413. https://doi.org/10.1192/bjp.bp.108.058925

Alegría-Torres, J. A., Baccarelli, A., & Bollati, V. (2011). Epigenetics and lifestyle. *Epigenomics, 3*(3), 267–277. https://doi.org/10.2217/epi.11.22

Allred, S. (2009). Reframing Asperger syndrome: Lessons from other challenges to the diagnostic and statistical manual and ICIDH approaches. *Disability & Society, 24*(3), 343–355. https://doi.org/10.1080/09687590902789511

Almeida, J., Johnson, R. M., Corliss, H. L., Molnar, B. E. & Azrael, D. (2009). Em otional distress among LGBT youth: The influence of perceived discrimination based on sexual orientation. *Journal of Youth & Adolescence, 38*, 1001–1014. doi:10.1007/s10964-009-9397-9

Amad, A., Ramoz, N., Thomas, P., Jardri, R., & Gorwood, P. (2014). Genetics of borderline personality disorder: Systematic review and proposal of an integrative model. *Neuroscience and Biobehavioral Reviews, 40*, 6–19. https://doi.org/10.1016/j.neubiorev.2014.01.003

American Psychiatric Association. (1952). *Diagnostic and statistical manual of mental disorders.*

American Psychiatric Association. (1968). *Diagnostic and statistical manual of mental disorders* (2nd ed.).

American Psychiatric Association. (1980). *Diagnostic and statistical manual of mental disorders* (3rd ed.).

American Psychiatric Association. (1987). *Diagnostic and Statistical Manual of Mental Disorders* (3rd ed., text rev.).

American Psychiatric Association. (1994). *Diagnostic and statistical manual of mental disorders* (4th ed.).

American Psychiatric Association. (2000). *Diagnostic and statistical manual of mental disorders* (4th ed., text rev.).

American Psychiatric Association. (2013). *Diagnostic and statistical manual of mental disorders* (5th ed.). https://doi.org/10.1176/appi.books.9780890425596

American Psychological Association. (2017). *Multicultural guidelines: An ecological approach to context, identity, and intersectionality.* http://www.apa.org/about/policy/multicultural-guidelines.pdf

Amianto, F., Ottone, L., Abbate Daga, G., & Fassino, S. (2015). Binge-eating disorder diagnosis and treatment: a recap in front of DSM-5. *BMC Psychiatry, 70.* DOI 10.1186/s12888-015-0445-6

Andersen, S. L., & Teicher, M. H. (2000). Sex differences in dopamine receptors and their relevance to ADHD. *Neuroscience and Biobehavioral Reviews, 24*(1), 137–141. http://dx.doi.org/10.1016/S0149-7634(99)00044-5

Applegate, J. S., & Shapiro, J. R. (2005). *Neurobiology for clinical social work: Theory and practice.* W. W. Norton & Company.

Anda, R., Williamson, D., Jones, D., Macera, C., Eaker, E., Glassman, A., & Marks, J. (1993). Depressed affect, hopelessness, and the risk of ischemic heart disease in a cohort of U.S. adults. *Epidemiology, 4, 285–294.10.1097/00001648-199307000-00003*

Anello, A., Reichenberg, A., Luo, X., Schmeidler, J., Hollander, E., Smith, C. J., Puleo, C M., Kryzak, L. A., & Silverman, J. M., (2009). Brief report: parental age and the sex ratio in autism. *Journal of Autism and Developmental Disorders, 39,* 1487–1492. DOI 10.1007/s10803-009-0755-y

Arcelus, J., Mitchell, A. J., & Wales, J. (2011). Mortality rates in patients with anorexia nervosa and other eating disorders: A meta-analysis of 36 studies. *JAMA Psychiatry, 68*(7), 724–731. doi:10.1001/archgenpsychiatry.2011.74

Arens, E. A., Stopsack M., Spitzer C., Appel K., Dudeck M., Völzke H., Grabe, H. J., & Barnow, S. (2013). Borderline Personality Disorder in four different age groups: a cross sectional study of community residents in Germany. *Journal of Personality Disorders, 27,* 196–207. https://doi.org/10.1521/pedi_2013_27_072

Arnett, A. B., Pennington, B. F., Willcutt, E. G., DeFries, J. C., & Olson, R. K. (2015). Sex differences in ADHD symptom severity. *The Journal of Child Psychology and Psychiatry, 56*(6), 632–639. https://doi.org/10.1111/jcpp.12337

Axelson, D. A., Findling, R. L., Fristad, M. A., Kowatch, R. A., Youngstrom, E. A., Horwitz, S .M., Arnold, L. E., Frazier T, W., Ryan,. N, Demeter, C., Gill, M .K., Hauser–Harrington, J. C, Depew, J., Kennedy, S. M., Gron, B. A., Rowles, B. M, & Birmaher, B. (2012). Examining the proposed disruptive mood dysregulation disorder diagnosis in children in the longitudinal assessment of manic symptoms study. *Journal of Clinical Psychiatry 73,* 1342–1350.

Baer, J. S., Sampson, P. D., Barr, H. M., Connor, P. D., & Streissguth, A. P. (2003). A 21-year longitudinal analysis of the effects of prenatal alcohol exposure on young adult drinking. *Archives of General Psychiatry, 60*(4), 377–385. https://doi.org/10.1001/archpsyc.60.4.377

Baily, R. K., (2005). Diagnosis and treatment of attention-deficit/hyperactivity disorder (ADHD) in African – American and Hispanic patients. *Journal of the American Medical Association, 97*(10 suppl), 3s-4s.

Baio, J., Wiggins, L., Christensen, D. L., Maenner, M. J. Daniels, J., Warren, Z., Kurzius-Spencer, M., Zahorodny, W., Robinson Rosenberg, R. White, T., Durkin, M. S., Imm, P. Nikolaou, L., Yeargin-Allsopp, M., Lee, L-C.,Harrington, R., Lopez, M.,Fitzgerald, R. T., Hewitt, A., Pettygrove, S., Constantino, J., Vehorn, A., Shenouda, J., Jennifer Hall-Lande, J., Van Naarden Braun, K., & Dowling, K. (2018). Prevalence of Autism Spectrum Disorder Among Children Aged 8 Years—Autism and Developmental Disabilities Monitoring Network, 11 Sites, United States, 2014*MMWR Surveillance Summaries 67*(6)**,** 1–23

Baker, H., Mitchell, K. S., Neale, M. C., & Kendler, K. S. (2010). Eating Disorder Symptomatology and Substance Use Disorders: Prevalence and Shared Risk in a Population Based Twin Sample. *International Jounral of Eating Disorders, 43,* 648–658

Baldwin, D. S., Aitchison, K., Bateson, A., Curran, H. V., Davies, S., Leonard, B., Nutt, D. J., Stephens, D. N., & Wilson, S. (2013). Benzodiazepines: Risk and benefits. A reconsideration. *Journal of Psychopharmacology, 27,* 967–971.

Bandelow, B., Krause, J., Wedekind, D., Broocks, A., Hajak, G., & Rüther, E., (2005). Early traumatic life events parental attitudes family history and birth risk factors in patients with borderline personality disorder and healthy controls. *Psychiatry Research* 134, 169–179. ttps://doi.org/10.1016/j.psychres.2003.07.008

Bandura, A. (1977) Social Learning Theory. New York. General Learning Press. P. 1–46

Bang, L., Kristensen, U. B., Wisting, L., Stedal, K., Garte, M., Minde, A., & Ro, O. (2020). Presence of eating disorder symptoms in patients with obsessive-compulsive disorder. *BMC Psychiatry, 20,* (36). https://doi.org/10.1186/s12888-020-2457-0

Bangasser, D. A., & Valentino, R. J. (2014). Sex differences in stress-related psychiatric disorders: Neurobiological perspectives. *Frontiers in Neuroendocrinology, 35*(3), 303–319. https://doi.org/10.1016/j.yfrne.2014.03.008

Barker, R. L. (1995). *The social work dictionary.* NASW Press.

Barkus, E., & Murray, R. M. (2010). Substance use in adolescence and psychosis: Clarifying the relationship. *Annual Review of Clinical Psychology, 6*(1), 365–389. https://doi.org/10.1146/annurev.clinpsy.121208.131220

Barzega, G., Maina, G., Venturello, S., & Bogetto, F. (2008). Gender-related differences in the onset of panic disorder. *ACTA Psychiatrica Scandinavica, 103*(3), 189–195. https://doi.org/10.1034/j.1600-0447.2001.00194.x

Barnard-Brak, L., Roberts, B., & Valenzuela, E. (2020). Examining breaks and resistance in medication adherence among adolescents with ADHD as associated with school outcomes. *Journal of Attention Disorders, 24*(8), 1148–1155. https://doi.org/10.1177/1087054718763738

Barsky, A. (2019). DSM-5 and the ethics of diagnosing. *The New Social Worker.* https://www.socialworker.com/feature-articles/ethics-articles/dsm-5-and-ethics-of-diagnosis/

Baumeister, D., Akhtar, R., Ciufolini, S, Pariante, C. M., & Mondelli, V. (2016). Childhood trauma and adulthood inflammation: A met-analysis of peripheral C-reactive protein, interleukin-6 and tumor necrosis factor-α. *Molecular Psychiatry*, 21, 642-649. https://doi.org/10.1038/mp.2015.67

Baxter, A. J., Brugha, T. S., Erskine, H. E., Scheurer, R. W., Vos, T., & Scott, J. G. (2015). The epidemiology and global burden of autism spectrum disorders. *Psychological Medicine, 45*(3), 601–13. doi: 10.1017/S003329171400172X.

Beals, J., Spicer P., Mitchell, C. M., Novins, D. K., Manson, S. M., the AI-SUPERPFP Team (2003). Racial disparities in alcohol use: Comparison of two American Indian reservation populations with national data. *American Journal of Public Health, 93*(10), 1683–1685. https://doi.org/10.2105/AJPH.93.10.1683

Beauvais, F., Jumper-Thurman, P., & Burnside, M. (2008). The changing patterns of drug use among American Indian students over the past thirty years. *American Indian Alaskan Native Ment Health Research: Journal of the National Center,15*(2), 15–24.

Beek, T. F., Cohen-Kettenis, P. T., & Kreukels, B. P. C. (2016). Gender incongruence/gender dysphoria and its classification history. *International Review of Psychiatry, 28*(1), 5–12. https://doi.org/10.3109/09540261.2015.1091293

Bergh, C., & Sodersten, P. (1996). Anorexia nervosa, self-starvation and the reward of stress. *Nature Medicine, 2*(1), 21–22. DOI: 10.1038/nm0196-21

Begeer, S., Mandell, D., Wijnker-Holmes, B., Venderbosch, S., Rem, D., Stekelenburg, F., & Koot, H. M. (2013). Sex Differences in the Timing of Identification Among Children and Adults with Autism Spectrum Disorders. *Journal of Autism and Developmental Disorders, 43,* 1151–1156

Bélanger, L., Morin, C. M., Langlois, F., & Ladouceur, R. (2004). Insomnia and generalized anxiety disorder: Effects of cognitive behavior therapy for gad on insomnia symptoms. *Journal of Anxiety Disorders, 18*(4), 561–571. https://doi.org/10.1016/S0887-6185(03)00031-8

Bender, D., Skodol A., I.R D, Markowitz, J., Shea, M., Yen, S. (2007) Ethnicity and mental health utilization by patients with personality disorders. *Journal of Consulting and Clinical Psychology, 75*(6), 992–999.

Benseñor, I. M., Tófoli, L. F., & Andrade, L. (2003). Headache complaints associated with psychiatric comorbidity in a population-based sample. *Brazilian Journal of Medical and Biological Research, 36*(10), 1425–1432. https://doi.org/10.1590/S0100-879X2003001000021

Berends, T., Boonstra, N., & van Elburg, A. (2018). Relapse in anorexia nervosa: A systematic review and meta-analysis. *Current Opinion in Psychiatry, 31*(6), 445–455. https://doi.org/10.1097/YCO.0000000000000453

Bertelsen, A., Harvald, B., & Hauge, M. (1977). A Danish Twin Study of Manic-Depressive Disorders. *British Journal of Psychiatry,* 130(4), 330-351. doi:10.1192/bjp.130.4.330

Bertsch, K., Schmidinger, I., Neumann, I. D., & Herpetz, S. C. (2013). Reduced plasma oxytocin levels in female patients with borderline personality disorder. *Hormones and Behavior , 63*(3), 424–9. https://doi.org/10.1016/j.yhbeh.2012.11.013

Bjornsson, A. S., Didie, E. R., Grant, J. E., Menard, W., Stalker, E., & Phillips, K. A. (2013). Age at onset and clinical correlates in body dysmorphic disorder. *Comprehensive Psychiatry, 54*, 893–903. https://doi.org/10.1016/j.comppsych.2013.03.019

Black, D. W., Gunter, T., Allen, J., Blum, N., Arndt, S., Wenman, G., & Sieleni, B. (2007). Borderline personality disorder in male and female offenders newly committed to prison. *Comprehensive Psychiatry, 48*(5), 400–405. https://doi.org/10.1016/j.comppsych.2007.04.006

Blader, J. C., & Carlson, G. A. (2007). Increased rates of bipolar disorder diagnoses among U.S. child, adolescent, and adult inpatients, 1996–2004. *Biological Psychiatry, 62*(2), 107–114. https://doi.org/10.1016/j.biopsych.2006.11.006

Blanco, C., Compton, W. M., Saha, T. D., Goldstein, B. I., Ruan, W. J., Huang, B., & Grant, B. F. (2017). Epidemiology of DSM-5 bipolar I disorder: Results from the national epidemiologic survey on alcohol and related conditions—III. *Journal of Psychiatric Research, 84*, 310–317. https://doi.org/10.1016/j.jpsychires.2016.10.003

Blashfield, R. K., Keeley, J. W., Flanagan, E. H., & Miles, S. R. (2014). The cycle of classification: DSM-I through DSM-5. *Annual Review of Clinical Psychology, 10*(1), 25–51. https://doi.org/10.1146/annurev-clinpsy-032813-153639

Blasi, V., Young, A. C., Tansy, A. P., Petersen, S. E., Snyder, A. Z., & Corbetta, M. (2002). Word retrieval learning modulates right frontal cortex in patients with left frontal damage. *Neuron, 36*(1), 159–170.

Bogetto, F., Venturello, S., Albert, U., Maina, G., & Ravizza, L. (1999). Gender-related clinical differences in obsessive-compulsive disorder. *European Psychiatry, 14*(8), 434–441. https://doi.org/10.1016/S0924-9338(99)00224-2

Bolanos, S. H., Khan, D. A, Hanczyc, M., Bauer, M .S., Dhanani, N., Brown, E. S. (2004). Assessment of mood states in patients receiving long-term corticosteroid therapy and in controls with patient-rated and clinician-rated scales. *Annals of Allergy and Asthma Immunology, 92*, 500–505.

Boerema, Y. E., de Boer, M. M., van Blakom, A. J. L. M., Eikelenboom, M., Visser, H. A., & van Oppen, P. (2019). Obsessive compulsive disorder with and without hoarding symptoms: Characterizing differences. Journal of Affective Disorders, 246, 652–658. https://doi.org/10.1016/j.jad.2018.12.115

Bortolato, B., Köhler, C. A., Evangelou, E., León-Caballero, J., Solmi, M., Stubbs, B., Belbasis, L., Pacchiarotti, I., Kessing, L. V., Berk, M., Vieta, E., & Carvalho, A. F. (2017). Systematic assessment of environmental risk factors for bipolar disorder: An umbrella review of systematic reviews and meta-analyses. *Bipolar Disorders, 19*(2), 84–96. https://doi.org/10.1111/bdi.12490

Bosch, A., Bierens, M., de Wit, A. G., Ly, V., van der Velde, de Boer, H., van Beek, G., Appelman, A., Visser, S., Bos, L., van der Meer, J., Kamphuis, N., Draaisma, J. M. T., Donders, R., van de Loo-Neus, G. H. H., Hoekstra, P. J., Bottelier, M., Arias-Vasquez, A., Klip, H., Buitelaar, J. K., van den Berg, S. W., & Rommelse, N. N. (2020). A two arm randomized controlled trial comparing the short and long term effects of an elimination diet and a healthy diet in children with ADHD (TRACE study). Rationale, study design and methods. *BMC Psychiatry, 20*, 262 https://doi.org/10.1186/s12888-020-02576-2

Bosworth, H. B., Voils, C. I., Potter, G. G., & Steffens, D. C. (2008). The effects of antidepressant medication adherence as well as psychosocial and clinical factors on depression outcome among older adults. *International Journal of Geriatric Psychiatry, 23*(2), 129–134. https://doi.org/10.1002/gps.1852

Bourgeron, T. (2015). From the genetic architecture to synaptic plasticity in autism spectrum disorder. *National Review of Neuroscience, 25,* 341–347.

Breitbart, W., Stiefel, F., Kornblith, A. B., & Pannullo, S. (1993). Neuropsychiatric disturbance in cancer patients with epidural spinal cord compression receiving high dose corticosteroids: a prospective comparison study. *Psychooncology, 2,* 233–245

Breslau, J., Kendler, K., Su, M., Gaxiola-Aguilar, S., & Kessler, R. (2005). Lifetime risk and persistence of psychiatric disorder across ethnic group in the United States. *Psychological Medicine, 35*(3), 317–327. doi:10.1017/S0033291704003514

Brown, M. A., Comtois, K. A., Linehan, M. M. (2002). Reasons for suicide attempts and nonsuicidal self-injury in women with borderline personality disorder. *Journal of Abnormal Psychology, 111*(1), 198–202. https://doi.org/10.1037/0021-843X.111.1.198

Buckley, P. F., Miller, B. J., Lehrer, D. S., & Castle, D. J. (2009). Psychiatric Comorbidities and Schizophrenia. *Schizophrenia Bulletin, 35*(2), 383–402. Doi:10.1093.schbul/sbn135

Buhlmann, U., Winter, A., & Norbert, K. (2013). Emotion recognition in body dysmorphic disorder: Application of the reading of the mind in the eyes task. *Body Image, 10*(2), 247–250. http://dx.doi.org/10.1016/j.bodyim.2012.12.001

Bulik, C. M., Hebebrand, J., Keski-Rahkonen, A., Klump, K. L., Reichborn-Kjennerud, T., Mazzeo, S. E., & Wade, T. D. (2007). Genetic epidemiology, endophenotypes, and eating disorder classification. *International Journal of Eating Disorders, 40*(S3), S52–S60. https://doi.org/10.1002/eat.20398

Bulik, C. M., Thornton, L., Pinheiro, A. P., Plotnicov, K., Klump, K. L., Brandt, H., Crawford, S., Fichter, M. M., Halmi, K. A., Johnson, C., Kaplan, A. S., Mitchell, J., Nutzinger, D., Strober, M., Treasure, J., Woodside, D. B., Berrettini, W. H., & Kaye, W. H. (2008). Suicide attempts in anorexia nervosa. *Psychosomatic Medicine, 70*(3), 378–383. https://doi.org/10.1097/PSY.0b013e3181646765

Breslau, J., Aguilar-Gaxiola, S., Kendler, K. S., Su, M., William, D., & Kessler, R. C. (2006). Specifying race-ethnic differences in risk for psychiatric disorder in a USA national sample. *Psychological Medicine, 36*(1), 57–68. DOI: https://doi.org/10.1017/S0033291705006161

Calikusu, C., Kucukgoncu S., Tecer, O., & Bestepe, E. (2012). Skin picking in Turkish students: Prevalence, characteristics and gender differences. *Behavior Modification, 36*, 49–66. https://doi.org/10.1016/S0896-6273(02)00936-4

Canetta, S. E., Bao, Y., Co, M. D. T., Ennis, F. A., Cruz, J., Terajima, M., Shen, L., Kellendonk, C., Schaefer, C. A., & Brown, A. S. (2014). Serological documentation of maternal influenza exposure and bipolar disorder in adult offspring. *American Journal of Psychiatry, 171*(5), 557–563. https://doi.org/10.1176/appi.ajp.2013.13070943

Canino, G., Polanczyk, G., Bauermeister, J. J., Rohde, L. A., & Frick, P. J. (2010). Does the prevalence of CD and ODD vary across cultures? *Social Psychiatry and Psychiatric Epidemiology, 45*(7), 695–704. https://doi.org/10.1007/s00127-010-0242-y

Carabotti, M., Scirocco, A., Maselli, M. A., & Severi, C. (2015). The gut–brain axis: Interactions between enteric microbiota, central and enteric nervous systems. *Annals of Gastroenterology: Quarterly Publication of the Hellenic Society of Gastroenterology, 28*(2), 203–209.

Carta, M. G., Balestrieri, M., Murru, A., & Hardoy, M. C. (2009). Adjustment Disorder: epidemiology, diagnosis, and treatment. *Clinical Practice and Epidemiology in Mental Health, 5*(1), 1–15.

Cass, K., McGuire, C., Bjork, I., Sobotka, N., Walsh, K., & Mehler, P. S. (2020). Medical complications of anorexia nervosa. *Psychosomatics, 61*(6), 625–631. https://doi.org/10.1016/j.psym.2020.06.020

Castillo, M., & Weiselberg, E. (2017). Bulimia nervosa/purging disorder. *Current Problems in Pediatric and Adolescent Health Care, 47*(4), 85–94. https://doi.org/10.1016/j.cppeds.2017.02.004

Cath, D., Nizar, K., Boomsma, D., & Mathews, C. A. (2017). Age-specific prevalence of hoarding and obsessive-compulsive disorder: A population-based study. *American Journal of Geriatric Psychiatry, 25* (3), 245–255. https://doi.org/10.1016/j.jagp.2016.11.006

Centers for Disease Control (2018). Autism and Developmental Disabilities Monitoring Network (ADDM). https://www.cdc.gov/ncbddd/autism/addm.html

Centers for Disease Control (2019). Data and Statistics about ADHD https://www.cdc.gov/ncbddd/adhd/data.html

Chavira, D. A., Grilo, C., Shea, M., Yen, S., Gunderson, J., Morey, L. (2003). Ethnicity and four personality disorders. *Comprehensive Psychiatry, 44*(6), 483–91.

Chandra, S., Radwan, M. M., Majumdar, C. G., Church, J. C., Freeman, T. P., & ElSohly, M. A. (2019). New trends in cannabis potency in USA and Europe during the last decade (2008–2017). *European Archives of Psychiatry and Clinical Neuroscience, 269*(1), 5–15. https://doi.org/10.1007/s00406-019-00983-5

Chanen, A. M., Jackson H. J., McGorry, P. D., Allot, K. A., Clarkson, V., & Yuen, H. P. (2004). Two-year stability of personality disorder in older adolescent outpatients. *Journal of Personality Disorders, 18*(6), 526–541. https://doi.org/10.1521/pedi.18.6.526.54798

Celano, C. M., Freudenreich, O., Fernandez-Robles, C., Stern, T. A., Caro, M. A., & Huffman, J. C. (2011). Depressogenic effects of medications: a review. *Dialogues in clinical neuroscience, 13*(1), 109–125. https://doi.org/10.31887/DCNS.2011.13.1/ccelano

Chen, C.-Y., O'Brien, M. S., & Anthony, J. C. (2005). Who becomes cannabis dependent soon after onset of use? Epidemiological evidence from the United States: 2000–2001. *Drug and Alcohol Dependence, 79*(1), 11–22. https://doi.org/10.1016/j.drugalcdep.2004.11.014

Chen, J. A., Penagarikano, O., Belgard, T. G., Swarup, V. & Geschwind, D. H., (2015). The emerging picture of autism spectrum disorder: genetics and pathology. *Annual Review of Pathology, 10,* 111–144. https//doi.org/10.1146/annurev-pathol-012414-040405

Cheon, K.-A. Ryu, Y. H., Kim, Y.-K., Namkoong, K., Kim, C.-H., & Lee, J. D. (2003). Dopamine transporter density in the basal ganglia assessed with [123I]IPT SPET in children with attention deficit hyperactivity disorder. *European Journal of Nuclear Medicine and Molecular Imaging, 30*(2), 306–311. doi: 10.1007/s00259-002-1047-3.

Cera, S., Botessi, G., Grisham, J. R., Ghisi, M. (2018). Body dysmorphic disorder and its associated psychopathological features in an Italian community sample. *International Journal of Psychiatry in Clinical Practice, 22* (3), 206–214.

Cheslack-Postova, K., Liu, K., & Bearman, P. S. (2011). Closely spaced pregnancies are associated with increased odds of autism in California sibling births. *Pediatrics, 127,* 246–253. http://dx.doi.org/10.1542/peds.2010-2371

Cheslack-Postova, K., Suominen, A., Jokiranta, E., Lehti, V., McKeague, I. W., Sourander, A., & Brown, A. S. (2014). Increased risk of autism spectrum disorders at short and long interpregnancy intervals in Finland. *Journal of the American Academy of Child & Adolescent Psychiatry, 53*(10), 1074–1081. http://dx.doi.org/10.1016/j.jaac.2014.06.009

Cheung, A. S., Leemaqz, S. Y., Wong, J. W. P., Chew, D., Ooi, O., Cundill, P., Silberstein, N., Locke, P., Zwickl, S., Grayson, R., Zajac, J. D., & Pang, K. C. (2020). Non-binary and binary gender identity in Australian trans and gender diverse individuals. *Archives of Sexual Behavior, 49*(7), 2673–2681. https://doi.org/10.1007/s10508-020-01689-9

Christensen, D. L., Baio, J., Braun, K. V., Bilder, D., Charles, J Constantino, J. N., Daniels, J., Durkin, M. S., Fitzgerald, R. T., Kurzius-Spencer, M., Lee, L-C., Pettygrove, S., Robinson, C., Schulz, E., Wells, C., Wingate, M. S., Zahorodny, W., Yeargin-Allsopp, M. (2016). Prevalence and characteristics of autism spectrum disorder among children aged 8 years- autism and developmental disabilities monitoring network, 11 sites, United States, 2012. *MMWR Surveillance Summary, 65,* 1–23

Chu, R. K., Rosic, T., & Samaan, Z. (2017). Adult ADHD: Questioning diagnosis and treatment in a patient with multiple psychiatric comorbidities. *Case Repots in Psychiatry, 2017,* doi: 10.1155/2017/1364894.

Clacey, J., Goldacre, M., & James, A. (2015). Paediatric bipolar disorder: International comparisons of hospital discharge rates 2000–2010. *British Journal of Psychiatry Open, 1*(2), 166–171. https://doi.org/10.1192/bjpo.bp.115.001933

Coccaro, E. F. (2019). Psychiatric comorbidity in intermittent explosive disorder. In E. F. Coccaro & M. S. McCloskey (Eds.), *Intermittent explosive disorder: Etiology, assessment, and treatment.* (pp. 67–84). Elsevier Academic Press. https://doi.org/10.1016/B978-0-12-813858-8.00004-8

Coccaro, E. F., Solis, O., Fanning, J., & Lee, R. (2015). Emotional intelligence and impulsive aggression in intermittent explosive disorder. *Journal of Psychiatric Research, 61,* 135–140. https://doi.org/10.1016/j.jpsychires.2014.11.004

Coccaro, E. F. (2012). Intermittent explosive disorder as a disorder of impulsive aggression for DSM-5. *American Journal of Psychiatry, 169*(6), 577–588. https://doi.org/10.1176/appi. ajp.2012.11081259

Coccaro, E. F., Schmidt, C. A., Samuels, J. F., & Nestadt, G. (2004). Lifetime and 1-month prevalence rates of intermittent explosive disorder in a community sample. *Journal of Clinical Psychiatry, 65*(6), 820–824. https://doi.org/10.4088/jcp.v65n0613.

Cochran, S. D., Ackerman, D., Mays, V. M. & Ross, M. W. (2004). Prevalence of non-medical drug use and dependence among homosexually active men and women in the. *U.S. population. Addiction, 99,* 989–998. doi:10.llll/j.1360–0443.2004.00759.x

Comas-Díaz, L., Hall, G. N., & Neville, H. A. (2019). Racial trauma: Theory, research, and healing: Introduction to the special issue. *American Psychologist, 74*(1), 1–5. https://doi. org/10.1037/amp0000442

Conner, B. T., & Lochman, J. E. (2010). Comorbid conduct disorder and substance use disorders. *Clinical Psychology: Science and Practice, 17*(4), 337–349. https://doi. org/10.1111/j.1468-2850.2010.01225.x

Coo, H., Ouellette-Kuntz, H., Lam, Y.-M., Brownell, M., Flavin, M. P. & Roos, L. L. (2015). The association between the interpregnancy interval and autism spectrum disorder in a Canadian cohort. *Canadian Journal of Public Health, 106*(2), e36–42.

Copeland, V. C. (2005). African Americans: Disparities in health care access and utilization. *Health & Social Work, 30*(3), 265–270.

Corcoran, J., & Walsh, J. (2015). *Mental health in social work: A case book on diagnosis and strengths based assessment, with DSM 5 update* (2nd ed.). Pearson Education.

Corrigan, P. (2004). How stigma interferes with mental health care. *American Psychologist, 59*(7), 614–625. https://doi.org/10.1037/0003-066X.59.7.614

Corrigan, P. W., Davidson, L., Schomerus, G., Shuman, V. (2019). How does the public understand recovery from severe mental illness versus substance use disorder. *Psychiatric Rehabilitation Journal, 42*(4). 341–349. http://dx.doi.org/10.1037/prj0000380

Cozolino, L. (2002). *The neuroscience of psychotherapy: Building and rebuilding the human brain.* W. W. Norton & Company.

Crane, A. M., Roberts, M. E., & Treasure, J. (2007). Are obsessive–compulsive personality traits associated with a poor outcome in anorexia nervosa? A systematic review of randomized controlled trials and naturalistic outcome studies. *International Journal of Eating Disorders, 40,* 581–588. https://doi.org/10.1002/eat.20419

Crenshaw, K. (1991). Mapping the margins: Intersectionality, identity politics, and violence against women of color. *Stanford Law Review, 43*(6), 1241–1299. https://doi.org/ 10.2307/1229039

Crow, S. J., Peterson, C. B., Swanson, S. A., Raymond, N. C., Specker, S., Eckert, E. D., & Mitchell, J. E. (2009). Increased mortality in bulimia nervosa and other eating disorders. *American Journal of Psychiatry, 166*(12), 1342–1346. https://doi.org/10.1176/appi. ajp.2009.09020247

Crow, S. J., Swanson, S. A., le Grange, D., Feig, E. H., & Merikangas, K. R. (2014). Suicidal behavior in adolescent and adults with bulimia nervosa. *Comprehensive Psychiatry, 55,* 1534–1539. Doi:10.1016/j.comppsych.2014.05.021

Culbert, K. M., Racine, S. E., & Klump, K. L. (2015). Research review: What we have learned about the causes of eating disorders—a synthesis of sociocultural, psychological, and biological research. *Journal of Child Psychology and Psychiatry, 56*(11), 1141–1164. https://doi.org/10.1111/jcpp.12441

Degenhardt, L., Bharat, C., Glantz, M. D., Sampson, N. A., Scott, K., Lim, C. C. W., Aguliar-Gaziola, S., Al-Hamzawi, A., Alonso, J., Andrade, L. H., Broment, E. J., Bruffaerts, R., Bunting, B., de Girolamo, G, Gureje, O., Haro, J. M., Harris, M. G., He, Y., de Jonge, P., Karam, E. G., Karam, G. E., Kiejna, A., Lee, S., Lepine, J. P., & Kessler, R. C. (2019). The epidemiology of drug use disorders cross-nationally: Findings from the WHO's world mental health surveys. *International Journal of Drug Policy, 71,* 103–112. https://doi.org/10.1016/j.drugpo.2019.03.002

De Genna, N. M., & Feske, U. (2013). Phenomenology of borderline personality disorder: The role of race and socioeconomic status. *Journal of Nervous and Mental Disease, 201*(12), 1027–1034. https://doi.org/10.1097/NMD.0000000000000053

DeGruy, J. (2005). Post Traumatic Slave Syndrome: America's Legacy of Enduring Injury and Healing: Milwaukee, WI: Uptone Press

de Giambattista, C., Ventura, P., Trerotoli, P., Margari, M., Palumbi, R., & Margari, L. (2019). Subtyping the autism spectrum disorder: Comparison of children with high functioning autism and Asperger syndrome. *Journal of Autism & Developmental Disorders, 49*(1), 138–150. https://doi.org/10.1007/s10803-018-3689-4

Dell'Osso, L., Abelli, M., Carpita, B., Pini, S., Castellini, G., Carmassi, C., & Ricca, V. (2016). Historical evolution of the concept of anorexia nervosa and relationships with orthorexia nervosa, autism, and obsessive–compulsive spectrum. *Neuropsychiatric Diseases and Treatment, 12,* 1651–1660. https://doi.org/10.2147/NDT.S108912

Dell'Osso, B., Berlin, H. A., Serati, M., & Altamura, A. C. (2010). Neuropsychobiological aspects, comorbidity patterns and dimensional models in borderline personality disorder. *Neuropsychobiology, 61*(4), 169–79. https://doi.org/10.1159/000297734

de Vries, A. L. C., Doreleijers, T. A. H., Steensma, T. D., & Cohen, K. P. T. (2011). Psychiatric comorbidity in gender dysphoric adolescents. *Journal of Child Psychology and Psychiatry, 52*(11), 1195–1202. https://doi.org/10.1111/j.1469-7610.2011.02426.x

de Vries, A. L. C., Noens, I. L. J., Cohen-Kettenis, P. T., van Berckelaer-Onnes, I. A., & Doreleijers, T. A. (2010). Autism spectrum disorders in gender dysphoric children and adolescents. *Journal of Autism and Developmental Disorders, 40*(8), 930–936.

Dunn, N. R., Freemantle, S. N, Mann, R. D. (1999). Cohort study on calcium channel blockers, other cardiovascular agents, and the prevalence of depression. *British Journal of Clinical Pharmacology, 48*(2), 230–233.

Devaux, M., & Sassi, F. (2013). Social inequalities in obesity and overweight in 11 OECD countries. *European Journal of Public Health, 23*(3), 464–469. https://doi.org/10.1093/eurpub/ckr058

DeVylder, J. E. (2013). The fall and rise of Adolf Meyer's Psychogenic etiology of dementia praecox (schizophrenia): 1903–1910 and beyond. *Smith College Studies in Social Work, 83*(1), 2–17. DOI: 10.1080/00377317.2013.746919

Diflorio, A., & Jones, I. (2010). Is sex important? Gender differences in bipolar disorder. *International Review of Psychiatry, 22*(5), 437–452. https://doi.org/10.3109/09540261.20 10.514601

Dilsaver, S. C. (2011). An estimate of the minimum economic burden of bipolar I and II disorders in the United States: 2009. *Journal of Affective Disorders, 129*(1), 79–83. https://doi.org/10.1016/j.jad.2010.08.030

Dishion, T. J., Nelson, S. E., & Kavanagh, K. (2003). The family check-up with high-risk young adolescents: Preventing early-onset substance use by parent monitoring. *Behavior Therapy, 34*(4), 553–571. https://doi.org/10.1016/S0005-7894(03)80035-7

Dobrova-Krol, N. A., Bakermans-Kranenburg, M. J., Van Ijzendoorn, M. H., & Juffer, F. (2010). The importance of quality of care: Effects of perinatal HIV infection and early institutional rearing on preschoolers' attachment and indiscriminate friendliness. *Journal of Child Psychology and Psychiatry, 51*(12), 1368–1376.

Doctor, R. M., & Shiromoto, F. N. (2010). *The encyclopedia of trauma and traumatic stress disorders.* Facts on File.

Dodds, L., Fell, D. B., Shea, S., Armson, B. A., Allen, A. C., & Bryson, S. (2011). The role of prenatal, obstetric and neonatal factors in the development of autism. *Journal of Autism and Developmental Disorders, 41,* 891–902. http://dx.doi.org/10.1007/s10803-010-1114-8

Dodge, K. A., Bates, J. E., & Pettit, G. S. (1990). Mechanisms in the cycle of violence. *Science, 250*(4988), 1678–1683. https://doi.org/10.1126/science.2270481

Dong, X. Q., Simon, M., Mosqueda, L., & Evans, D. A. (2012). The prevalence of elder self-neglect in a community-dwelling population: Hoarding, hygiene and environmental hazards. *Journal of Aging and Health, 23* (4), 507–24. https://doi.org/10.1177/0898264311425597

Drabble, L., Midanik, L. T. and Trocki, K. (2005). Reports of alcohol consumption and alcohol related problems among homosexual, bisexual, and heterosexual respondents: Results from the 2000 National Alcohol Survey. *Journal of Studies on Alcohol, 66,* 111–120.

Dougherty, L. R., Smith, V. C., Bufferd, S. J., Carlson, G. A., Stringaris, A., Leibenluft, E., & Klein, D. N., (2014). DSM-5 disruptive mood dysregulation disorder: correlates and predictors in young children. *Psychological Medicine, 44*(1), 2339–2350.

Duke, D. C., Keeley, M. L., Geffken, G. R., & Storch, E. A. (2010). Trichotillomania: A current review. *Clinical Psychology Review, 30,* 181–193. https://doi.org/10.1016/j.cpr.2009.10.008

Duke, D. C., Keeley, M. L., Ricketts, E. J., Geffken, G. R., & Storch, E. A. (2010). The phenomenology of hairpulling in college students. *Journal of Psychopathology and Behavioral Assessment, 32,* 281–292. https://doi.org/10.1007/s10862-009-9150-4

Eddy, K. T., Dorer, D. J., Franko, D. L., Tahilani, K., Thompson-Brenner, H., & Herzog, D. B. (2008). Diagnostic crossover in anorexia nervosa and bulimia nervosa: Implications for DSM-V. *American Journal of Psychiatry, 165*(2), 245–250. https://doi.org/10.1176/appi.ajp.2007.07060951

Eisen, J. L., Pinto, A., Mancebo, M. C., Dyck, I. R., Orlando, M. E., & Rasmussen, S. A. (2010). A 2-year prospective follow-up study of the course of obsessive- compulsive disorder. *The Journal of Clinical Psychiatry, 71* (8), 1033–1039.

Ellis, E. E., Yilanli, M., & Saadabadi, A. (2021, May 12). Reactive attachment disorder. In *StatPearls*. StatPearls Publishing. https://www.ncbi.nlm.nih.gov/books/NBK537155/

Enander, J., Ivanov, V. Z., Mataix-Cols, D., Kuja-Halkola, R., Ljotsson, B., Lundstrom, S., Perez-Vigil, A., Monzani, B., Lichtenstein, P., & Ruck, C. (2018). Prevalence and heritability of body dysmorphic symptoms in adolescents and young adults: A population-based nationwide twin study. *Psychological Medicine, 48,* 2740–2747.

Ennis-Cole, D., Durodoye, B. A., Harris, H. L. (2013). The impact of culture on autism diagnosis and treatment: Considerations for counselors and other professionals. *The Family Journal, 21*(3), 279–287. https://doi.org/10.1177/1066480713476834

Eskild-Johnson, M., Stoving, R. L., Flindt, C. F., & Sjogren, M. (2020). Comorbid depression as a negative predictor of weight gain during treatment of anorexia nervosa: A systematic scoping review. *European Eating Disorders Review, 28,* 605–619. DOI: 10.1002/erv.2787

Espel-Huynh, H. M., Muratore, A. F., & Lowe, M. R. (2018). A narrative review of the construct of hedonic hunger and its measurement by the power of food scale. *Obesity Science & Practice, 4*(3), 238–249. https://doi.org/10.1002/osp4.161

Etain, B., Henry, C., Bellivier, F., Mathieu, F., & Leboyer, M. (2008). Beyond genetics: Childhood affective trauma in bipolar disorder. *Bipolar Disorders, 10*(8), 867–876. https://doi.org/10.1111/j.1399-5618.2008.00635.x

Eubig, P. A., Aguiar, A., & Schantz, S. L. (2010). Lead and PCBs as risk factors for attention deficit/hyperactivity disorder. *Environmental Health Perspectives, 118,* 1654–1667

Faith, M. S., Butyrn, M., Wadden, T. A., Fabricatore, A., Nguyen, A. M., & Heymsfield, S. B. (2011). Evidence for prospective associations among depression and obesity in population – based studies. *Obesity Reviews, 12, e438–e453.* doi: 10.1111/j.1467-789X.2010.00843.x

Faraone, S., Biederman, J., Monteaux, M., Doyle, A., & Seidman, L. (2001) A psychometric measure of learning disability predicts educational failure four years later in boys with Attention- Deficit/Hyperactivity Disorder. *Journal of Attention Disorders, 4*(4), 220–30.

Fawcett, E. J., Power, H., & Fawcett, J. M. (2020). Women are at greater risk of OCD than men: a metal-analytic review of OCD prevalence worldwide. *Journal of Clinical Psychiatry, 81*(4). https://doi.org/10.4088/jcp.19r13085

Fayet, F., Petocz, P., & Samman, S. (2012). Prevalence and correlates of dieting in college women: A cross-sectional study. *International Journal of Women's Health, 4,* 405–411. https://doi.org/10.2147/IJWH.S33920

Fein, D., Barton, M., Eigsti, I. M., Kelley, E., Naigles, L., Schultz, R. T., Stevens, R. T., Helt, M., Orintstein, A., Rosenthal, M., Troyb, E., & Tyson, K. (2013). Optimal outcome in individuals with a history of autism. *Journal of Child Psychology and Psychiatry, 54(2),* 195–205.

Ferentinos, P., Preti, A., Veroniki, A. A., Pitsalidis, K. G., Theofilidis, A. T., Antoniou, A., & Fountoulakis, K. N., (2020). Comorbidity of obsessive-compulsive disorder in bipolar spectrum disorders: systematic review and meta-analysis of its prevalence. *Journal of Affective Disorders, 263,* 193–208.

Fincham, D., Grimsrud, A., Corrigall, J., Williams, D. R., Seedat, S., Stein, D. J., & Myer, L. (2009). Intermittent explosive disorder in South Africa: Prevalence, correlates and the role of traumatic exposures. *Psychopathology, 42*(2), 92–98. https://doi.org/10.1159/000203341

Flessner, C. A., Lochner, C., M., Stein, D. J., Woods, D. W., Franklin, M. E., & Keuthen, N. J. (2010). Age of onset of trichotillomania symptoms: Investigating clinical correlates. *Journal of Nervous Mental Disorders, 198,* 896–900. doi: 10.1097/NMD.0b013e3181fe7423

Fombonne, E. (2003). Epidemiological Surveys of Autism and Other Pervasive Developmental Disorders: An Update. *Journal of Autism Developmental Disorders* **33,** 365–382. https://doi.org/10.1023/A:1025054610557

Fornano, M., Gabrielli, F., Albano, C., Fornano, S., Rizzto, S., Mattei, C., Solano, P., Vinciguerra, V., & Fornaro, P. (2009). Obsessive-compulsive disorder and related disorders: a comprehensive survey. *Annals of General Psychiatry, 8*(13). doi:10.1186/1744-859X-8-13

Forcano, L., Álvarez, E., Santamaría, J. J., Jimenez-Murcia, S., Granero, R., Penelo, E., Alonso, P., Sánchez, I., Menchón, J. M., Ulman, F., Bulik, C. M., & Fernández-Aranda, F. (2011). Suicide attempts in anorexia nervosa subtypes. *Comprehensive Psychiatry, 52*(4), 352–358. https://doi.org/10.1016/j.comppsych.2010.09.003

Forte, A., Buscajoni, A., Fiorillo, A., Pompili, M., & Baldessarini, R. J. (2019). Suicidal risk following hospital discharge: A review. *Harvard Review of Psychiatry, 27*(4), 209–216. https://doi.org/10.1097/HRP.0000000000000222

Freedland, K. E., Rich, M. W, Skala, J. A., Carney, R. M., Davila-Roman, V. G., Jaffe,. A. S. (2003). Prevalence of depression in hospitalized patients with congestive heart failure. *Psychosomatic Medicine, 65,* 119–128. doi: 10.1097/01.PSY.0000038938.67401.85

Frick, P. J. (2006). Developmental pathways to conduct disorder. *Child and Adolescent Psychiatric Clinics of North America, 15,* 311–331. Doi: 10.1016/j.chc.2005.11.003

Friedman, L. A., & Rapoport, J. L. (2015). Brain development in ADHD. *Current Opinions in Neurobiology, 30,* 106–111. doi: 10.1016/j.conb.2014.11.007.

Fuller-Thomson, E., & Ryckman, K. (2020). Achieving complete mental health despite a history of generalized anxiety disorders: Findings from a large, nationally representative Canadian survey. *Journal of Affective Disorders, 265,* 687–694. https://doi.org/10.1016/j.jad.2019.12.004

Gadsby, S. (2017). Distorted body representations in anorexia nervosa. *Consciousness and Cognition, 51,* 17–33. https://doi.org/10.1016/j.concog.2017.02.015

Galetto, V., & Sacco, K. (2017). Neuroplastic changes induced by cognitive rehabilitation in traumatic brain injury: A review. *Neurorehabilitation and Neural Repair, 31*(9), 800–813. https://doi.org/10.1177/1545968317723748

Galmiche, M., Dechelotte, P., Lambert, G., & Tavolacci, M. P. (2019). Prevalence of eating disorders over the 2000–2018 period: a systematic literature review. *American Journal of Clinical Nutrition, 109,* 1402–1413. https://doi.org/10.1093/ajcn/nqy342

Garno, J. L., Goldberg, J. F., Ramirez, P. M., & Ritzler, B. A. (2005). Impact of childhood abuse on the clinical course of bipolar disorder. *British Journal of Psychiatry, 186*(2), 121–125. https://doi.org/10.1192/bjp.186.2.121

Gary, F. A. (2005). Stigma: Barrier to mental health care among ethnic minorities. *Issues in Mental Health Nursing, 26*(10), 979–999. https://doi.org/10.1080/01612840500280638

Gaub, M., & Carlson, C. L. (1997). Gender differences in ADHD: A meta-analysis and critical review. *Journal of the American Academy of Child & Adolescent Psychiatry, 36*(8), 1036–1045

Gaudio, S., Brooks, S. J., & Riva, G. (2014). Nonvisual multisensory impairment of body perception in anorexia nervosa: A systematic review of neuropsychological studies. *PLOS ONE, 9*(10), e110087. https://doi.org/10.1371/journal.pone.0110087

Gearhardt, A. N., Davis, C., Kuschner, R., & Brownell, K. D. (2011). The addiction potential of hyperpalatable foods. *Current Drug Abuse Reviews, 4*(3), 140–145. https://doi.org/10.2174/1874473711104030140

Ghaemi, S. N., & Vohringer, P. A. (2011). The heterogeneity of depression: an old debate renewed. *ACTA Psychiatrica Scandinavica, 124*(6), 497. https://doi.org/10.1111/j.1600-0447.2011.01746.x

Ghorayeb, I., Gamas, A., Mazurie, Z., & Mayo, W. (2017). Attention-deficit hyperactivity and obsessive-compulsive symptoms in adult patients with primary restless legs syndrome: Different phenotypes of the same disease? *Behavioral Sleep Medicine, 17*(3), 246–253. https://doi.org/10.1080/15402002.2017.1326919

Gibbs, T. A., Okuda, M., Oquendo, M. A., Lawson, W. B., Wang, S., Thomas, Y. F., & Blanco, C. (2013). Mental Health of African Americans and Caribbean Blacks in the United States: Results from the National Epidemiological Survey on Alcohol and Related Conditions. *American Journal of Public Health, 103*(2), 330–338.

Giordano, A. L., Clarke, P. B., & Furter, R. T. (2013). Predicting substance abuse relapse: The role of social interest and social bonding. *Journal of Addictions & Offender Counseling, 35*, 114–127.

Giordano, A. L., Clarke, P. B., & Furter, R. T. (2014). Predicting substance abuse relapse: The role of social interest and social bonding. *Journal of Addictions & Offender Counseling, 35*(2), 114–127. https://doi.org/10.1002/j.2161-1874.2014.00030.x

Gjevik, E., Eldevik, Fjaeran-Granum, T., & Sponheim, E. (2011). Kiddie-SADS reveals high rates of DSM-IV disorders in children and adolescents with autism spectrum disorder. *Journal of Autism and Developmental Disorders, 41*, 761–769. DOI 10.1007/s10803-010-1095-7

Gleason, M. M., Fox, N. A., Drury, S. S., Smyke, A. T., Nelson, C. A., & Zeanah, C. H. (2014). Indiscriminate behaviors in previously institutionalized young children. *Pediatrics, 133*(3), e657–e665.

Godart, N., Radon, L., Curt, F., Duclos, J., Perdereau, F., Lang, F., Venisse, J. L., Halfon, O., Bizouard, P., Loas, G., Corcos, M., Jeammet, Ph., & Flament, M. F. (2015). Mood disorders in eating disorder patients: Prevalence and chronology of ONSET. *Journal of Affective Disorders, 185*, 115–122. https://doi.org/10.1016/j.jad.2015.06.039

Goeree, M. S., Ham, J. C., Iorio, D. (2011). Race, social class, and bulimia nervosa Goeree, Michelle Sovinsky and Ham, John C. and Iorio, Daniela, Race, Social Class, and Bulimia Nervosa. IZA Discussion Paper No. 5823, Available at SSRN: https://ssrn.com/abstract=1877636

Goisman, R. M., Allworth, B. A., Rogers, M. P., Warshaw, M. G., Goldenberg, I., Vasile, R. G., Rodriguez-Villa, F., Mallya, G. & Keller, M. B. (1998). Simple phobia as a comorbid anxiety disorder. *Depression and Anxiety* 7 (3), 105–112. https://doi.org/10.1002/ (SICI)1520-6394(1998)7:3<105::AID-DA2>3.0.CO;2-A

Goldberg, J. F., & Garno, J. L. (2009). Age at onset of bipolar disorder and risk for co-morbid borderline personality disorder. *Bipolar Disorders*, *11*(2), 205–208. https://doi.org/10.1111/j.1399-5618.2008.00653.x

Goldfarb, W. (1947). Variations in adolescent adjustment of institutionally reared children. *American journal of Orthopsychiatry*, *17*(3), 449.

Gottesman, I. I., Laursen, T. M., Bertelsen, A., Mortensen, P. B. (2010). Severe Mental Disorders in Offspring With 2 Psychiatrically Ill Parents. *Archives of General Psychiatry*, *67*(3), 252–257. doi:10.1001/archgenpsychiatry.2010.1

Gradus, J. L., Qin, P., Lincoln, A. K., Miller, M., Lawler, E., Sørensen, H. T., & Lash, T. L. (2010). Posttraumatic stress disorder and completed suicide. *American Journal of Epidemiology*, *171*, 721–727. https://doi.org/10.1093/aje/kwp456

Graetz, B. W., Sawyer, M. G., & Baghurst, P. (2005). Gender differences among children with DSM-IV ADHD in Australia. *Journal of the American Academy of Child & Adolescent Psychiatry*, *44*(2), 159–168. https://doi.org/10.1097/00004583-200502000-00008

Grant, B. F., Chou, S. P., Goldstein, R. B., Huang, B., Stinson, F. S., Saha, T. D., Smith, S. M., Dawson, D. A., Pulay, A. J., Pickering, R. P., & Ruan, W. J. (2008). Prevalence, correlates, disability, and comorbidity of DSM-IV borderline personality disorder: Results from the Wave 2 National Epidemiologic Survey on Alcohol and Related Conditions. *Journal of Clinical Psychiatry*, *69*(4), 533–545. https://doi.org/10.4088/JCP.v69n0404

Grant, J. E., Chamberlain, S. R. (2017). Trichotillomania. *American Journal of Psychiatry*, *179*, (9), 868–874. http://dx.doi.org/10.1186/s12888-021-03209-y

Grant, B. F, Chou, S. P., Goldstein, R. B., Huang, B., Stinson, F. S., Saha, T. D., et al. (2008). Prevalence, correlates, disability, and comorbidity of DSM-IV borderline personality disorder: results from the wave 2 National Epidemiologic Survey on alcohol and related conditions. *Journal of Clinical Psychiatry*, *69*, 533–45.

Grant, J. E., Menard, W., Phillips, K. A. (2006). Pathological skin picking in individuals with body dysmorphic disorder. *General Hospital Psychiatry*, *28*, 487–493. https://doi.org/10.1016/j.genhosppsych.2006.08.009

Green, K. E. & Feinstein, B. A. (2012). Substance use in lesbian, gay, and bisexual populations: An update on empirical research and implications for treatment. *Psychology of Addictive Behaviors*, *26*, 265–278. doi:10.1037/a0025424

Griffiths, S., Mond, J. M., Murray, S. B., & Touyz, S. (2014). Young peoples' stigmatizing attitudes and beliefs about anorexia nervosa and muscle dysmorphia. *International Journal of Eating Disorders*, *47*(2), 189–195. https://doi.org/10.1002/eat.22220

Griffiths, S., Mond, J. M., Murray, S. B., & Touyz, S. (2015). The prevalence and adverse associations of stigmatization in people with eating disorders. *International Journal of Eating Disorders*, *48*(6), 767–774. https://doi.org/10.1002/eat.22353

Gronberg, T. K., Schendel, D. E., & Partner, E. T. (2013). Recurrence of autism spectrum disorders in full-and half-siblings and trends over time: A population-based cohort study. *JAMA Pediatrics*, *167*(10), 947–953.

Grothe, D. R., Scheckner, B., & Albano, D. (2004). Treatment of pain syndromes with venlafaxine. *Pharmacotherapy: The Journal of Human Pharmacology and Drug Therapy, 24*(5), 621–629. https://doi.org/10.1592/phco.24.6.621.34748

Gunderson, J. G. (2010). Revising the borderline diagnosis for DSM-V: an alternative proposal. *Journal of Personality Disorders, 24* (6), 694–708. https://doi.org/10.1159/000297734

Gunderson, J. G., Morey, L. C., Stout, R. L., Skodol, A. E., Shea, T., McGlashan, T. H., Zanarini, M. C., Grilo, C. M., Sanislow, C. A., Yen, S., Daversa, M. T., & Bender, D. S. (2004). Major depressive disorder and borderline personality disorder revisited: longitudinal interactions. *Journal of Clinical Psychiatry, 65*, 1049–1056.

Gunderson, J. G., Stout, R. L., McGlashan, T. H., Shea, T., Morey, L. C., Grilo, C. Zanarini, M. C., M. Yen, S., Markowitz, J. C., Sanislow, C., Ansell, E., Pinto, A., Skodol, A. E. (2011). Ten-year course of borderline personality disorder: psychopathology and function from the Collaborative Longitudinal Personality Disorders study. *Archives of General Psychiatry, 68*(8),827–837. doi:10.1001/archgenpsychiatry.2011.37

Gunderson, J. G., Zanarini, M. C., Choi-Kain, L. W., Mitchell, K. S., Jang, K. L., Hudson, J. I., (2011). Family study of borderline personality disorder and its sectors of psychopathology. *Archives of General Psychiatry 68*(7), 753–762. doi:10.1001/archgenpsychiatry.2011.65

Gunderson, J. G., & Lyons-Ruth, K., (2008). BPD's interpersonal hypersensitivity phenotype: a gene–environment-developmental model. *Journal of Personality Disorders, 22*, 22–41. https://doi.org/10.1521/pedi.2008.22.1.22

Gunnes, N., Suren, P., Bresnahan, M., Hornig, M., Lie, K. K., Lipkin, W. I., Magnus, P., M., Nilsen, R. M., Reichborn-Kjennerud, T., Schjolberg, S., Susser, E. S., Oyen, A.-S., & Stoltenber, C. (2013). Interpregancy interval and risk of autistic disorder. *Epidemiology, 24*(6), 906–912. DOI: 10.1097/01.ede.0000434435.52506.f5

Gunstad, J., & Phillips, K. A. (2003). Axis I comorbidity in body dysmorphic disorder. *Comprehensive Psychiatry, 44* (4), 270–276. https://doi.org/10.1016/S0010-440X(03)00088-9

Hallas. J. (1996). Evidence of depression provoked by cardiovascular medication: a prescription sequence symmetry analysis. *Epidemiology, 7*(5), 78–484.

Hallett, V., Lecavalier, L., Sukhodolsky, D. G., Cipriano, N., Aman, M. G., McCracken, J. T., McDougle, C. J., Tierney, E., King, B. H., Hollander, E., Sikich, L., Bregman, J., Anagnoustou, E., Donnellly, C., Katsovich, L., Vitiello, K., Benedetto, B., Gadow, K., & Scahill, L. (2013). Exploring the manifestations of anxiety in children with autism spectrum disorders. *Journal of Autism and Developmental Disorders, 43*, 2341–2352

Hankin, B. L., Abramson, L. Y., Moffitt, T. E., Silvan, P. A., McGee, R., & Angell, K. E., (1998). Development of depression from pre adolescence to young adulthood: Emerging gender differences in a 10-year longitudinal study. *Journal of Abnormal Psychology, 107,* 128–140. *Doi:10.1037/0021-843x.107.1.128*

Harvard Medical School, 2007. National Comorbidity Survey (NCS). (2017, August 21). https://www.hcp.med.harvard.edu/ncs/index.php. Data Table 1: Lifetime prevalence DSM-IV/WMH-CIDI disorders by sex and cohort.

Hasin, D. S., Sarvet, A. L., Meyers, J. L., Saha, T. D., Ruan, W. J., Stohl, M., & Grant, B. F. (2018). Epidemiology of adult DSM-5 major depressive disorder and its specifiers in the United States. *JAMA Psychiatry, 75* (4), 336–346. https://doi.org/10.1001/jamapsychiatry.2017.4602

Hautala, L., Junnila, J., Helenius, H., Vaananen, A., Liuksila, P., Raiha, H., Valimaki, M., & Saarijarvi, S. (2008). Towards understanding gender differences in disordered eating among adolescents. *Journal of Clinical Nursing, 17*(13), 1803–1813. https://doi.org/10.1111/j.1365-2702.2007.02143.x

Haek, M., Coulter, R. W. S., Egan, J. E., Fish, S., Friedman, M. R., Tula, M. & Kinsky, S. (2017). Harm reduction principles for healthcare settings, *Harm Reduction Journal, 17*(70). DOI 10.1186/s12954-017-0196-4

Hayes, S. L., Storch, E. A., & Berlanga, L. (2009). Skin picking behaviors: an examination of the prevalence and severity in a community sample. *Journal of Anxiety Disorders, 23* (3), 314–319. https://doi.org/10.1016/j.janxdis.2009.01.008

He, H., Hu, C., Ren, Z., Bai, L., Gao, F., & Lyu, J. (2020). Trends in the incidence and DALYs of bipolar disorder at global, regional, and national levels: Results from the Global Burden of Disease Study 2017. *Journal of Psychiatric Research, 125*, 96–105. https://doi.org/10.1016/j.jpsychires.2020.03.015

Heaner, M. K., & Walsh, B. T. (2013). A history of the identification of the characteristic eating disturbances of bulimia nervosa, binge eating disorder and anorexia nervosa. *Appetite, 71*, 445–448. https://doi.org/10.1016/j.appet.2013.06.001

Hedegaard, H., Chen, L.-H., & Warner, M. (2015). Drug-poisoning deaths involving heroin: United States, 2000–2013. *NCHS Data Brief, 190*, 1–8.

Herpertz, S. C., & Bertsch, K. (2015). A new perspective on the pathophysiology of borderline personality disorder: a model of the role of oxytocin. *American Journal of Psychiatry, 172*(9), 840–51. https://doi.org/10.1176/appi.ajp.2015.15020216

Heston, L. (1966). Psychiatric disorders in foster home reared children of schizophrenic mothers. *British Journal of Psychiatry, 112(*489), 819–825. Doi:101192bjp.112.489.819

Hilbert, A. (2019). Binge-eating disorder. *Psychiatric Clinics of North America, 42*(1), 33–43. https://doi.org/10.1016/j.psc.2018.10.011

Hilty, D. M., Brady, K. T., & Hales, R. E. (1999). A review of bipolar disorder among adults. *Psychiatric Services, 50*(2), 201–213. https://doi.org/10.1176/ps.50.2.201

Hirsch, J. A., Nicola, G., McGinty, G., Liu, R. W., Barr, R. M., Chittle, M. D., & Manchikanti, L. (2016). ICD-10: History and context. *American Journal of Neuroradiology, 37*(4), 596–599. https://doi.org/10.3174/ajnr.A4696

Hodges, L. M., Fyer, A. J., Weissman, M. M., Logue, M. W., Haghighi, F., Evgrafov, O., Rotondo, A., Knowles, J. A., & Hamilton, S. P. (2014). Evidence for linkage and association of GABRB3 and GABRA5 to panic disorder. *Neuropsychopharmacology, 39*, 2423–2431.

Holloway, V., Gadian, D. G., Vargha-Khadem, F., Porter, D. A., Boyd, S. G., & Connelly, A. (2000). The reorganization of sensorimotor function in children after hemispherectomy: A functional MRI and somatosensory evoked potential study. *Brain, 123*(12), 2432–2444. https://doi.org/10.1093/brain/123.12.2432

Hoek, H. W., van Harten, P. N., Hermans, K. M., Katzman, M. A., Matroos, G. E., & Susser, E. S. (2005). The incidence of anorexia nervosa on Curacao. *American Journal of Psychiatry*, *162*(4), 748–752.

Hollander, E., Stein, D. J., Kwon, J. H., Rowland, C. M., Wong, J., Broatch, J., & Himelein, C. (1997). Psychosocial function and economic cost of obsessive-compulsive disorder. *CNS Spectrums*, *2*, 16–25. DOI: https://doi.org/10.1017/S1092852900011068

Horesh, N., & Iancu, I. (2010). A comparison of life events in patients with unipolar disorder or bipolar disorder and controls. *Comprehensive Psychiatry*, *51*(2), 157–164. https://doi.org/10.1016/j.comppsych.2009.05.005

Hoshiai, M., Matsumoto, Y., Sato, T., Ohnishi, M., Okabe, N., Kishimoto, Y., Terada, S., & Kuroda, S. (2010). Psychiatric comorbidity among patients with gender identity disorder. *Psychiatry & Clinical Neurosciences*, *64*(5), 514–519. https://doi.org/10.1111/j.1440-1819.2010.02118.x

Hudson, C. G. (2005). Socioeconomic status and mental illness: Tests of the social causation and selection hypotheses. *American Journal of Orthopsychiatry*, *75*(1), 3–18. https://doi.org/10.1037/0002-9432.75.1.3

Hudson, J., Hiripi, E., Pope, H. and Kessler, R. 2007. The prevalence and correlates of eating disorders in the national comorbidity survey replication. *Biological Psychiatry*, 61: 348–358. https://doi.org/10.1016/j.biopsych.2006.03.040

Hsu, C. W., Lee, S. Y., & Wang, L. J. (2019). Gender differences in the prevalence, co-morbidities and antipsychotic prescription of early-onset schizophrenia: A nationwide population-based study in Taiwan. *European Journal of Adolescent Psychiatry, 28*, 759–767. https://doi.org/10.1007/s00787-018-1242-9

Hung, C. I. ((2014). Factors predicting adherence to antidepressant treatment. Current Opinions in Psychiatry, 27, 344–9. http://dx.doi.org/10.1371/journal.pone.0185119

Iliachenko, E. K., Ragazan, D. C., Eberhard, J., & Berge, J. (2020). Suicide mortality after discharge from inpatient care for bipolar disorder: A 14-year Swedish national registry study. *Journal of Psychiatric Research*, *127*, 20–27. https://doi.org/10.1016/j.jpsychires.2020.05.008

Ishigooka, J., Iwao, M., Suzuki, M., Fukuyama, Y., Murasaki, M., & Miura, S. (1998). Demographic features of patients seeking cosmetic surgery. *Psychiatry & Clinical Neurosciences*, *52*(3), 283–287. https://doi.org/10.1046/j.1440-1819.1998.00388.x

Ivanova, A., Zaidel, E., Salamon, N., Bookheimer, S., Uddin, L. Q., & de Bode, S. (2017). Intrinsic functional organization of putative language networks in the brain following left cerebral hemispherectomy. *Brain Structure and Function*, *222*(8), 3795–3805. https://doi.org/10.1007/s00429-017-1434-y

Iwasaki, Y., Matsunaga, H., Kiriike, N., Tanaka, H., & Matsui, T. (2000). Comorbidity of axis I disorders among eating-disordered subjects in Japan. *Comprehensive Psychiatry*, *41*(6), 454–460. https://doi.org/10.1053/comp.2000.16561

Jagielska, G. & Kacperska, I. (2017). Outcome, comorbidity and prognosis in anorexia nervosa. *Psychiaria Polska, 51*(2), 205-2018. DOI: https://doi.org/10.12740/PP/64580

Jiang, W., Glassman, A., Krishnan, R., O'Connor, C. M., & Califf, R. M. (2005) Depression and ischemic heart disease: what have we learned so far and what must we do in the future? *American Heart Journal, 150,* 54–78. DOI 10.1016/j.ahj.2005.04.012

Johnson, C. P., Follmer, R. L., Oguz, I., Warren, L. A., Christensen, G. E., Fiedorowicz, J. G., Magnotta, V. A. & Wemmie, J. A. (2015). Brain abnormalities in bipolar disorder detected by quantitative T1ρ mapping. *Molecular Psychiatry, 20*(2), 201–206.

Jones, D. R., Macias, C., Barreira, P. J. Fisher, W. H., Hargreaves, W. A., & Harding, C. M. (2004). Prevalence, severity and co-occurrence of chronic physical health problems of persons with serious mental illness. *Psychiatric Services, 55,*(11), 1250–1257. https://doi.org/10.1176/appi.ps.11.1250

Jonkman, C. S., Oosterman, M., Schuengel, C., Bolle, E. A., Boer, F., & Lindauer, R. J. (2014). Disturbances in attachment: inhibited and disinhibited symptoms in foster children. *Child and adolescent psychiatry and mental health, 8*(1), 1–7.

Jones-Smith, E. (2018). *Culturally diverse counseling: Theory and practice.* SAGE Publications.

Joseph, N. T., Myers, H. F., Schettino, J. R., Olmos, N. T., Bingham-Mira, C., Lesser, I. M., & Poland, R. E. (2011). Support and undermining in interpersonal relationships are associated with symptom improvement in a trial of antidepressant medication. *Psychiatry: Interpersonal and Biological Processes, 74*(3), 240–254. https://doi.org/10.1521/psyc.2011.74.3.240

Joshi, G., Petty, C., Wozniak, J., Henin, A., Fried, R., Galdo, M., Kotarski, M., Walls, S., & Biederman, J. (2010). The heavy burden of psychiatric comorbidity in youth with autism spectrum disorders: A large comparative study of a psychiatrically referred population. *Journal of Autism and Developmental Disorders, 40,* 1361–1370.

Joshi, S. V. (2002). ADHD, growth deficits, and relationships to psychostimulant use. *Pediatrics in Review, 23,* 67–68. Doi: 10.1542/pir.23-2-67

Julien, D., O'Connor, K. P., & Aardema, F. (2007). Intrusive thoughts, obsessions, and appraisals in obsessive–compulsive disorder: A critical review. *Clinical Psychology Review, 27,* 366–383. https://doi.org/10.1016/j.cpr.2006.12.004

Karadaĝ, F., Oguzhanoglu, N. K., Özdel, O., Ateşci, F. Ç., & Amuk, T. (2006). OCD symptoms in a sample of Turkish patients: A phenomenological picture. *Depression and Anxiety, 23*(3), 145–152. https://doi.org/10.1002/da.20148

Kawa, S., & Giordano, J. (2012). A brief historicity of the diagnostic and statistical manual of mental disorders: Issues and implications for the future of psychiatric canon and practice. *Philosophy, Ethics, and Humanities in Medicine, 7*(1), 2. https://doi.org/10.1186/1747-5341-7-2

Kazdin, A. E. (1997). Practitioner review: Psychosocial treatments for conduct disorder in children. *Journal of Child Psychology and Psychiatry, 38*(2), 161–178. https://doi.org/10.1111/j.1469-7610.1997.tb01851.x

Keel, P. K., & Brown, T. A. (2010). Update on course and outcome in eating disorders. *International Journal of Eating Disorders, 43*(3), 195–204. https://doi.org/10.1002/eat.20810

Keel, P. K., & Klump, K. L. (2003). Are eating disorders culture-bound syndromes? Implications for conceptualizing their etiology. *Psychological Bulletin, 129*(5), 747–769. https://doi.org/10.1037/0033-2909.129.5.747

Kendler, K. S., Ohlsson, H., Lichtenstein, P., Sundquist, J., & Sundquist, K. (2018). The genetic epidemiology of treated major depression in Sweden. *American Journal of Psychiatry, 175*(11), 1137–1144. https://doi.org/10.1176/appi.ajp.2018.17111251

Kerner, B. (2015). Comorbid substance use disorders in schizophrenia: A latent class approach. *Psychiatry Research, 225,*(3), 395–401. https://doi.org/10.1016/j.psychres.2014.12.006

Kessler, R. C. (2001). Epidemiology of women and depression. *Journal of Affective Disorders, 74*, 51–13. Doi: 10.1016/s0165-0327(02)00426-3

Kessler, R. C., Berglund, P. A., Chiu, W. T., Deitz, A. C., Hudson, J. I., Shahly, V., Aguilar-Gaxiola, S., Alonso, J., Angermeyer, M. C., Benjet, C., Bruffaerts, R., de Girolamo, G., de Graaf, R., Maria Haro, J., Kovess-Masfety, V., O'Neill, S., Posada-Villa, J., Sasu, C., Scott, K., Viana, M., C., & Xavier, M. (2013). The prevalence and correlates of binge eating disorder in the World Health Organization World Mental Health Surveys. *Biological Psychiatry, 73*(9), 904–914. https://doi.org/10.1016/j.biopsych.2012.11.020

Kessler, R. C., Berglund, P. A., Demler, O. R. Jin, R. Walters, E. E. (2005). Lifetime Prevalence and Age-of-Onset Distributions of DSM-IV Disorders in the National Comorbidity Survey Replication (NCS-R). *Archives* of *General Psychiatry 62*(6), 593–602. doi:10.1001/archpsyc.62.6.593

Kessler, R. C., Chiu, W. T., Jin, R., Ruscio, A. M., Shear, K., & Walters, E. E. (2006). The epidemiology of panic attacks, panic disorder, and agoraphobia in the national comorbidity survey replication. *Archives of General Psychiatry, 63*(4), 415–424. https://doi.org/10.1001/archpsyc.63.4.415

Kessler, R. C., Coccaro, E. F., Fava, M., Jaeger, S., Jin, R., & Walters, E. (2006). The prevalence and correlates of DSM-IV intermittent explosive disorder in the national comorbidity survey replication. *Archives of General Psychiatry, 63*(6), 669–678. https://doi.org/10.1001/archpsyc.63.6.669

Kessler, R. C., McGonagle, K. A., Zhao, S., Nelson, C. B., Hughes, M., Eshleman, S., Wittchen, H.-U., & Kendler, K. S. (1994). Lifetime and 12-month prevalence of DSM-III-R psychiatric disorders in the United States: Results from the National Comorbidity Survey. *Archives of General Psychiatry, 51*(1), 8–19. https://doi.org/10.1001/archpsyc.1994.03950010008002

Kernberg, O. (1967). Borderline personality organization. *Journal of the American Psychoanalytic Association 15*(3), 641–685. https://doi.org/10.1177/000306516701500309

Kety, S. S. (1988). Schizophrenic Illness in the families of schizophrenic adoptees: Findings from the Danish National Sample, *Schizophrenia Bulletin*, 14(2), 217–222. https://doi.org/10.1093/schbul/14.2.217

Kim, S. H., Macari, S., Koller, J., & Chawarska, K. (2016). Examining the phenotypic heterogeneity of early autism spectrum disorder: Subtypes and short-term outcomes. *Journal of Child Psychology & Psychiatry, 57*(1), 93–102. https://doi.org/10.1111/jcpp.12448

Kirk, A. (2005). Critical perspectives. In S. A. Kirk (Ed.), *Mental health disorder in the social environment: Critical perspectives*. Columbia University Press. 1–19.

Kirmayer, L. J., Gomez-Carillo, A., Vissiere, S. (2017). Culture and depression in global mental health: an ecological approach to the phenomenology of psychiatric disorders, *Social Science & Medicine, 183,* 163–168. http://dx.doi.org/10.1016/j.socscimed.2017.04.034

Kjaer, J. N., Biskin, R., Vestergaard, C., Gustafsson, N., & Munk-Jorgensen, P. (2016). The clinical trajectory of patients with borderline personality disorder. *Personality and Mental Health, 10,* 181–190. https://doi.org/10.1002/pmh.1337

Koenigsberg, H. W., Denny, B. T, Fan. J., Liu, X., Guerreri, S., Mayson, S. J., Rimsky, L., New, A. S., Goodman, M., & Siever, L. J. (2014). The neural correlates of anomaloushabituation to negative emotional pictures in borderline and avoidant personality disorder patients. *American Journal of Psychiatry, 171*(1), 82–90. https://doi.org/10.1176/appi.ajp.2013.13070852

Koenen, K. C., Ratanatharathorn, A., Ng, L., McLaughlin, K. A., Bromet, E. J., Stein, D. J., Karam, E. G., Ruscio, A. M., Benjet, C., Scott, K., Atwoli, L., Petukhova, M., Lim, C. C. W., Aguilar-Gaxiola, S., Al-Hamzawi, A., Alonso, J., Bunting, B., Ciutan, M., de Girolamo, G., Degenhardt, L., Gureje, O., Haro, J. M., Huang, Y., … Kessler, R. C. (2017). Posttraumatic stress disorder in the World Mental Health Surveys. *Psychological Medicine, 47*(13), 2260–2274. https://doi.org/10.1017/S0033291717000708

Kolb, B., & Whishaw, I. Q. (2016). *An introduction to brain and behavior* (5th ed.). Worth Publishers.

Koran, L. M., Abujaoude, E., Large, M. D., & Serpe, R. T. (2008). The prevalence of body dysmorphic disorder in the United States adult population. *CNS Spectrums, 13*(4), 316–322.

Krauss Whitbourne, S. (2013). What the DSM-5 changes mean for you: The good, the bad and the indifferent in the DSM-5. *Psychology Today.* https://www.psychologytoday.com/us/blog/fulfillment-any-age/201305/what-the-dsm-5-changes-mean-you

Kunitz S. J. (2008). Risk factors for polydrug use in a Native American population. *Substance Use Misuse, 43,* 331–339. https://doi.org/10.1080/10826080701202783

Lahey, B. B., Loeber, R., Burke, J., Rathouz, P. J., & McBurnett, K. (2002). Waxing and waning in concert: Dynamic comorbidity of conduct disorder with other disruptive and emotional problems over 17 years among clinic-referred boys. *Journal of Abnormal Psychology, 111*(4), 556–567. https://doi.org/10.1037/0021-843X.111.4.556

Lao, M. C., Lombardo, M. V., & Auyeung, B. (2015). Sex/gender differences in autism: setting the scene for future research. *Academy of Child and Adolescent Psychiatry, 54*(1), 11–24.

Lamers, F., van Oppen, P., Comijs, H. C., Smit, J. H., Spinhoven, P., van Balkom, A. J., L. M., Nolen W. A., Zitman, F. G., Beekman, A. T. F., & Penninx, B. W. J. H. (2011). Comorbidity patterns of anxiety and depressive disorders in a large cohort study: the Netherlands study of depression and anxiety (NESDA). *Journal of Clincial Psychiatry, 72*(3), 341–348.

Lang, K. W., Reichl, S., Lange, K. M., Tucha, L, & Tucha, O. (2010). The history of attention deficit hyperactivity disorder. *Attention Deficit and Hyperactivity Disorders, 2*(4), 241.255.

Lefebvre, A., Beggiato, A., Bourgeron, T., Toro, R. (2015). Neuroanatomical Diversity of Corpus Callosum and Brain Volume in Autism: Meta-analysis, Analysis of the Autism Brain Imaging Data Exchange Project, and Simulation. *Biological Psychiatry, 78*(2), 126–134. https://doi.org/10.1016/j.biopsych.2015.02.010

Lemke, M. R., Depressive symptoms in Parkinson's disease. *European Journal of Neurology, 15*(1), 21.25. https://doi.org/10.1111/j.1468-1331.2008.02058.x

Lenzenweger, M. F., Lane, M. C., Loranger, A. W., & Kessler, R. C. (2007). DSM-IV personality disorders in the National Comorbidity Survey Replication. *Biological Psychiatry 62* (6),553–564. https://doi.org/10.1016/j.biopsych.2006.09.019

Leslie, M., Turton, R., Burgess, E., Nazar, B. P., & Treasure, J. (2018). Testing the addictive appetite model of binge eating: The importance of craving, coping, and reward enhancement. *European Eating Disorders Review, 26*(6), 541–550. https://doi.org/10.1002/erv.2621

Leung, A., & Chue, P. (2000). Sex differences in schizophrenia, a review of the literature. *Acta Psychiatrica Scandinavica, 101*(401), 3–38. https://doi.org/10.1111/j.0065-1591.2000.0ap25.x

Levinson, C. A., Zerwas, S. C., Brosof, L. C., Thornton, L. M., Strober, M., Pivarunas, B., Crowley, J. J., Yilmaz, Z., Berrettini, W. H., Brandt, H., Crawford, S., Fichter, M. M., Halmi, K. A., Johnson, C., Kaplan, A. S., Via, M. L., Mitchell, J., Rotondo, A., Woodside, D. B., Kaye, W. H., & Bulik, C. M. (2018). Associations between dimensions of anorexia nervosa and obsessive–compulsive disorder: An examination of personality and psychological factors in patients with anorexia nervosa. *European Eating Disorders Review, 27*(2), 161–172. https://doi.org/10.1002/erv.2635

Lewinsohn, P. M. (1974). *A behavioral approach to depression.* In R. J. Friedman & M. M. Katz (Eds.), The psychology of depression: Contemporary theory and research. (pp. 157–174). Oxford: Wiley.

Lewis-Fernancez, R., Hinton, D. E., Amaro, L., Patterson, E. H, Hofmann, S. G., Craske, M. G., Stein, D. J., Asnaai, A., & Liao, B. (2010). Culture and the anxiety disorders: Recommendations for DSM-V. *Depression and Anxiety, 27*(2), 212–229. http://dx.doi.org/10.1002/da.20647

Lichtman, J. H., Bigger, J. T, Blumenthal, J. A., Frasure- Smith, N., Kaufman, P. G., Lesperance, F., Mark, D. B., Sheps, D. S., Barr Taylor, C., & Sivarajan Froelicher, E. S. (2008). Recommendations for Screening, Referral, and Treatment: A Science Advisory From the American Heart Association Prevention Committee of the Council on Cardiovascular Nursing, Council on Clinical Cardiology, Council on Epidemiology and Prevention, and Interdisciplinary Council on Quality of Care and Outcomes Research: *Endorsed by the American Psychiatric Association. Circulation, 21*(17), 1768–1775. https://doi.org/10.1161/CIRCULATIONAHA.108.190769

Lindberg, G., Bingefors, K., Ranstam, J., et al. Use of calcium channel blockers and risk of suicide: ecological findings confirmed in population based cohort study. *British Medical Journal, 316, 741–745.* doi: https://doi.org/10.1136/bmj.316.7133.741

Lindberg, S. M., Grabe, S., & Hyde, J. S. (2007). Gender, pubertal development, and peer sexual harassment predict objectified body consciousness in early adolescence, *Journal of Research on Adolescence, 17, 723–742. Doi:10.1111/j.1532-7795.2007.00544.x*

Link, B. G., Phelan, J. C., Bresnahan, M., Stueve, A., & Pescosolido, B. A. (1999). Public conceptions of mental illness: Labels, causes, dangerousness, and social distance. *American Journal of Public Health*, *89*(9), 1328–1333. https://doi.org/10.2105/AJPH.89.9.1328

Lochman, J. E., Evans, S. C., Burke, J. D, Roberts, M. C., Fite, P. J., Reed, G. M., de la Pena, F. R., Matthys, W., Ezpeleta, L., Siddiqui, S., Garralda, M. E. (2015) An empirically based alternative to DSM-5's disruptive mood dysregulation disorder for ICD-11. *World Psychiatry* 14:30–33. Doi: 10.1002/wps.20176

Lochner, C., Hemmings, S. M. J., Kinnear, C. J., Moolman-Smook, J. C., Corfield, V. A., Knowles, J. A., Niehaus, D. J. H., & Stein, D. J. (2004). Gender in obsessive–compulsive disorder: clinical and genetic findings. *European Neuropsychopharmacology*, *14*(2), 105–113. https://doi.org/10.1016/S0924-977X(03)00063-4

Loeber, R., Burke, J. D., Lahey, B. B., Winters, A., & Zera, M. (2000). Oppositional defiant and conduct disorder: A review of the past 10 years, part I. *Journal of the American Academy of Child & Adolescent Psychiatry*, *39*(12), 1468–1484. https://doi.org/10.1097/00004583-200012000-00007

Lorberboym, M., Watemberg, N., & Nissenkorn, A. (2004). Technetium 99m Ethylcysteinate Dimer Single-Photon Emission Computed Tomography (SPECT) During Intellectual Stress Test in Children and Adolescents With Pure Versus Comorbid Attention-Deficit Hyperactivity Disorder (ADHD). *Journal of Child Neurology*, *19*(2), 91–96. https://doi.org/10.1177/08830738040190020201

Luppino, F. S., de Wit, L. M., Bouvy, P. F., Stijnen, T., Cuijpers, P., Penninx, B. W. J. H., & Zitman, F. G. (2010). Overweight, obesity, and depression: A systematic review and meta-analysis of longitudinal studies. *Archives of General Psychiatry*, *67*(3), 220–229. https://doi.org/10.1001/archgenpsychiatry.2010.2

Lyall, K., Croen, L., Daniels, J., Fallin, M. D., Ladd-Acosta, C., Lee, B. K., Park, B. Y., Snyder, N. W., Schendel, D., Volk, H., Windham, G. C., & Newschaffer, C. (2017). The changing epidemiology of autism spectrum disorders. *Annual Review of Public Health*, *38*(1), 81–102. https://doi.org/10.1146/annurev-publhealth-031816-044318

Mandy, W., Chilvers, R., Chowdhury, U., Salter, G., Seigal, A., & Skuse, D. (2012). Sex differenced in autism spectrum disorder: Evidence from a large sample of children and adolescents. *Journal of Autism and Developmental Disorders*, *42*, 1304–1313.

Marcos-Vidal, L., Martinez,-Garcia, M., Pretus, C., Garcia-Garcia, D., Martinez, K., Janssen, J., Vilarroya, O., Castellanos, F. X., Desco, M., Sepulcre, J., & Carmona, S. (2018). Local functional connectivity suggests functional immaturity in children with attention-deficit/hyperactivity disorder. *Human Brain Mapping*, *39*(6), 2422–2454. doi: 10.1002/hbm.24013

Marder, S. R. & Cannon, T. D. (2019). Schizophrenia. *The New England Journal of Medicine*, *381*, 1753–1761. DOI: 10.1056/NEJMra1808803

Marinangeli, M. G., Butti, G., Scinto, A., Di Cicco, L., Petruzzi, C., Daneluzzo, E., & Rossi, A. (2000). Patterns of comorbidity among DSM-III-R personality disorders. *Psychopathology*, *33*(2), 69–74. doi:10.1159/000029123

Mathews, C. A., Delucchi, K., Cath, D. C., Willemsen, G., Boomsma, D. I. (2014) Partitioning the etiology of hoarding and obsessive-compulsive symptoms. *Psychological Medicine, 44*(13), 2867–2876. DOI: https://doi.org/10.1017/S0033291714000269

Matthews, C. R. & Selvidge, M. M. D. (2005). Lesbian, gay, and bisexual clients' experiences in treatment for addiction. *Journal of Lesbian Studies, 9,* 79–90. doi:10.1300/J155v09n03_08

Maurex, L., Zaboli, G., Wiens, S., Asberg, M., Leopardi, R., Ohman, A., 2009. Emotionally controlled decision-making and a gene variant related to serotonin synthesis in women with borderline personality disorder. *Scandinavian. Journal of Psychology 50,* 5–10. https://doi.org/10.1111/j.1467-9450.2008.00689.x

May, H. T., Horne, B. D., Knight, S., Knowlton, K. U., Bair, T. L., Lappe, D. L., Le, V. T., & Muhlstein, J. B. (2017). The association of depression at any time to the risk of death following coronary artery disease diagnosis. *Quality of Care and Clinical Outcomes, 3*(4), 296–302. Https:/10.1093/ehjqcco/qcx017

Mayes, S. D., Waxmonsky, J. D., Calhoun, S. L., & Bixler, E. O. (2016). Disruptive Mood Dysregulation Disorder Symptoms and Association with Oppositional Defiant and Other Disorders in a General Population Child Sample. Journal of Child and Adolescent Psychopharmacology, 26(2), 101–106. DOI: 10.1089/cap.2015.0074

Mayhew, A. J., Pigeyre, M., Couturier, J., & Meyre, D. (2018). An evolutionary genetic perspective of eating disorders. *Neuroendocrinology, 106*(3), 292–306. https://doi.org/10.1159/000484525

McCabe, S. E., Hughes, T. L., Bostwick, W. B., West, B. T. & Boyd, C. J. (2009). Sexual orientation, substance use behaviors and substance dependence in the United States. *Addiction, 104,* 1333–1345. doi:10.1111/j.1360-0443.2009.02596.x

McClellan, A. T. (2017). Substance misuse and substance use disorders: Why do they matter in healthcare? *Transactions of the American Clinical and Climatological Association, 128,* 112–130.

McCormick, B., Blum, N., Hansel, R., Franklin, J. A., St. John, D., Pfohl, B., Allen, J., & Black, D. W. (2007). Relationship of sex to symptom severity, psychiatric comorbidity, and health care utilization in 163 subjects with borderline personality disorder. *Comprehensive Psychiatry, 48*(5), 406–412. https://doi.org/10.1016/j.comppsych.2007.05.005

McElroy, S. L, Soutullo, C. A, Beckman, D. A, Taylor, P. Jr., & Keck P. E. Jr. (1998). DSM-IV intermittent explosive disorder: A report of 27 cases. *Journal of Clinical Psychiatry, 59,* 203–210. https://doi.org/10.4088/jcp.v59n0411

McGilloway, A., Hall, R. E., Lee, T., & Bhui, K. S. (2010). A systematic review of personality disorder, race and ethnicity: prevalence, aetiology and treatment. *BMC Psychiatry 10*(33). https://doi.org/10.1186/1471-244X-10-33

McLean, C. P., Asnaani, A., Litz, B. T., & Hofmann, S. G. (2011). Gender differences in anxiety disorders: Prevalence, course of illness, comorbidity and burden of illness. *Journal of Psychiatric Research, 45*(8), 1027–1035. Doi: 10.1016/jpsychires.2011.03.006

McLean, C. P., & Anderson, E. R. (2009). Brave men and timid women? A review of the gender differences in fear and anxiety. *Clinical Psychology Review, 29*(6), 496–505. https://doi.org/10.1016/j.cpr.2009.05.003

Medicode (Firm). (1996). *ICD-9-CM: International classification of diseases, 9th revision, clinical modification*. Salt Lake City, Utah: Medicode.

Meichenbaum D. (1976) Toward a Cognitive Theory of Self-Control. In: Schwartz G. E., Shapiro D. (eds) Consciousness and Self-Regulation. Springer, Boston, MA. https://doi.org/10.1007/978-1-4684-2568-0_6

Meron Ruscio, A., Hallion, L. S., Lim, C. C. W. Aguilar-Gaxiola, S., Al-Hamzawi, A., Alonso, J. Andrade, L. H., Borges, G., Bromet, E. G., Bunting, B., Caldas de Almeida, J. M., Demyttenaere, K., Florescu, S., de Girolamo, G., Gureje, O., Haro, J. M. He, Y., Hinkov, H. Hu, H., de Jong, P., Karam, E. G., Lee, S., Lepine, J. P. … Scott, K. M. (2017). Cross-sectional Comparison of the Epidemiology of *DSM-5* Generalized Anxiety Disorder Across the Globe. *JAMA Psychiatry, 74(5),* 465–475. doi:10.1001/jamapsychiatry.2017.0056

Meyer, J. H. (2013). Neurochemical imaging and depressive behaviours. *Current Topics in Behavioral Neurosciences, 28*(14), 101–134. https://doi.org/10.1007/7854_2012_219

Miller, T. W., Nigg, J. T., & Miller, R. L. (2009). Attention deficit hyperactivity disorder in African American children: What can be concluded from the past ten years. *Clinical Psychology Review, 29*(1), 77–86.

Mirin, S. M., Batki, S. L., Oscar, B., Gonzales, P. I., Kleber, H., Schottenfeld, R. S., Weiss, R. D., & Yandown, V. W. (2002). Practice guidelines for the treatment of patients with substance use disorders: Alcohol, cocaine, opioids. In N. C. Numerous Contributors (Ed.), *American Psychiatric Association practice guidelines for the treatment of psychiatric disorders: Compendium 2002* (pp. 249–348). American Psychiatric Association.

Mitchell, C. M., Beals, J., Novins, D. K., Spicer P., & the AI-SUPERPFP Team. Drug use among two American Indian populations: Prevalence of lifetime use and DSM-IV substance use disorders. Drug Alcohol Depend 2003; 69:29–41.

Mitchell, A. J., Vancampfort, D., Sweers, K., van Winkel, R., Yu, W., & De Hert, M. (2013). Prevalence of Metabolic Syndrome and Metabolic Abnormalities in Schizophrenia and Related Disorders—A Systematic Review and Meta-Analysis. *Schizophrenia Bulletin: The Journal of Psychoses and Related Disorders, 39*(2), 306–318. https://doi.org/10.1093/schbul/sbr148

Mitchell, J. E. (2016). Medical comorbidity and medical complications associated with binge-eating disorder. *International Journal of Eating Disorders, 49*(3), 319–323. https://doi.org/10.1002/eat.22452

Mitsis, E. M., McKay, K. E., Shulz, K. P., Newcorn, J. H., & Halperin, J. M. (2000). Parent-teacher concordance for DSM-IV attention-deficit/hyperactivity disorder in a clinic-referred sample. *Journal of the American Academy of Child & Adolescent Psychiatry, 39*(3), 308–313. https://doi.org/10.1097/00004583-200003000-00012

Miller, J. M, Kustra, R. P., Vuong, A., Hammer, A. E., Messenheimer, J. A. (2008). Depressive symptoms in epilepsy: prevalence, impact, aetiology, biological correlates and effect of treatment with antiepileptic drugs. *Drugs, 68,* 1493-509

Minzenberg, M. J., Fan, J., New, A. S, Tang, C. Y., & Siever, L. J. (2008). Frontolimbic structural changes in borderline personality disorder. *Journal of Psychiatric Research, 42*(9), 727–33.

Mizushima, J., Sakurai, H., Mizuno, Y., Shinfuku, M., Tani, H., Yoshida, K., Ozawa, Ch., Serizawa, A., Kodashiro, N., Koide, S., Minamisawa, A., Mutsumoto, E., Nagain, N., Tachino, G., Takashiaski, T., Takeuchi, H., Kikuchi, T., Uchida, H., Watanabe, K., Kocha, H., & Mimura, M. (2013). Melancholic and reactive depression: a reappraisal of old categories. *BMC Psychiatry, 13*. Doi: 10.1186/1471-244x-12-311.

Mohammadi, M. R., Salmanian, M., Hooshyari, Z., Shakiba, A., Alavi, S. S., Ahmadi, A., Khaleghi, A., Zarafshan, H., Mostafavi, S. A., Alaghmand, A., Molavi, P., Mahmoudi-Gharaei, J., Kamali, K., Ghanizadeh, A., Nazari, H., Sarraf, N., Ahmadipour, A., Derakhshanpour, F., Riahi, F., Golbon, A., Kousha, M., Yazdi, A. S. H., Shahrbarbaki, M. E., ... Ahmadi, N. (2019). Lifetime prevalence, sociodemographic predictors, and comorbidities of oppositional defiant disorder: The national epidemiology of Iranian Child and Adolescent Psychiatric Disorders (IRCAP). *Brazilian Journal of Psychiatry, 42*(2), 162–167. https://doi.org/10.1590/1516-4446-2019-0416

Monzani, B., Rijsdijk, F., Harris, J., & Mataix-Cols, D. (2014). The structure of genetic and environmental risk factors for dimensional representations of DSM-5 obsessive-compulsive spectrum disorders. *JAMA Psychiatry, 71*(2), 182–189. oi:10.1001/jamapsychiatry.2013.3524

Moreno, C., Laje, G., Blanco, C., Jiang, H., Schmidt, A. B., & Olfson, M. (2007). National trends in the outpatient diagnosis and treatment of bipolar disorder in youth. *Archives of General Psychiatry, 64*(9), 1032–1039. https://doi.org/10.1001/archpsyc.64.9.1032

Moret, C., & Briley, M. (2011). The importance of norepinephrine in depression. *Neuropsychiatric Disease and Treatment, 7*(Suppl 1), 9–13. https://doi.org/10.2147/NDT.S19619

Morneau-Vaillancourt, G., Coleman, J. R. I., Purves, K. L., Cheesman, R., Rayner, C., Breen, G., & Eley, T. C. (2019). The genetic and environmental hierarchical structure of anxiety and depression in the UK Biobank. *Depression and Anxiety, 37*(6), 512–520. https://doi.org/10.1002/da.22991

Mosner, M. G., Kinard, J. L., Shah, J. S., McWeeny, S., Greene, R. K., Lowery, S. C., Mazefsky, C. A., & Dichter, G. S. *(2019).* Rates of Co-occurring Psychiatric Disorders in Autism Spectrum Disorder Using the Mini International Neuropsychiatric Interview. *Journal of Autism and Developmental Disorders* 49, 3819–3832. https://doi.org/10.1007/s10803-019-04090-1

Mueller, N. T., Bakacs, E., Combellick, J., Grigoryan, Z., & Dominguez-Bello, M. G. (2015). The infant microbiome development: Mom matters. *Trends in Molecular Medicine, 21*(2), 109–117. https://doi.org/10.1016/j.molmed.2014.12.002

Muise, A. M., Stein, D. G., & Arbess, G. A. (2003). Eating disorders in adolescent boys: a review of the adolescent and young adult literature. *Journal of Adolescent Health, 33*(6), 427–435.

Mukherjee, S., & Manahan-Vaughan, D. (2013). Role of metabotropic glutamate receptors in persistent forms of hippocampal plasticity and learning. *Neuropharmacology, 66*, 65–81. https://doi.org/10.1016/j.neuropharm.2012.06.005

Mula, M., Sander, J. W. (2007). Negative effects of antiepileptic drugs on mood in patients with epilepsy. *Drug Safety, 30*, 555–567

Munkvold, L., Lundervold, A., Lie, S. A., & Manger, T. (2009). Should there be separate parent and teacher-based categories of ODD? Evidence from a general population. *Journal of Child Psychology & Psychiatry, 50*(10), 1264–1272. https://doi.org/10.1111/j.1469-7610.2009.02091.x

Munkvold, L., Lundervold, A., Manger, T. (2011) Oppositional Defiant Disorder—Gender Differences in Co-occurring Symptoms of Mental Health Problems in a General Population of Children. *Journal of Abnormal Psychology, 39,* 577–587. https://doi.org/10.1007/s10802-011-9486-6

Munn-Chernoff, M. A., & Baker, J. H. (2016). A primer on the genetics of comorbid eating disorders and substance use disorders. *European Eating Disorders Review, 24*(2), 91–100. https://doi.org/10.1002/erv.2424

Munn-Chernoff, M. A., Keel, P. K., Klump, K. L., Grant, J. D., Bucholz, K. K., Madden, P. A. F., Heath, A. C., & Duncan, A. E. (2015). Prevalence of and familial influences on purging disorder in a community sample of female twins. *International Journal of Eating Disorders, 48*(6), 601–606. https://doi.org/10.1002/eat.22378

Murch, S. H., Andrew, A., Casson D. H., Malik, M., Berelowitz, M., Dhillon, A. P., Thomson, M. A., Valentine, A., Davies, S. E., Walker-Smith, J. A. (2004). Retraction of an interpretation. *Lancet, 363*(9411), 759.

Murry, R. M., Bhavsar, V., Tipoli, G., & Howes, O. 30 years on: how the neurodevelopmental hypotheses of schizophrenia morphed into the developmental risk factor model of psychosis. *Schizophrenia Bulletin, 43*(6), 1190–1196. https://doi.org/10.1093/schbul/sbx121

Murray, D. W., Kollins, S. H., Hardy, K. K., Abikoff, H. B., Swanson, J. M:, Cunningham, C., Vitiello, B., Riddle. M. A., Davies, M., Greenhill, L. L., McCracken J. T., McGough J. J., Posner, K., Skrobala, A. M., Wigal, T., Wigal, S. B., Ghuman, J. K., & Chuang, S. Z. (2007). Parent versus Teacher Ratings of Attention-Deficit/Hyperactivity Disorder Symptoms in the Preschoolers with Attention-Deficit/Hyperactivity Disorder Treatment Study (PATS). *Journal of Child and Adolescent Psychopharmacology, 17*(5), 605–619. https://doi.org/10.1089/cap.2007.0060

Nadal, K. L. (2018). *Microaggressions and traumatic stress: Theory, research, and clinical treatment.* American Psychological Association.

Nadeem, E., Lange, J. M., Edge, D., Fongwa, M., Belin, T., & Miranda, J. (2007). Does stigma keep poor young immigrant and U.S.-born Black and Latina women from seeking mental health care? *Psychiatric Services, 58*(12), 1547–1554. https://doi.org/10.1176/ps.2007.58.12.1547

Nagendra, A., Halverson, T. F., Pinkham, A. E., Harvey, P. D., Jarskog, L. F., Weisman de Mamani, A., & Penn, D. L. (2020). Neighborhood socioeconomic status and racial disparities in schizophrenia: An exploration of domains of functioning. *Schizophrenia Research, 224,* 95–101. https://doi.org/10.1016/j.schres.2020.09.020

Narad, M. E., Garner, A. A., Peugh, J. L., Tamm, L., Antonini, T. N., Kingery, K. M., Simon, J. O., Epstein, J. N. (2015). *Psychological Assessment, 27*(1), 239–248.

National Association of Social Workers. (2021). Preamble to the code of ethics. https://www.socialworkers.org/About/Ethics/Code-of-Ethics/Code-of-Ethics-English

National Institute of Drug Addictions (2020). Dopamine Neurons Signal Rich Information About Unexpected Events. https://www.drugabuse.gov/news-events/science-highlight/dopamine-neurons-signal-rich-information-about-unexpected-events

National Institutes of Health. (2021, March 11). *Opioid overdose crisis*. National Institute on Drug Abuse. https://www.drugabuse.gov/drug-topics/opioids/opioid-overdose-crisis

National Institute for Health and Care Excellence (2009). Borderline Personality Disorder: Treatment and Management (NICE Clinical Guideline CG78). NICE

National Institute of Mental Health. (2019). *Transforming the understanding and treatment of mental illness*. https://www.nimh.nih.gov/health/statistics/mental-illness.shtml#part_154785

Newcomb, E. T, & Hagopian, L. P. (2018). Treatment of severe problem behaviour in children with autism spectrum disorder and intellectual disabilities, *International Review of Psychiatry, 30* (1), 96–109, DOI: 10.1080/09540261.2018.1435513

Nock, M. K., Kazdin, A. E., Hiripi, E., & Kessler, R. C. (2007). Lifetime prevalence, correlates, and persistence of oppositional defiant disorder: Results from the national comorbidity survey replication. *Journal of Child Psychology and Psychiatry, 48*(7), 703–713. https://doi.org/10.1111/j.1469-7610.2007.01733.x

Novick, D. , Montogomery, W., Aguado, J., Kadziola, Z., Peng, X., Brugnoli, R., Haro. J. P. (2013). Which symptoms are associated with an unfavorable course in Asian patients with major depressive disorder? *Journal of Affective Disorders, 149,* 182–188. https://doi.org/10.1016/j.jad.2013.01.020

Nigg, J. T, Lewis, K., Edinger, T., Falk, M. (2012). Meta-analysis of attention-deficit/hyperactivity disorder or attention-deficit/hyperactivity disorder symptoms, restriction diet, and synthetic food color additives. *Journal of the American Academy of Child Psychiatry, 51*(1):86–97.

Norman, R. M. G., Malla, A. K., Manchanda, R., Harricharan, R., Takhar, J., & Northcott, S. (2005). Social support and three-year symptom and admission outcomes for first episode psychosis. *Schizophrenia Research, 80, 277–234.* https://doi.org/10.1016/j.schres.2005.05.006

Oakely, P. K. S., Baxter, A., Harris, M., Desoe, J., Dziouba, A., & Siskind, D. (2018). Increased mortality among people with schizophrenia and other non-affective psychotic disorders in the community: A systematic review and meta-analysis. *Journal of Psychiatric Research, 102*, 245–253. https://doi.org/10.1016/j.jpsychires.2018.04.019

OCDUK (2021). The history of OCD. https://www.ocduk.org/ocd/history-of-ocd/

Obsessive Compulsive Cognitions Work Group (1997). Cognitive assessment of obsessive-compulsive disorder. *Behaviour Research and Therapy, 35*(7), 667–681. https://doi.org/10.1016/S0005-7967(97)00017-X

Odgers, C. L., Caspi, A., Broadbent, J. M., Dickson, N., Hancox, R. J., Harrington, H., Poulton, R., Sears, M. R., Thomson, W. M., & Moffitt, T. E. (2007). Prediction of differential adult health burden by conduct problem subtypes in males. *Archives of General Psychiatry, 64*(4), 476–484. https://doi.org/10.1001/archpsyc.64.4.476

Odgers, C. L., Moffitt, T. E., Broadbent, J. M., Dickson, N., Hancox, R. J., Harrington, H., Poulton, R., Sears, M. R., Thomson, W. M., & Caspi, A. (2008). Female and male antisocial trajectories: From childhood origins to adult outcomes. *Development and Psychopathology, 20*(2), 673–716. https://doi.org/10.1017/S0954579408000333

Odlaug, B. L., Lust, K., Schreiber, L. R., Christenson, G., Derbyshire, K., & Grant, J. E., (2013). Skin picking disorder in university students: Health correlates and gender differences. *General Hospital Psychiatry, 35,* 168–173. https://doi.org/10.17744/mehc.38.4.01

Oldham, J. M. (2006). Borderline personality disorder and suicidality. *American Journal of Psychiatry, 163,* 20–6. https://doi.org/10.1176/appi.ajp.163.1.20

Olguin, P., Fuentes, M., Gabler, G., Guerdjikova, A. I., Keck, P. E., & McElroy, S. L. (2017). Medical comorbidity of binge eating disorder. *Eating and Weight Disorders—Studies on Anorexia, Bulimia and Obesity, 22*(1), 13–26. https://doi.org/10.1007/s40519-016-0313-5

O'Neil, K. A., Conner, B. T., & Kendall, P. C. (2011). Internalizing disorders and substance use disorders in youth: Comorbidity, risk, temporal order, and implications for intervention. *Clinical Psychology Review, 31*(1), 104–112. https://doi.org/10.1016/j.cpr.2010.08.002

Orinstein, A. J., Suh, J., Porter, K., De Yoe, K. A., Tyson, K. E., Troyb, E., Barton, M., Eigsti, M.-I., Stevens, M. C., & Fein, D. A. (2015). Social function and communication in optimal outcome children and adolescents with an autism history on structured test measures. *Journal of Autism and Developmental Disorders, 45*(8), 2443–2463.

Orlovska, S., Vestergaard, C. H., Hammer Bech, B., Nordentoft, M., Vestergaard, M., & Eriksen Benros, M. (2017). Association of streptococcal throat infection with mental disorders: Testing key aspects of the PANDAS hypothesis in a nationwide study, *JAMA Psychiatry, 74* (7), 740–746. doi:10.1001/jamapsychiatry.2017.0995

Ortega, A. N., Canino, G., & Alegria, M. (2008). Lifetime and 12-month intermittent explosive disorder in Latinos. *American Journal of Orthopsychiatry, 78*(1), 133–139. https://doi.org/10.1037/0002-9432.78.1.133

Osland, S., Arnold, P. D., & Pringsheim, T. (2018). The prevalence of diagnosed obsessive compulsive disorder and associated comorbidities: A population-based Canadian study. *Psychiatry Research, 268,* 137–142. https://doi.org/10.1016/j.psychres.2018.07.018

Otto, M. W., Perlman, C. A., Wernicke, R., Reese, H. E., Bauer, M. S., & Pollack, M. H. (2004). Posttraumatic stress disorder in patients with bipolar disorder: A review of prevalence, correlates, and treatment strategies. *Bipolar Disorders, 6*(6), 470–479. https://doi.org/10.1111/j.1399-5618.2004.00151.x

Ouhaz, Z., Fleming, H., and Mitchell, A. S. (2018). Cognitive functions and neurodevelopmental disorders involving the prefrontal cortex and mediodorsal thalamus. *Frontiers in Neuroscience, 12*(33), 1–18. doi: 10.3389/fnins.2018.00033

Packer, A. (2016). Neocortical neurogenesis and the etiology of autism spectrum disorder. *Neuroscience & Biobehavioral Reviews, 64,* 185–195. https://doi.org/10.1016/j.neubiorev.2016.03.002

Palmer, B. A., Pankratz, V. S. & Bostwick, J. M. (2005) The lifetime risk of suicide in schizophrenia: a reexamination. *Archives of General Psychiatry 62,* 247–253. doi:10.1001/archpsyc.62.3.247

Paniagua, F. A. (2014). *Assessing and treating culturally diverse clients: A practical guide* (4th ed.). SAGE. https://doi.org/10.4135/9781506335728

Papageourgiou, V., Kalyva, E., Dafoulis, V., & Vostanis, P. (2008). Differences in parents' and teachers' ratings of ADHD symptoms and other mental health problems. *The European Journal of Psychiatry,* 22(4).

Parboosing, R., Bao, Y., Shen, L., Schaefer, C. A., & Brown, A. S. (2013). Gestational influenza and bipolar disorder in adult offspring. *JAMA Psychiatry, 70*(7), 677–685. https://doi.org/10.1001/jamapsychiatry.2013.896

Paris, J., 1998. Does childhood trauma cause personality disorders in adults? *Canadian Journal of Psychiatry, 43,* 148–153. https://doi.org/10.1177/070674379804300203

Paris, J. & Zweig-Frank, H. (2001). A twenty-seven year follow-up of borderline patients. *Comprehensive Psychiatry 42(6),* 482–487. https://doi.org/10.1053/comp.2001.26271

Parker, G., Fink, M., Shorter, E., Taylor, M. A., & Akiskal, H. (2010). Issues for the DSM-5: whither melancholia? The case for its classification as a distinct mood disorder. *American Journal of Psychiatry, 167*(7), 745–747.

Parry, P., Allison, S., & Bastiampillai, T. (2018). 'Paediatric bipolar disorder' rates are lower than claimed—a reexamination of the epidemiological surveys used by a meta-analysis. *Child and Adolescent Mental Health, 23*(1), 14–22. https://doi.org/10.1111/camh.12231

Pasterski, V., Gilligan, L., & Curtis, R. (2014). Traits of autism spectrum disorders in adults with gender dysphoria. *Archives of Sexual Behavior, 43*(2), 387–393. https://doi.org/10.1007/s10508-013-0154-5

Patel, R. S., Amarvadi, N., Bhullar, H., Lekireddy, J., & Win, H. (2018). Understanding the demographic predictors and associated comorbidities in children hospitalized with conduct disorder. *Behavioral Sciences, 8*(9), 80. https//doi:10.3390/bs8090080

Peña, C. J., Bagot, R. C., Labonté, B., & Nestler, E. J. (2014). Epigenetic signaling in psychiatric disorders. *Journal of Molecular Biology, 426*(20), 3389–3412. https://doi.org/10.1016/j.jmb.2014.03.016

Pelsser, L. M., Frankena, K., Toorman, J., Pereira, R. R. (2017). Diet and ADHD, reviewing the evidence: a systematic review of meta-analyses of double-blind placebo-controlled trials evaluating the efficacy of diet interventions on the behavior of children with ADHD. *PLoS One. 12*(1), e0169277.

Perocco Zanatta, D., Rondinoni, C., Garrido Salmon, C. E., & Del Ben, C. M. (2019). Brain alterations in first episode depressive disorder and resting state fMRI: A systematic review. *Psychology & Neuroscience, 12*(4), 407–429. Doi: 10.1037/pne0000165

Pesce, L., van Neen, T., Carlier, I., van Noorden, M. S., van der Wee, N. J. A., van Hemet, A. M, & Giltay, E. J. (2016). Gender differences in outpatients with anxiety disorder: The Leiden Routine Outcome Monitoring Study. *Epidemiology and Psychiatric Services, 25*(3). http://dx.doi.org/10.1017/S2045796015000414

Peterson, C. M., Baker, J. H., Thornton, L. M., Trace, S. E., Mazzeo, S. E., Neale, M. C., Munn-Chernoff, M. A., Lichtenstein, P., Pedersen, N. L, & Bulik, C. M. (2016). Genetic and environmental components to self-induced vomiting. *International Journal of Eating Disorders, 49*(4), 421–427. https://doi.org/10.1002/eat.22491

Phillips, K. A., Quinn, G., & Stout, R. L. (2008). Functional impairment in body dysmorphic disorder: A prospective follow-up study. *Journal of Psychiatric Research, 42, 701–707.* doi:10.1016/j.jpsychires.2007.07.010

Polderman, T. J., Benyamin, B., de Leeuw, C. A., Sullivan, P. F., van Bochoven, A., Visscher, P. M., & Posthuma, D. (2015). Meta-analysis of the heritability of human traits based on fifty years of twin studies. *Nature Genetics, 47,* 702–709, http://dx.doi.org/10.1038/ng.3285.

Pompili, M., Gonda, X., Serafini, G., Innamorati, M., Sher, L., Amore, M., Rihmer, Z., & Girardi, P., (2013). Epidemiology of suicide in bipolar disorders: a systematic review of the literature. *Bipolar Disorders,* 15, 457–490. https://doi.org/10.1111/bdi.12087

Ponterotto, J. G., Casas, J. M., Suzuki, L. A., & Alexander, C. M. (Eds.). (2010). *Handbook of multicultural counseling* (3rd ed.). SAGE.

Pope, H. G., Jr., Gruber, A. J., Mangweth, B., Bureau, B., deCol, C., Jouvent, R., & Hudson, J. I. (2000). Body image perception among men in three countries. *American Journal of Psychiatry, 157*(8), 1297–1301. https://doi.org/10.1176/appi.ajp.157.8.1297

Pope-Davis, D. B., & Coleman, H. L. K. (1997). *Multicultural counseling competencies: Assessment, education and training, and supervision.* SAGE. https://doi.org/10.4135/9781452232072

Poran, M. A. (2002). Denying diversity: Perceptions of beauty and social comparison processes among Latina, Black, and White women. *Sex Roles, 47*(1), 65–81. https://doi.org/10.1023/A:1020683720636

Post, R. M., & Kalivas, P. (2013). Bipolar disorder and substance misuse: Pathological and therapeutic implications of their comorbidity and cross-sensitisation. *British Journal of Psychiatry, 202*(3), 172–176. https://doi.org/10.1192/bjp.bp.112.116855

Postlewhwaite, A., Kellett, S., Mataix-Cols, D. (2019). Prevalence of hoarding disorder: A systematic review and meta-analysis. *Journal of Affective Disorders, 256*(1), 309–316. https://doi.org/10.1016/j.jad.2019.06.004

Poudel, A., & Gautam, S. (2017). Age of onset of substance use and psychosocial problems among individuals with substance use disorders. *BMC Psychiatry, 17*(1), 10. https://doi.org/10.1186/s12888-016-1191-0

Prioleau, B. (2016). *Reflecting on JFK's legacy of community-based care.* https://www.samhsa.gov/homelessness-programs-resources/hpr-resources/jfks-legacy-community-based-care

Probst, B. (2013). "Walking the tightrope": Clinical social workers' use of diagnostic and environmental perspectives. *Clinical Social Work Journal, 41*(2), 184–191. https://doi.org/10.1007/s10615-012-0394-1

Puccio, F., Fuller-Tyszkiewicz, M., Ong, D., & Krug, I. (2016). A systematic review and meta-analysis on the longitudinal relationship between eating pathology and depression. *International Journal of Eating Disorders, 49*(5), 439–454. https://doi.org/10.1002/eat.22506

Purves D., Augustine G. J., Fitzpatrick D., Hall, W. C., LaMntia, A. S., White, L. E., Mooney, R. D., & Piatt, M. L. (Eds.). (2001). *Neuroscience* (2nd ed.). Sineuar Associates.

Qin, J., Li, R., Raes, J., Arumugam, M., Burgdorf, K. S., Manichanh, C., Nielsen, T., Pons, N., Levenez, F., Yamada, T., Mende, D. R., Li, J., Xu, J., Li, S., Li, D., Cao, J., Wang,

B., Liang, H., Zheng, H., Xie, Y., Tap, J., Lepage, P., Bertalan, M., ... Wang, J. (2010). A human gut microbial gene catalogue established by metagenomic sequencing. *Nature, 464*(7285), 59–65. https://doi.org/10.1038/nature08821

Rabinowitz, J., Levine, S., Garibaldi, G., Bugarski-Kirola, D., Galani Berardo, C., & Kapur, S. (2012). Negative symptoms have greater impact on functioning than positive symptoms in schizophrenia: Analysis of CATIE data

Rabinowitz, J., Levine, S., Hafner, H. (2006). A Population based elaboration of the role of age of onset on the course of schizophrenia. *Schizophrenia Research, 88* (1–3), 96–101. https://doi.org/10.1016/j.schres.2006.07.007

Rachman, S. (1998). A cognitive theory of obsessions: elaborations. *Behaviour Research and Therapy, 36*(4). 385–401. https://doi.org/10.1016/S0005-7967(97)10041-9

Radwan, K., & Coccaro, E. F. (2020). Comorbidity of disruptive behavior disorders and intermittent explosive disorder. *Child and Adolescent Psychiatry and Mental Health, 14*(1), 1–10. https://doi.org/10.1186/s13034-020-00330-w

Rapaport, M. H., Clary, C., Fayyad, R., & Endicott, J. (2005). Quality of life impairment in depressive and anxiety disorders. *American Journal of Psychiatry, 162*, 1171–1178. https://doi.org/10.1176/appi.ajp.162.6.1171

Rao, S., & Broadbear, J. (2019). Borderline personality disorder and depressive disorder. *Australasian Psychiatry, 27*(6), 573–577. https://doi.org/10.1177/1039856219878643

Rector N. A., Cassin, S. E, Richter, M. A., & Burroughs E. (2009). Obsessive beliefs in first-degree relatives of patients with OCD: a test of the cognitive vulnerability model. *Journal of Anxiety Disorders, 23*, 145–149. https://doi.org/10.1016/j.janxdis.2008.06.001

Reed, E., Prado, G., Matsumoto, A. & Amaro, H. (2010). Alcohol and drug use and related consequences among gay, lesbian and bisexual college students: Role of experiencing violence, feeling safe on campus, and perceived stress. *Addictive Behaviors*, 35, 168–171.

Reichenberg, A., Gross, R., Weiser, M., Bresnahan, M., Silverman, J., Harlap, S., Rabinowitz, J. S., Shulman, C., Malaspina, D., Lubin, G., Knobler, H. Y., Davidson, M., & Ezra, S. (2006). Advancing paternal age and autism. *Archives in General Psychiatry, 63*, 1026–1032

Reichborn, K. T., Bulik, C. M., Kendler, K. S., Røysamb, E., Maes, H., Tambs, K., & Harris, J. R. (2003). Gender differences in binge-eating: A population-based twin study. *Acta Psychiatrica Scandinavica, 108*(3), 196–202. https://doi.org/10.1034/j.1600-0447.2003.00106.x

Rhebergen, D., Lamers, F., Spijker, J., De Graaf, R., Beekman, A. T., Penninx, B. W. (2012). Course trajectories of unipolar depressive disorders identified by latent class growth analysis. Psychological *Medicine, 42*, 1383–1396.

Ricciardelli, L. A., McCabe, M. P., Ball, K., & Mellor, D. (2004). Sociocultural influences on body image concerns and body change strategies among indigenous and non-indigenous Australian adolescent girls and boys. *Sex Roles: A Journal of Research, 51*(11–12), 731–741. https://doi.org/10.1007/s11199-004-0722-1

Richler, J., Bishop, S. L., Kleinke J. R., Lord, C. (2007). Restricted and repetitive behaviors in young children with autism spectrum disorders. *Journal of Autism and Developmental Disorders, 37*, 73–85.

Rief, W., Buhlmann, U., Wilhelm, S., Borkenhagen, A., & Brähler, E. (2006). The prevalence of body dysmorphic disorder: A population-based survey. *Psychological Medicine, 36*(6), 877–885. https://doi.org/10.1017/S0033291706007264

Risso, G., Martoni, R. M., Erzegovesi, S., Bellodi, L., & Baud-Bovy, G. (2020). Visuo-tactile shape perception in women with anorexia nervosa and health women with and without body concerns. *Neuropsychologia, 149,* https://doi.org/10.1016/j.neuropsychologia.2020.107635

Robbins, S. P. (2014). From the editor-The DSM-5 and its role in social work assessment and research. *Journal of Social Work Education, 50*(2), 201–205. https://doi.org/10.1080/1043 7797.2014.885363

Robinson, A., Kosmerly, S., Mansfield-Green, S., & Lafrance, G. (2014). Disordered eating behaviours in an undergraduate sample: Associations among gender, body mass index, and difficulties in emotion regulation. *Canadian Journal of Behavioural Science, 46*(3), 320–326. https://doi.org/10.1037/a0031123

Robinson, S. M., & Adinoff, B. (2016). The classification of substance use disorders: Historical, contextual, and conceptual consideration, *Behavioral Sciences, 6*(18). doi:10.3390/bs6030018

Rodriguez, B. F., Weisberg, R. B., Pagano, M. E., Burce, S. E., Spencer, M. A., Culpepper, L., & Keller, M. B. (2006). Characteristics and predictors of full and partial recovery from generalized anxiety disorder in primary care patients. *Journal of Nervous and Mental Disorders, 194* (2), 91–97.

Roest, A. M., de Vried, Y. A., Lim C. C. W., Wittchen, H.-U., Stein, D. J., Adamowski, T., Al-Hamzawi, A., Bromet, E. J., Viana, M. C., de Girolamo, G., Demyttenaere, K., Florescu, S., Gureje, O., Haro, J. M., Hu, C., Karam, E. G., Caldas-de-Almeida, J. M., Kawakami, N., Lepine, J. P., Levinson, D., Medina-Mora, M. E., Navarro-Mateu, F., O'Neill, S. ... de Jong, P. (2018). A comparison of DSM-5 and DSM- IV agoraphobia in the world Mental health surveys. *Depression and Anxiety 36,* 499–510. DOI: 10.1002/da.22885

Root, M. P. (1992). Reconstructing the impact of trauma on personality. In L. S. Brown & M. Ballou (Eds.), Personality and psychopathology: Feminist reappraisals (pp. 229–265). New York: Guilford.

Rothe, E. M. (2005). Considering cultural diversity in the management of ADHD in Hispanic patients. *Journal of the American Medical Association, 97* (10 suppl), 17s–23s.

Ruscio, A. M., Stein, D. J., & Kessler, R. C. (2010). The epidemiology of obsessive compulsive disorder in the National Comorbidity Survey Replication. *Molecular Psychiatry, 15,* 53–63. https://doi.org/10.1038/mp.2008.94

Rytwinski, N. K., Scur, M. D., Feeny, N. C., & Youngstrom, E. A. (2013). The co-occurrence of major depressive disorder among individuals with posttraumatic stress disorder: A meta-analysis. *Journal of Traumatic Stress, 26*(3), 299–309. https://doi.org/10.1002/jts.21814

Sacco, R., Gabriele, S., & Persico, A. M. (2015). Head circumference and brain size in autism spectrum disorder. A systematic review and meta-analysis. *Psychiatry Research, 234,* 239–251.

Sadock, B. J., Sadock, V. A., & Ruiz, P. (2015). *Synopsis of psychiatry: Behavioral sciences/clinical psychiatry* (11th ed.). Wolters Kluwer.

Salk, R. H., Hyde, J. S., Abramson L. Y. (2017). Gender differenced in depression in representative national samples: Meta-analyses of diagnoses and symptoms. *Psychological Bulletin, 148(8), 783–822.* Doi:10.10.7/bul.0000102

Salkever, D. S., Karakus, M. C., Slade, E, P., Harding, C. M., Hough, R. L., Rosenheck, M. D., Swartz, M. S., Barrio, C. & Yamada, A. M. (2007). Measures and predictors of community-based employment and earnings of persons with schizophrenia in a multisite study. *Psychiatric Services, 58*(3), 315–324

Salvatore, J. E. & Dick, D. M. (2018). Genetic influences on conduct disorder. *Neuroscience and Biobehavioral Reviews, 91,* 91–101. https://doi.org/10.1016/j.neubiorev.2016.06.034

Substance Abuse and Mental Health Service Administration (2020). Key substance use and mental health indicators in the United States: Results from the 2019 National Survey on Drug Use and Health (HHS Publication No. PEP20-07-01-001, NSDUH Series H-55). Rockville, MD: Center for Behavioral Health Statistics and Quality, Substance Abuse and Mental Health Services Administration. Https://www.samhsa.gov/data.

Samuels J., Eaton, W. W., Bienvenu, O. J., Brown, C. H., Costa, P. T., & Nestadt, G. (2002). Prevalence and correlates of personality disorders in a community sample. *British Journal of Psychiatry, 180,* 536–42. doi:10.1192/bjp.180.6.536

Sánchez-Villegas, A., Henríquez, P., Figueiras, A., Ortuño, F., Lahortiga, F. & Martínez-González, M. A. (2007). Long chain omega-3 fatty acids intake, fish consumption and mental disorders in the SUN cohort study. *European. Journal of Nutrition, 46,* 337– 346. DOI 10.1007/s00394-007-0671-x

Sathyanarayana Rao, T. S., & Andrade, C. (2011). The MMR vaccine and autism: Sensation, refutation, retraction and fraud. *Indian Journal of Psychiatry, 53* (2), 95–96.

Sawchuck, C. N., Roy-Byrne, P., Noonan, C., Craner, J. R., Goldberg, J., Manson, S., Buchwald, D., & the Al-SUPERPFP Team (2017). Panic attack and panic disorder in the American Indian community. *Journal of Anxiety Disorder, 48,* 6–12. https://doi.org/10.1016/j.janxdis.2016.10.004

Schaumberg, K., Jangmo, A., Thornton, L. M., Birgegård, A., Almqvist, C., Norring, C., Larsson, H., & Bulik, C. M. (2019). Patterns of diagnostic transition in eating disorders: A longitudinal population study in Sweden. *Psychological Medicine, 49*(5), 819–827. https://doi.org/10.1017/S0033291718001472

Schertz, M., Adesman, A. R., Alfieri, N. E. & Bienkowski, R. S. (1996). Predictors of weight loss in children with attention deficit hyperactivity disorder treated with stimulant medication. *Pediatrics, 98*(4), 763–769.

Schiepek G., Tominschek I., Karch S., Mulert C., Pogarell O. (2007). Neuroimaging and the neurobiology of obsessive-compulsive disorder. *Psychotherapy and Psychosomatic Medicine in Psychology,* (57) 379–394. DOI: 10.1055/s-2006-952021

Seidel, M., Ehrlich, S., Breithaupt, L., Welch, E., Wiklund, C., Hübel, C., Thornton, L. M., Savva, A., Fundin, B. T., Pege, J., Billger, A., Abbaspour, A., Schaefer, M., Boehm, I., Zvrskovec, J., Rosager, E. V., Hasselbalch, K. C., Leppä, V., Sjögren, M., Nergårdh, R., Feusner, J. D., Ghaderi, A., & Bulik, C. M. (2020). Study Protocol of Comprehensive Risk Evaluation for Anorexia Nervosa in Twins (CREAT): A study of discordant monozygotic twins with anorexia nervosa. *BMC Psychiatry, 20*(1), 507. https://doi.org/10.1186/s12888-020-02903-7

Schwartz, J. H. (2002). Neurotransmitters. In V. S. Ramachandran (ed.), Encyclopedia of the Human Brain (2nd ed. pp. 601–611). Academic Press

Senreich, E. (2012). Lesbian, Gay, and Bisexual Clients in a Substance Abuse Treatment Program Serving a Mostly Black and Hispanic Population. *Journal of LGBT Issues in Counseling, 6* (4), 310–336. https://doi.org/10.1080/15538605.2012.730474

Serap Monkul, E., Malhi, G. S., & Soares, J. C. (2005). Anatomical MRI abnormalities in bipolar disorder: do they exist and do they progress? *Australian & New Zealand Journal of Psychiatry, 39*(4), 222–226. https://doi.org/10.1080/j.1440-1614.2005.01571.x

Shameer Nijam, M. N., Thambirajah, N., Vithanawasam, D., Vithanage, K., Liyanage, D. S., Gooneratne, I. K., & Senanayake, S. (2019). Phencyclidine: a rare cause of saccadic intrusions. *Annal of Indian Academy of Neurology, 22*(4), 503–505. Doi: 10.4103sianAIAN_174_18

Shelton, J. F., Tancredi, D. J., & Hertz-Picciotto, I. (2010). Independent and dependent contributions of advance maternal and paternal ages to autism risk. *Autism Research, 3,* 30–39.

Shern, D. L., Blanch, A. K., & Steverman, S. M. (2016). Toxic stress, behavioral health, and the next major era in public health. *American Journal of Orthopsychiatry, 86*(2), 109.

Shimada-Sugimoto, M., Otowa, T., & Hettema, J. M. (2017). Genetics of anxiety disorders: Genetic epidemiological and molecular studies in humans. *Psychiatry and Clinical Neurosciences, 69*(7), 388–401. https://doi.org/10.1111/pcn.12291

Shingleton, R. M., Thompson-Brenner, H., Thompson, D. R., Pratt, E. M., & Franko, D. L. (2015). Gender differences in clinical trials of binge eating disorder: An analysis of aggregated data. *Journal of Consulting and Clinical Psychology, 83*(2), 382–386. https://doi.org/10.1037/a0038849

Sibley, M. H., Pelham, W. E., Molina, B. S. G., Nagy, E. M., Waschbusch, D. A., Garefino, A. C., Kuriyan, A. B., Babinski, D. E., & Karch, K. M. (2012). Diagnosing ADHD in adolescence. *Journal of Consulting and Clinical Psychology, 80*(1), 139–150.

Siddiqui, E. U., Naeem, S. S., Naqvi, H., & Ahmed, B. (2012). Prevalence of body-focused repetitive behavior in three large medical colleges of Karachi: A cross-sectional study. *BMC Research Notes, 5,* 614–619. https://doi.org/10.1016/j.genhosppsych.2014.07.008

Siegel, D. J. (1999). *The developing mind: toward a neurobiology of interpersonal experience.* Guilford Press.

Silverman, M. H., Frankenburg, F. R., Reich, D. B. (2012). The course of anxiety disorders other than PTSD in patients with borderline personality disorder and axis II comparison subjects: a 10 year follow up study. *Journal of Personality Disorders, 26*(5), 804–814. https://doi.org/10.1521/pedi.2012.26.5.804

Simpson, H. B., Wetterneck, C. T., Cahill, S. P., Steinglass, J. E., Franklin, M. E., Leonard, R. C., Weltzin, T. E., & Riemann, B. C. (2013). Treatment of obsessive-compulsive disorder complicated by comorbid eating disorders. *Cognitive Behaviour Therapy, 42*(1), 64–76. https://doi.org/10.1080/16506073.2012.751124

Skoog G., & Skoog I. (1999). A 40-year follow-up of patients with obsessive compulsive disorder. *Archives of General Psychiatry,* 56, 121–127. doi:10.1001/archpsyc.56.2.121

Skodol, A., Pagano, R. M., Bender, D., Shea, M. T., Gunderson, J. G., Yen, S., Stout, R. L., Morey, L. C., Sanislow, C. A., Grilo, C. M., Zanarini, M. C., & McGlashan, T. H. (2005). Stability of functional impairment in patients with schizotypal, borderline, avoidant or obsessive-compulsive personality disorder over two years. *Psychological Medicine, 35*(3), 443–451. Doi: 10.1017/S003329170400354X

Slane, J. D., Burt, S. A., & Klump, K. L. (2011). Genetic and environmental influences on disordered eating and depressive symptoms. *International Journal of Eating Disorders, 44*(7), 605–611. https://doi.org/10.1002/eat.20867

Steinhausen, H.-C., & Weber, C. P. (2009). The outcome of bulimia nervosa: Findings from one-quarter century of research. *The American Journal of Psychiatry, 166*(12), 1331341. https://doi.org/10.1176/appi.ajp.2009.09040582

Stuyt, E. (2018). The problem with the current high potency THC marijuana from the perspective of an addiction psychiatrist. *Missouri Medicine, 115*(6), 482–486.

Smeets, M. A. M., Klugkist, I. G., Rooden, S., van Anema, H. A., & Postma, A. (2009). Mental body distance comparison: A tool for assessing clinical disturbances in visual body image. *Acta Psychologica, 132*(2), 157–165. https://doi.org/10.1016/j.actpsy.2009.03.011

Smith, I., Reichow, B., & Volkmar, F. (2015). The effects of DSM-5 criteria on number of individuals diagnosed with autism spectrum disorder: A systematic review. *Journal of Autism & Developmental Disorders, 45*(8), 2541–2552. https://doi.org/10.1007/s10803-015-2423-8

Smith, W. A. (2004). Black faculty coping with racial battle fatigue: The campus racial climate in a post-civil rights era. In D. Cleveland (Ed.), *A long way to go: Conversations about race by African American faculty and graduate students* (pp. 171–190). Peter Lang Publishing.

Smith, W. A., Yosso, T. J., & Solórzano, D. G. (2006). Challenging racial battle fatigue on historically White campuses: A critical race examination of race-related stress. In C. A. Stanley (Ed.), *Faculty of color: Teaching in predominantly white colleges and universities* (pp. 299–327). Anker Publishing.

Smoller, J.W. and Finn, C.T. (2003), Family, twin, and adoption studies of bipolar disorder. Am. J. Med. Genet., 123C: 48-58. https://doi.org/10.1002/ajmg.c.2001

Snyder, S. H., & Ferris, C. D. (2000). Novel neurotransmitters and their neuropsychiatric relevance. *American Journal of Psychiatry, 157*(11), 1738–1751

Spencer, T., Biederman, J., & Wilens, T. (1998). Growth deficits in children with attention deficit hyperactivity disorder. *Pediatrics, 102*(suppl 3), 501–506.

Sobin, C., Blundell, M., Weiller, F., Gavigan, C., Haiman, C., & Karayiorgou, M. (1999). Phenotypic characteristics of obsessive-compulsive disorder ascertained in adulthood. *Journal of Psychiatric Research, 33*(3), 265–273. https://doi.org/10.1016/S0022-3956(98)00061-2

Sollie, H., Larsson, B., & Morch, W.-T. (2012). Comparison of mother, father, and teacher reports of ADHD core symptoms in a sample of child psychiatric outpatients. *Journal of Attention Disorder, 17*(8), 699–710.https://doi.org/10.1177/1087054711436010

Soloff, P. H., Fabio, A., Kelly, T. M. (2005). High-lethality status in patients with borderline personality disorder. Journal of Personality Disorders, 19, 386–99. https://doi.org/10.1521/pedi.2005.19.4.386

Spicer, P., Beals, J., Croy, C. D., Mitchell, C. M., Novins, D. K., Moore, L., & Manson, S. M., The American Indian Service Utilization, Psychiatric Epidemiology, Risk Protective Factors Project Team. (2003). The prevalence of DSM-III-R alcohol dependence in two American Indian populations. *Alcoholism: Clinical and Experimental Research*, *27*(11), 1785–1797. https://doi.org/10.1097/01.ALC.0000095864.45755.53

Spitoni, G. F., Serino, A., Cotugno, A., Mancini, F., Antonucci, G., & Pizzamiglio, L. (2015). The two dimensions of the body representation in women suffering from anorexia nervosa. *Psychiatry Research*, *230*(2), 181–188. https://doi.org/10.1016/j.psychres.2015.08.036

Squarcina, L., Fagnani, C., Bellani, M., Altumura, C. A., & Brambilla, P. (2016). Twin studies for the investigation of the relationships between genetic facto and brain abnormalities in bipolar disorder, *Epidemiology and Psychiatric Sciences, 25*(6), 515–520. Doi.10.1017/s2045796016000615

Stanley, B., Gameroff, M. J., Michalsen, V., & Mann, J. (2011) Are suicide attempters who self-mutilate a unique population? *American Journal of Psychiatry, 158*, 427–32. https://doi.org/10.1176/appi.ajp.158.3.427

Steensma, T. D., McGuire, J. K., Kreukels, B. P. C., Beekman, A. J., & Cohen-Kettenis, P. T. (2013). Factors associated with desistence and persistence of childhood gender dysphoria: A quantitative follow-up study. *Journal of the American Academy of Child & Adolescent Psychiatry*, *52*(6), 582–590. https://doi.org/10.1016/j.jaac.2013.03.016

Steffensmeier, J. J., Ernst, M. E, Kelly, M., & Hartz, A. J. (2006). Do randomized controlled trials depression. A Second look at propranolol and depression. *Pharmacotherapy, 26*, 162–167. https://doi.org/10.1592/phco.26.2.162

Stein, D. J., Lim, C. C. W., Roest, A. M., de Jonge, P., Aguilar-Gaxiola, S., Al-Hamzawi, A., Alonso, J., Benjet, C., Bromet, E. J., Bruffaerts, R., de Girolamo, G., Florescu, S., Gureje, O., Haro, J. M., Harris, M. G., He, Y., Hinkov, H., Horiguchi, I., Hu, C., Karam, A., Karam, E. G., Lee, S., Lepine, J., … WHO World Mental Health Survey Collaborators. (2017). The cross-national epidemiology of social anxiety disorder: Data from the world mental health survey initiative. *BMC Medicine, 15*(1), 1–21. https://doi.org/10.1186/s12916-017-0889-2

Steiner, H., & Remsing, L. (2007). Practice parameter for the assessment and treatment of children and adolescents with oppositional defiant disorder. *Journal of the American Academy of Child & Adolescent Psychiatry*, *46*(1), 126–141. https://doi.org/10.1097/01.chi.0000246060.62706.af

Stevens, T., Peng, L., & Barnard-Brak, L. (2016). The comorbidity of ADHD in children diagnosed with autism spectrum disorder. *Research in Autism Spectrum Disorders, 31*, 11–18. https://doi.org/10.1016/j.rasd.2016.07.003

Stinson, F. S., Dawson, D. A., Chou S. P., Smith, S., Goldstein R. B., Ruan W. J., & Grant, B. F. (2007). The epidemiology of DSM-IV specific phobia in the USA: results from the national epidemiological survey on alcohol and related conditions. *Psychological Medicine, 37*, 1047–1059. DOI: https://doi.org/10.1017/S0033291707000086

Strober, M., Freeman, R., Lampert, C., Diamond, J., & Kaye, W. (2000). Controlled family study of anorexia nervosa and bulimia nervosa: Evidence of shared liability and transmission of partial syndromes. *The American Journal of Psychiatry, 157*(3), 393–401. https://doi.org/10.1176/appi.ajp.157.3.393

Su, J., Chun Kuo, S. I., Aliev, F., Guy, M. C., Derlan, C. L., Edenberg, H. J., Nurnberger, J. I., Kramer, J. R., Bucholz, K. K., Salvatore, J. E., & Dick, D. M. (2018). Influence of parental alcohol dependence symptoms and parenting on adolescent risky drinking and conduct problems: A family systems perspective. *Alcoholism Clinical & Experimental Research, 42*(9), 1783–1794. https://doi.org/10.1111/acer.13827

Substance Abuse and Mental Health Services Administration (2018). *Key Substance Use and Mental Health Indicators in the United States: Results from the 2017 National Survey on Drug Use and Health.* https://www.samhsa.gov/data/report/2017-nsduh-annual-national-report

Substance Abuse and Mental Health Service Administration (2018). Key substance use and mental health indicators in the United States: Results from the 2018 National Survey of Drug Use and Health Releases. https://www.samhsa.gov/data/sites/default/files/cbhsq-reports/NSDUHNationalFindingsReport2018/NSDUHNationalFindingsReport2018.pdf

Sue, D. W., Capodilupo, C. M., Torino, G. C., Bucceri, J. M., Holder, A., Nadal, K. L., & Esquilin, M. (2007). Racial microaggressions in everyday life: implications for clinical practice. *American psychologist, 62*(4), 271.

Sukel, K. (2018). *Beyond emotion: Understanding the amygdala's role in memory.* https://www.dana.org/article/beyond-emotion-understanding-the-amygdalas-role-in-memory/

Sullivan, P. F., Bulik, C. M., Kendler, K. S. (1998). Genetic epidemiology of binging and vomiting. *British Journal of Psychiatry, 173,* 75–79. https://doi.org/10.1192/bjp.173.1.75

Surace, T., Fusar-Poli, L., Vozza, L., Cavone, V., Arcidiacono, C., Mammano, R., Basile, L., Rodolico, A., Bisicchia, P., Caponnetto, P., Signorelli, M. S., & Aguglia, E. (2020). Lifetime prevalence of suicidal ideation and suicidal behaviors in gender non-conforming youths: A meta-analysis. *European Child & Adolescent Psychiatry.* https://doi.org/10.1007/s00787-020-01508-5

Surmeier, D. J., & Graybiel, A. M. (2012). A feud that wasn't: Acetylcholine evokes dopamine release in the striatum. *Neuron, 75*(1), 1–3. https://doi.org/10.1016/j.neuron.2012.06.028

Swanson, J. M., Kraemer, H. C., Hinshaw, S. P., Arnold, L. E., Conners, K., Abikoff, H. B., Clevenger, W., Davies, M., Elliott, G. R., Greenhill, L. L., Hechtman, L., Hoza, B., Jensen, P. S., March, J. S., Newcorn, J. H., Owens, E. B., Pelham, W., Schiller, E., Severe, J. E., Simpson, S., Vittiello, B., Wells, K., Wigal, T., Wu. M. (2001). Clinical relevance of the primary findings of the MTA: Success rates based on severity of ADHD and ODD symptoms at the end of treatment. *Journal of the American Academy of Child and Adolescent Psychiatry, 40*(2), 168–179.

Svanborg, C., Baarnhielm, S., Wistedt, A. A., & Lutzen, K. (2008). Helpful and hindering factors for remission in dysthymia and panic disorder at 9-year follow up: a mixed methods study. *BioMed Central Psychiatry, 8*(52). doi:10.1186/1471-244X-8-52

Tadić, A., Wagner, S., Hoch, J., Başkaya, Ö., von Cube, R., Skaletz, C., Lieb, K., & Dahmen, N. (2009). Gender differences in axis I and axis II comorbidity in patients with borderline personality disorder. *Psychopathology, 42*(4), 257–263. https://doi.org/10.1159/000224149

Tandon, M., Pergika, A. (2017). Attention deficit hyperactivity disorder in preschool-age children. *Child & Adolescent Psychiatric Clinics, 26*(3), 523–538. DOI: https://doi.org/10.1016/j.chc.2017.02.007

Taqui, A. M., Shaikh, M., Gowani, S. A., Shahid, F., Khan, A., Tayyeb, S. M., Satti, M., Vaqar, T., Shahid, S., Shamsi, A., Ganatra, H. A., & Naqvi, H. A. (2008). Body dysmorphic disorder: Gender differences and prevalence in a Pakistani medical student population. *BMC Psychiatry, 8*, 1–10. https://doi.org/10.1186/1471-244X-8-20

Tiihonen, J., Wahlbeck, K., Lonnqvist,. J, et al. (2006). Effectiveness of antipsychotic treatments in a nationwide cohort of 2230 patients in community care after first hospitalisation due to schizophrenia and schizoaffective disorder: Observational follow up study. *British Medical Journal 333,* 224. doi: https://doi.org/10.1136/bmj.38881.382755.2F

Tizard, B., & Rees, J. (1975). The effect of early institutional rearing on the behaviour problems and affectional relationships of four-year-old children. *Journal of child psychology and psychiatry, 16*(1), 61-73.

Tomko, R. L., Trull, T. J., Wood, P. K., & Sher, K. J. (2014). Characteristics of borderline personality disorder in a community sample: comorbidity, treatment utilization, and general functioning. *Journal of Personality Disorders, 28*, 734–50. https://doi.org/10.1521/pedi_2012_26_093

Torgersen, S., Czajkowski, N., Jacobson, K., Reichborn-Kjennerud, T., Røysamb, E., Neale, M. C., & Kendler, K. S. (2008). Dimensional representations of DSM-IV cluster B personality disorders in a population-based sample of Norwegian twins: a multivariate study. *Psychological Medicine. 38,* 1617–1625. doi:10.1017/S0033291708002924

Torgersen, S., Myers, J., Reichborn-Kjennerud, T., Røysamb, E., Kubarych, T. S., &., Kendler, K. S. (2012). The heritability of cluster B personality disorders assessed both by personal interview and questionnaire. *Journal of Personality Disorders*, 26, 848–866. https://doi.org/10.1521/pedi.2012.26.6.848

Torresan, R. C., de Abreu Ramos-Cerqueira, A. T., de Mathis, M. A., Diniz, J. B., Ferrão, Y. A., Miguel, E. C., & Torres, A. R. (2009). Sex differences in the phenotypic expression of obsessive-compulsive disorder: An exploratory study from Brazil. *Comprehensive Psychiatry, 50*(1), 63–69. https://doi.org/10.1016/j.comppsych.2008.05.005

Tozzi, F., Thornton, L. M., Klump, K. L., Fichter, M. M., Halmi, K. A., Kaplan, A. S., Strober, M., Woodside, D. B., Crow, S., Mitchell, J., Rotondo, A., Mauri, M., Cassano, G., Keel, P., Plotnicov, K. H., Pollice, C., Lilenfeld, L. R., Berrettini, W. H., Bulik, C. M., & Kaye, W. H. (2005). Symptom fluctuation in eating disorders: Correlates of diagnostic crossover. *American Journal of Psychiatry, 162*(4), 732–740. https://doi.org/10.1176/appi.ajp.162.4.732

Tripathi, A., Avasthi, A., Grover, S., Sharma, E., Lakdawala, B. M., Thirunavukarasu, M., Dan, A., Sinha, V., Sareen, H., Mishra, K. K., Rastogi, P., Srivastava, S., Dhingra, I., Behere, P. B., Solanki, R. K., Sinha, V. K., Desai, M., & Reddy, Y. C. J. (2018). Gender differences in obsessive-compulsive disorder: Findings from a multicentric study from India. *Asian Journal of Psychiatry, 37*, 3–9. https://doi.org/10.1016/j.ajp.2018.07.022

Trull, T. J., 2001. Relationships of borderline features to parental mental illness, childhood abuse, Axis I disorder, and current functioning. *Journal of Personality Disorders 15*, 19–32. https://doi.org/10.1521/pedi.15.1.19.18647

Tryon, P. A., Mayes, S. D., Rhodes, R. L., & Waldo, M. (2006). Can Asperger's disorder be differentiated from autism using DSM-IV criteria? *Focus on Autism and Other Developmental Disabilities, 21*(1), 2–6. https://doi.org/10.1177/10883576060210010101

Tsai, L., & Ghaziuddin, M. (2014). DSM-5 ASD moves forward into the past. *Journal of Autism & Developmental Disorders, 44*(2), 321–330. https://doi.org/10.1007/s10803-013-1870-3

Tsai, J., & Rosenheck, R. A. (2014). Psychiatric comorbidity among adults with schizophrenia: a latent class analysis. *Psychiatric Research, 210*(1), 16–20. Doi: 10.1016/j.psychres.2013.05.013

Tükel, R., Polat, A., Genç, A., Bozkurt, O., & Atlı, H. (2004). Gender-related differences among Turkish patients with obsessive-compulsive disorder. *Comprehensive Psychiatry, 45*(5), 362–366. https://doi.org/10.1016/j.comppsych.2004.06.006

Udo, T., & Grilo, C. M. (2018). Prevalence and correlates of DSM-5–defined eating disorders in a nationally representative sample of U.S. adults. *Biological Psychiatry, 84*(5), 345–354. https://doi.org/10.1016/j.biopsych.2018.03.014

Uchida, M., Spencer, T. J., Faraone, S. V., & Biederman, J. (2018). Adult outcome of ADHD: An overview of results from the NGH longitudinal family studies of pediatrically and psychiatrically referred youth with ad without ADHD of both sexes. *Journal of Attention Disorders, 22,* (6), 523–534.

Uher, R., & Swicker, A. (2017). Etiology in psychiatry: embracing the reality of poly-gene-environmntal causation of mental illness. *World Psychiatry*, 16 (2), 121-129. https://doi.org/10.1002/wps.20436

Underwood, M. D. Kassir, S. A., Bakalian, M. J., Galafyy, h., Dwork, A. J., Mann, J. J., & Arango, V. (2018). Serotonin receptors and suicide, major depression, alcohol use disorder and reported early life adversity. *Translational Psychiatry, 8*(1), 1–15. doi:10.1038/s41398-018-3909-1

United States Department of Health and Human Services (1980). International classification of diseases, 9th revision, clinical modification. Washington, DC: US Department of Health and Human Services.

Van Ameringen, M., Patterson, B., & Simpson, W. (2014). DSM-5 obsessive-compulsive and related disorders: clinical implications of new criteria. *Depression and Anxiety, 31,* 487–493. https://doi.org/10.1002/da.22259

Van der Miesen, A. I. R., de Vries, A. L. C., Steensma, T. D., & Hartman, C. A. (2018). Autistic symptoms in children and adolescents with gender dysphoria. *Journal of Autism and Developmental Disorders, 48*(5), 1537–1548. https://doi.org/10.1007/s10803-017-3417-5

Van Grootheest, D. S., Cath, D. C., & Beekman, A. T. (2005). Twin studies on obsessive-compulsive disorder: A review. *Twin Research and Human Genetics, 8*(5), 450–458. Doi:10.1375/twin.8.5.450

Van Lier, P. A. C., van der Ende, J., Koot, H. M., & Verhulst, F. C. (2007). Which better predicts conduct problems? The relationship of trajectories of conduct problems with ODD and ADHD symptom from childhood in to adolescence. *Journal of Child Psychology and Psychiatry, 48*(6), 601–608. https://doi.org/10.1111/j.1469-7610.2006.01724.x

Van Vliet, R., Roos, C., van der Mast, R. C., van den Broek, M., Westendorp, R. G. J., & de Craen A. J. M. (2009). Use of benzodiazepines, depressive symptoms and cognitive function in old age. *International Journal of Geriatric Psychiatry, 24,* 500–508. DOI: 10.1002/gps.2143

Vazey, E. M., & Aston-Jones, G. (2012). The emerging role of norepinephrine in cognitive dysfunctions of Parkinson's disease. *Frontiers in Behavioral Neuroscience, 6*(48), 1–6. https://doi.org/10.3389/fnbeh.2012.00048

Veale, D., Gledhill, L. J., Christodoulou, P., & Hodsoll, J. (2016). Body dysmorphic disorder indifferent settings: A systematic review and estimated weighted prevalence. *Body Image, 18,* 168–186. https://doi.org/10.1016/j.bodyim.2016.07.003

Virnig, B., Huang, Z., Lurie, N., Musgrave, D., McBean, A. M., & Dowd, B. (2004). Does Medicare managed care provide equal treatment for mental illness across races? *Archives of General Psychiatry, 61*(2), 201–205. https://doi.org/10.1001/archpsyc.61.2.201

Viswanath, B., Narayanaswmy, J. C., Rajkumar, R. P., Cherian, A. V., Kandavel, T., Math, S. B., & Reddy, J. (2012). Impact of depressive and anxiety disorder comorbidity on the clinical expression of obsessive-compulsive disorder. *Comprehensive Psychiatry, 53*(6), 775–782.

Vles, J. S., Feron, F. J., Hendriksen, J. G., Jolles, J., van Kroonenburgh, M. J., & Weber, W. E. (2003). Methylphenidate down-regulates the dopamine receptor and transporter system in children with attention deficit hyperkinetic disorder (ADHD). *Neuropediatrics 34*(2), 77–80. doi: 10.1055/s-2003-39602.

Volpe, U., Tortorella, A., Manchia, M., Monteleone, A. M., Albert, U., & Monteleone, P. (2016). Eating disorders: What age at onset? *Psychiatry Research, 238,* 225–227. https://doi.org/10.1016/j.psychres.2016.02.048

Votaw, V. R., Geyer, R., Rieselbach, M. M., & McHugh, R. K. (2019). The epidemiology of benzodiazepine misuse: A systematic review. *Drug and Alcohol Dependence, 200,* 95–114. https://doi.org/10.1016/j.drugalcdep.2019.02.033

Wakefield, A. J., Murch, S. H., Anthony, A., Linnell, J., Casson, D. M., Malik, M., Berelowitz, M., Dhillon, A. P., Thomson, M. A., Harvey, P., Valentine, A., Davies, S. E. & Walker-Smith, J. A. (1998). Ileal-lymphoid-nodular hyperplasia, non-specific colitis, and pervasive developmental disorder in children. *Lancet, 351,* 637–41.

Walder, D. J., Faraone, S. V., Glatt, S. J., Tsuang, M. T., & Seidman, L . J. (2014). Genetic liability , prenatal health, stress and family environment: Risk factors in the Harvard Adolescent Family High Risk for Schizophrenia Study. *Schizophrenia Research,* 157, 142-148. https://doi.org/10.1016/j.schres.2014.04.015

Walker, E., Kestler, L., Bollini, A., & Hochman, K. M. (2004). Schizophrenia: Etiology and Course. *Annual Review of Psychology, 55,* 401–430. DOI: 10.1146/annurev.psych.55.090902.141950

Walker, E. R., McGee, R. E., Druss, B. G. (2015). Mortality in Mental Disorders and Global Disease Burden Implications: A Systematic Review and Meta-analysis. *JAMA Psychiatry,* 72(4), 334–341. doi:10.1001/jamapsychiatry.2014.2502

Walton, Q., & Shepard Payne, L. (2016). Missing the mark: Cultural expressions of depressive symptoms among African-American women and men. *Social Work in Mental Health, 14,*(6), 637–657. https://doi.org/10.1080/15332985.2015.1133470

Ward, T., & Willis, G. (2010). Ethical issues in forensic and correctional research. *Aggression and Violent Behavior, 15*(6), 399–409. https://doi.org/10.1016/j.avb.2010.07.002

Weiner, D. B. (1992). Philippe Pinel's "Memoir on Madness" of December 11, 1794: A fundamental text of modern psychiatry. *American Journal of Psychiatry, 149*(6), 725–732. https://doi.org/10.1176/ajp.149.6.725

Wiersma, J. E., Hovens. J. G., Van Oppen P., Giltay, E. J., Van Schaik D. J., Beekman A. T., Penninx B. W. (2009). The importance of childhood trauma and childhood life events for chronicity of depression in adults. *Journal of Clinical Psychiatry 70,* 983–989.

Wetterborg, D., Långström, N., Andersson, G., & Enebrink, P. (2015). Borderline personality disorder: Prevalence and psychiatric comorbidity among male offenders on probation in Sweden. *Comprehensive Psychiatry, 62,* 63–70. https://doi.org/10.1016/j.comppsych.2015.06.014

White Hughto, J. M., Reisner, S. L., & Pachankis, J. E. (2015). Transgender stigma and health: A critical review of stigma determinants, mechanisms, and intervention. *Social Science & Medicine, 147,* 222–231. Doi: 10.1016/j.socscimed.2015.11.010

Wiesner, M., Elliott, M. N., McLaughlin, K. A., Banspach, S. W., Tortolero, S., & Shuster, M. A. (2015). Common versus specific correlates of fifth-grade conduct disorder and oppositional defiant disorder symptoms: Comparison of three racial/ethnic groups. *Journal of Abnormal Child Psychology, 43,* 985–998. Doi: 10.1007/s10802-014-9955-9

Wildes, J. E., Emery, R. E., Simons, A. D. (2001). The role of ethnicity and culture in the development of eating disturbance and body dissatisfaction: a meta-analytic review. *Clinical Psychology Review, 21*(4), 521–551. https://doi.org/10.1016/S0272-7358(99)00071-9

Williams, M. T., Rosen, D. C., & Kanter, J. W. (2019). *Eliminating Race-Based Mental Health Disparities: Promoting Equity and Culturally Responsive Care Across Settings.* New Harbinger Books. ISBN: 978-1-68403-196-2

Wing, L., Gould, J., & Gillberg, C. (2011). Autism spectrum disorders in the DSM-V: Better or worse than the DSM-IV? *Research in Developmental Disabilities, 32*(2), 768–773. https://doi.org/10.1016/j.ridd.2010.11.003

Winsper, C., Zanarini, M., & Wolke, D. (2012). Prospective study of family adversity and maladaptive parenting in childhood and borderline personality disorder symptoms in a non-clinical population at 11 years. *Psychological Medicine 42,* 2405–2420Doi:10.1017/S003329171200542

Winters, K. C., Tanner-Smith, E. E., Bresani, E., & Meyers, K. (2014). Current advances in the treatment of adolescent drug use. *Adolescent Health, Medicine and Therapeutics, 5,* 199–210. https://doi.org/10.2147/AHMT.S48053

Wolke, D., Lereya, S., Fisher, H., Lewis, G., & Zammit, S. (2014). Bullying in elementary school and psychotic experiences at 18 years: A longitudinal, population-based cohort study. *Psychological Medicine, 44*(10), 2199-2211. doi:10.1017/S0033291713002912

Wolraich, M. L., Lambert, W. E., Bickman, L., Simmons, T., Doffing, M. A., & Worley, K. (2004). Assessing the impact of parent and teach agreement on diagnosing attention-deficit hyperactivity disorder. *Journal of developmental & Behavioral Pediatrics, 25*(1), 41–47.

Woods, D. W., Flessner, C. A., Franklin, M. E., Keuthen, N. J., Goodwin, R. D., Stein, D. J., & Walther, M. R. (2006). The Trichotillomania Impact Project (TIP): Exploring phenomenology, functional impairment and treatment utilization. *Journal of Clinical Psychiatry, 67,* 1877–1888.

World Health Organization (1992). The ICD-10 classification of mental and behavioral disorders: Clinical descriptions and diagnostic guidelines. Geneva: World Health Organization

World Health Organization (2017). *Depression and other common mental disorders: Global health estimates.* https://apps.who.int/iris/bitstream/handle/10665/254610/WHO-MSD-MER-2017.2-eng.pdf

World Health Organization (2018). WHO/Europe brief-transgender health in the context of ICD-11. https://www.euro.who.int/en/health-topics/health-determinants/gender/gender-definitions/whoeurope-brief-transgender-health-in-the-context-of-icd-11

Wu, S., Wu, F., Ding, Y., Hour, J., Bi, J., & Zhang, Z. (2017). Advanced parental age and autism risk in children: a systematic review and meta- analysis. *ACTA Psychiatrica Scandinavica* 135 29–41

Yang, X., Fang, Y, Chen, H., Zhang, T., Yin, X., Man, J., Yang, L., & Lu, M. (2021). Global, regional and national burden of anxiety disorders from 1990–2019: results from the Global Burden of Disease Study 2019. *Epidemiology and Psychiatric Sciences, 30*(36), 1–11. https://doi.org/10.1017/ S2045796021000275

Yang, C. J., Gray, P., & Pope, H. G. (2005). Male body image in Taiwan versus the West: Yanggang Zhiqi meets the Adonis complex. *The American Journal of Psychiatry, 162,* 263–269. doi:10.1176/appi.ajp.162.2.263.

Yao, S., Larsson, H., Norring, C., Birgegård, A., Lichtenstein, P., D'Onofrio, B. M., Almqvist, C., Thornton, L. M., Bulik, C. M., & Kuja-Halkola, R. (2019). Genetic and environmental contributions to diagnostic fluctuation in anorexia nervosa and bulimia nervosa. *Psychological Medicine, 51*(1), 62–69. https://doi.org/10.1017/S0033291719002976

Yilmaz, Z., Hardaway, J. A., & Bulik, C. M. (2015). Genetics and epigenetics of eating disorders. *Advances in Genomics and Genetics, 5,* 131–150. https://doi.org/10.2147/AGG. S55776

Young, R. L., & Rodi, M. L. (2014). Redefining autism spectrum disorder using DSM-5: The implications of the proposed DSM-5 criteria for autism spectrum disorders. *Journal of Autism and Developmental Disorders, 44*(4), 758–765.

Yubero-Lahoz, S., Kuypers, K. P. C., Ramaekers, J. G., Langohr, K., Farre, M. & de la Torre, R. (2015). Changes in serotonin transporter (5- HTT) gene expression in peripheral blood cells after MDMA intake. *Psychopharmacology, 232,* 1921–1929. DOI 10.1007/ s00213-014-3827-4

Zablotsky, B., Black, L. I., Maenner, M. J., Schiever, L. A., Blumberg, S. J. (2015). Estimated prevalence of autism and other developmental disabilities following questionnaire changes in the 2014 National Health Interview Survey. *National Health Statistics Report, 87,* 1–20

Zaboli, G., Gizatullin, R., Nilsonne, A., Wilczek, A., Jönsson, E. G., Ahnemark, E., Asberg, M., Leopardi, R., 2006. Tryptophan hydroxylase-1 gene variants associate with a group of suicidal borderline women. *Neuropsychopharmacology 31,* 1982–1990. https://doi.org/10.1038/sj.npp.1301046

Zachor, D. A., & Ben-Itzchak, E. (2019). From toddlerhood to adolescence: Which characteristics among toddlers with autism spectrum disorder predict adolescent attention deficit/hyperactivity symptom severity? A long-term follow-up study. *Journal of Autism and Developmental Disorders, 49*(8), 3191–3202.

Zachor, D. A., & Ben-Itzhak, E. (2020). From toddlerhood to adolescence, trajectories and predictors of outcome: Long-term follow-up study in autism spectrum disorder. *Autism Research, 13, 1130–1143.*

Zanarini, M. C., Yong, L., Frankenburg, F. R., Hennen, J., Reich, D. B., Marino, M. F., Vujanovic, A. A., (2002). Severity of reported childhood sexual abuse and its relationship to severity of borderline psychopathology and psychosocial impairment among borderline inpatients. *Journal of. Nervous and Mental. Disorders. 190*(6), 381–387.

Zanarini, M. C., Frankenburg, F. R., Hennen, J., Reich, B. D., & Silk, K. R. (2004). Axis I comorbidity in patients with borderline personality disorder: 6 -year follow-up and prediction of time to remission. *American Journal of Psychiatry, 161,* 2018–2114.

Zanarini, M. C., Frankenburg, F. R., Hennen, J., Reich, B. D., & Silk, K. R. (2006). Prediction of the 10-year course of borderline personality disorder. *American Journal of Psychiatry, 163,* 827–832.

Zanarini, M. C., Frankenburg, F. R., Weingeroff, J. L, Reich, D. B., Fitzmaurice, G. M., & Weiss, R. D. (2011). The course of substance use disorders in patients with borderline personality disorder and Axis II comparison subjects: a 10-year follow-up study. *Addiction, 106* (2), 342–348. https://doi.org/10.1111/j.1360-0443.2010.03176.x

Zanatta, D. P., Rondinoni, C., Salmon, C. E. G., & Del Ben, C. M. (2019). Brain alterations in first episode depressive disorder and resting state fMRI: A systematic review. *Psychology & Neuroscience, 12*(4), 407–429. https://doi.org/10.1037/pne0000165

Zeanah, C. H., Scheeringa, M., Boris, N. W., Heller, S. S., Smyke, A. T., & Trapani, J. (2004). Reactive attachment disorder in maltreated toddlers. *Child Abuse & Neglect, 28*(8), 877–888. https://doi.org/10.1016/j.chiabu.2004.01.010

Zerbo, O., Yoshida, C., Gunderson, E. P., Dorward, K., Croen, L. A., (2015). Interpregancy interval and risk of autism spectrum disorder. *Pediatrics, 136*(4), 651–657. doi: 10.1542/peds.2015-1099

Zimmermann, P., Wittchen, H.-U., Höfler, M., Pfister, H., Kessler, R. C., & Lieb, R. (2003). Primary anxiety disorders and the development of subsequent alcohol use disorders: A 4-year community study of adolescents and young adults. *Psychological Medicine, 33*(7), 1211–1222. https://doi.org/10.1017/S0033291703008158

Zink, C. F., & Weinberger, D. R. (2010) Cracking the moody brain: The rewards of self starvation. *Nature Medicine, 16* (12), 1382–1383.

Zlotnick, C., Rothschild, L., & Zimmerman, M. (2002). The role of gender in the clinical presentation of patients with borderline personality disorder. *Journal of Personality Disorders, 16*(3), 277–282. https://doi.org/10.1521/pedi.16.3.277.22540

Zucker, K. J. (2010). The DSM diagnostic criteria for gender identity disorder in children. *Archives of Sexual Behavior, 39*(2), 477–498. https://doi.org/10.1007/s10508-009-9540-4

Zucker, K. J., & Lawrence, A. A. (2009). Epidemiology of gender identity disorder: Recommendations for the standards of care of the World Professional Association for Transgender Health. *International Journal of Transgenderism, 11*(1), 8–18.

Zucker, K. J., Lawrence, A. A., & Kreukels, B. P. C. (2016). Gender dysphoria in adults. *Annual Review of Clinical Psychology, 12,* 217–247. 10.1146/annurev-clinpsy-021815-093034

Zwicker, A., Denovan-Wright, E. M., & Uher, R. (2018). Gene-environment interplay in the etiology of psychosis. *Psychological Medicine, 48,* 1925–1936. https://doi.org/10.1014/s003329171700383x

Index